Attack

by
T/Sgt Richard G. Byers

Apollo Books, Inc.
107 Lafayette Street
Winona, Minnesota 55987

To Joseph Bugger who from another who was there and survived! Dick Byers

Copyright © 1984 by Richard G. Byers

ISBN # 0-916829-03-0

Manufactured by Apollo Books, 107 Lafayette, Winona, MN 55987

PRINTED IN THE UNITED STATES OF AMERICA

The
9th
Air Force
at War

376th BOMB GROUP
9th AIR FORCE

This War Diary is dedicated to ⌣

    Those who in time of national crisis—
when the veneer of our civilization was so
thin you could scratch it with your
fingernail—when the candle of liberty
flickered so low you could snuf it out with
your fingers—when man's inhumanity to
man reached proportions of unbelievable
beastiality—there were a select few and
they raised man's hopes from despotism's
dust and kept freedom's flag unfurled—laid
their lives on the altar of war to preserve
and transmit to posterity our cherished
principles of justice, freedom and
democracy—so that generations of people
in America could have the opportunity to
live as God has intended we live—freedom
from fear-want—freedom of speech-
religion—they fly forever from the great air
base in the sky in the blue skies over the
Middle East—may they find eternal peace
knowing that those of us who survived
have not forgotten their courage and
determination.

**GROUP AND PERSONAL
CITATIONS—MEDALS—RIBBONS
AWARDED TO
T/SGT RICHARD G. BYERS**

GROUP BATTLE STARS

★ Tunisia
★ Ploesti
★ Sicily
★ Naples—Foggia
★ Rome
★ Balkans

PRESIDENTIAL CITATIONS

★ Low Level Attack on the Ploesti Oil Refineries in Romania
★ Support of British 8th Army against Africa Corps

MEDALS AND RIBBONS

★ Distinguished Flying Cross
★ Air Medal with 8 Clusters
★ European-Africa-Middle East Campaigns
★ American Campaign
★ World War II Medal
★ Efficiency-Honor-Fidelity Medal

ACKNOWLEDGEMENTS

The author owes a great debt of thanks and deep appreciation to the following persons whose dedicated efforts made the publication of this World War II diary possible.

LOUISE ROIZER - Department of Foreign Languages, University of Arkansas for her translation of the leaflets which were tossed out of the waist windows over Italian and Greek cities.

SUE RUEHLE - Bella Vista, Arkansas for her untiring efforts in typing and preparing this manuscript for publication.

BRUCE MEYER PRODUCTIONS - Sioux City, Iowa for his photographic skills in preserving and preparing the old photographs for modern publication.

LARRY GREEN - Artist, Madison, South Dakota for his superior assistance in the preparation of the art work.

CORINNE BYERS - My wife, for her warm understanding, her gentle encouragement, her constant support, and, above all, her love.

B-24 called "Little Richard" —Serial number 240660.

FEBRUARY—1943

WEDNESDAY-FEBRUARY 24, 1943

Morrison Field—West Palm Beach, Florida—Port of Embarcation for B-24 crews for overseas combat duty—Middle East—or over the hump—Far East theaters. Our crew has been here for quite some time waiting for the final word to leave, but it seems everytime we were alerted, mechanical or structural failures were found in our ship we had named "Patches." A skeleton crew just previously flew her to Macon, Georgia where the tail structure was checked and reinforced, as in-flight tail flutters were causing serious flying problems on some ships.

We were scheduled to leave Monday with five other ships but at the last minute difficulties arose and we had to stay behind. Orders have just come down that all is 'go' for tomorrow. At 3:30 A.M. we were to leave by ourselves and go to South America—Ascension Islands—Africa and finally to Cairo where our sealed orders are to be opened and we'll finally know which theatre of air combat we're going to participate in. It's extremely exciting. Three of the crew members are married, Lear (Pilot), MacDonald (Co-pilot) and myself. All of the crew is busy packing. We've practically bought out the PX—boxes of candy, gum, mints, cigars, soap, shaving cream, etc. We loaded up on all the film we could get our hands on—also went over to Supply and checked out extra pieces of clothing—shoes, etc. Last minute briefing sessions for Pilot, Co-Pilot, Navigator and Radio Operator were of prime importance. Gregg, our Navigator, and I worked closely together. Emergency radio procedures were double-checked and re-checked. Anne has called her mother who is traveling to West Palm Beach. They will

1

return to Hibbing, Minnesota. I had the only car in the crew, a 1940 Olds sedan with hydromatic shift. The crew really loved it. I'm the oldest crew member—24 years old.

Late Wednesday night and early Thursday morning the crew gathered together. Those of us who were married said our final goodbyes. It was very sad and emotional. Some of us had the feeling we'd never return. This was a common thought among many crew members. We finally packed up all our gear, passed through the security gate, waved our final 'goodbye' and headed toward the ship silhouetted against base field floodlights and dark skies.

Our crew—standing left to right—Lt. Gregg,Navigator—Lt. Macdonald, Co-pilot—Lt. Gekas, Bombardier—kneeling left to right—S/Sgt Linderman, top turret gunner—S/Sgt Holbrook, right waist gunner—S/Sgt Keller, tail gunner—T/Sgt Byers, radio operator and left waist gunner—T/Sgt Fisher, Engineer and belly gunner.

THURSDAY, FEBRUARY 25, 1943

After carefully packing away all the gear and PX purchases and checking the ship over again, we finally got the signal from the tower to prepare for takeoff at approximately 3:30 A.M. We're heading for Waller Field, Trinidad about 1600 miles south. Takeoff was routine. We circled the field with all of us taking a longing last look at the good old United States and all of us mentally saying, "I'll be back."

The trip to Trinidad was uneventful. We flew about 3 to 5 thousand feet off the water. We landed in Trinidad about 2:30 P.M. Really not here. All of the crew retired early. Most of us made a few extra purchases at the base PX.

FRIDAY, FEBRUARY 26, 1943

After an early breakfast—after checking over the ship and gassing her up, we left Waller Field and headed for Zandrey Field, Paramaribo, Dutch Guiana about 550 miles from Trinidad. No problems in-flight. Crew in a good jovial mood. For many of the crew, this is the farthest they've been away from home. It's really getting hot here, as we approach the northern sections of the equator. All that's here is an airfield to service American combat planes on the way to the war zone. A few Dutch aircraft are here for Base protection. Crew relaxed. Looked over the ship, ate and went to bed.

SATURDAY, FEBRUARY 27, 1943

In the grayness of early dawn with a clear sky above, our B-24 rolled down the runway of Zandrey Field and headed south for Natel, Brazil, a distance of about 1,500 miles. Enroute we crossed the headwaters of the great Amazon River. It's about 100 miles across where the river flows into the Atlantic Ocean. Flying at about 700 to 1,000 feet we encountered the roughest turbulence I've ever flown in. Our faith in the B-24 certainly has been restored.

We've crossed the Equator and have landed at Natel, Brazil. Before we could leave the ship, we had to be fumigated. God! It was unbearable inside the ship! Guess this is just routine procedure. Went to an open-air theater on the base and saw "Hold That Ghost". Had a couple of Brazilian beers at the PX—good, just fair. All crews restricted to the Base. Popular songs of the day are: Sleepy Lagoon, Tangerine, Green Eyes, Beer Barrel Polka, Far Away Places, and Bugle Boy From Company 'B'.

SUNDAY, FEBRUARY 28, 1943

The weather here is terrific—hot and humid. Conditions are tough. Must use fine netting over your bunk to keep out flies, bugs, mosquitoes and all insects in general. Nothing cooking at all—ground crews getting ready to pull 100-hour inspection on the ship before we head East over the Atlantic to Ascension Islands. Laid around—went to PX with most of crew— had a few beers and generally talked of home and if we'd ever get back there again. Spirits high.

MARCH—1943

MONDAY, MARCH 1, 1943

Ground crews pulling 100-hour inspection on the ship. Hot and humid—bugs all over—food is terrible. As if that's not enough, we also have bedbugs which don't make very good sleeping partners. Everyone hopes we can leave the Natel Islands tomorrow. Everyone restricted to the base. Retired early as tomorrow will be a long day on the radio. Ascension is just a spot in the South Atlantic. Hopefully, Gregg and I can drop the ship right on target.

TUESDAY, MARCH 2, 1943

We all had an early breakfast, such as it was, and all of us were by the ship early as preparations for take-off were under way just as the sun was rising in the East. The sky was just beginning to light up as we began to taxi over to the runway for take-off clearance. A few seconds later we got the green light and roared down the runway, heading for Ascension Island. Fisher is sick and Pete isn't feeling too good. Everything enroute was OK. Made radio contact with Ascension—secured radio fix. Gregg used his navigational aids. Hit Ascension right on. Don't believe we were more than several miles off course. Ascension is 1,400 miles from South American coast line. We landed about 1:45 P.M. Ascension is a small island—about 2 miles by 4 miles and all rock. We had the ship immediately checked over and gassed as we plan to leave early in the morning for Accra, Gold Coast, Africa. Had a relaxing dinner—saw the show "Big Street." Fisher and Keller seem to be getting sicker. They did attend the open-air show with us. German U-boats are heavy in this area. They prey on shipping and sometimes on aircraft taking off either for Africa or South America. Tomorrow could be our first encounter with the enemy.

WEDNESDAY, MARCH 3, 1943

As daybreak came to Ascension, our crew was ready to go. Before we could take off, the literally thousands of birds that inhabit the island had to be cleared from the runway. They could affect engine performance—even cause an engine to be feathered. A beautiful sight. Finally got the clearance and took off in a northeasterly direction to the Gold Coast, over 1,400 miles away. Flying at 6,000 to 8,000 feet, we passed over many convoys with destroyers and cruisers patrolling the outlying areas giving protection to the slow-moving ships. Most were travelling in a northern direction—a positive reminder that we are getting closer to the battle zones. Landed at Accra about 4:15 P.M. Radio worked fine enroute. Heat here is terrific. The base here is British run—excellent facility. We sleep in army tents with wooden floors. A native valet is around at all times looking after our needs. The food is just great and the PX is well stocked. No apparent shortages. Bad news—Fisher and Keeler turned themselves in to the Base Hospital and will probably be there for ten days or more. We will go on without them and they'll have to catch up when released. Base Operations at Cairo will instruct them as to where we've been assigned. Many of the local blacks assist the British on the base— also American personnel are assigned here.

THURSDAY, MARCH 4, 1943

We've been informed we'll be here several days. Laid around taking things easy as did the rest of the crew. The vaccinations we previously received are getting the best of me— really painful. Crews come and go from this base all the time. It handles a lot of air traffic.

FRIDAY, MARCH 5, 1943

Early this morning we all got permission to go into town (Accra). It's unbelievable how filthy conditions are. A continuous odor hangs over the city which is caused by the extremely unsanitary conditions. The natives practically relieve themselves right in the street. Street stands are all over the place selling curios. They have a dozen different prices depending on how you argue. Bought several items for the folks back home. All the natives beg the American soldiers for money. Life seems to be very cheap in this area. They certainly have no morals whatsoever. We were all glad to get back to camp where the atmosphere is 100% different. Went to a show on base and saw Martha Raye. She is a Captain and had arrived from Dakar where she has been entertaining the troops. Great show. She did a grand job of entertaining all of us—takes your thoughts off the war. Local base personnel guard the ship at night but it's required that a member of the crew also be present. I was selected and slept out by our ship under a wing. The ship looks like a giant grasshopper silhouetted against the sky. Negro guards were all around. The night was uneventful but I was glad when the sun came up. Didn't sleep too well.

SATURDAY, MARCH 6, 1943

Left Accra early this morning and headed for Maiduguri, Nigeria some 1,000 miles distant. It's located in northern Nigeria near Lake Chad. Flying at about 800 to 1,000 feet, we passed over numerous native villages and also quite a stretch of the northern part of the jungle. Many, many herds of wild animals dashing through the jungle. The noise from our engines start them dashing every which way—quite a sight. Landed about 3:30 P.M. Certainly doesn't look like much of a place. There is a British section and an American section. What a surprise we all had—like stepping into the Waldorf Astoria dining room— beautiful. Certainly made one think of the good old USA. We had fantastic sleeping quarters. We strolled over to the British compound for a movie. It's apparent the two camps don't get along too well. The American PX had good old US beer and nice and cold, too. The PX was like a club room. The war seemed so far away. It cooled off considerably at night—had to wear our jackets. This place certainly is an oasis in the heart of the desert. For the personnel stationed here, not a bad way to live out the war.

Native drawing water out of well as they did for hundreds of years—near Lake Chad by Maidurqui in Nigeria, Africa—life was primitive.

Linderman and Fisher in dugout canoes at Lake Chad in Africa. Notice guns handy just in case.

SUNDAY, MARCH 7, 1943

The crew was up at 3:30 P.M. Had a great breakfast—eggs, bacon, toast, hashbrowns—almost like the last meal for the condemned. We rushed out to the ship for our next leg of the journey. Number 3 engine was running too rough during the pre-flight procedure so it was decided to spend another day here while ground crews worked on the engine. After lunch, some of the crew went out to Lake Chad and arranged for a ride in a native dugout canoe. Also took some very interesting photos. Native women are very scantily dressed—most walk around with exposed boobs—some not too bad—one catches himself staring now and then. The men also have cover but most children run around in their birthday suits, totally naked. Their method of farming or tilling the soil is most primitive. Later, some of us went to the show at the PX and saw the movie, "Star Spangled Rhythm." Several of the crew mixed it up a little with the base personnel playing poker.

Dress was very scant. Sometimes nothing but birth suits. Men dressed very brief. Notice grass huts. Many near Lake Chad.

MONDAY, MARCH 8, 1943

Seems we're always getting up at the crack of dawn. Ate and rushed out to the 24 and headed for Khartoum, Anglo Egyptian Sudan, around 1,400 miles distant. Most of the flight was over sandy, rocky desert land. All of our canteens are filled with water just in case something goes wrong. Each passing day brings us closer and closer to the field of operations. Angle Egyptian Sudan seems to be nothing but a vast land of rock and sand. We are approaching the Great French Sahara Desert—sand dunes and more sand dunes. We're flying at about 2,000 feet. Had to climb over 10,000 feet to get over a ridge of mountains. I didn't realize there were high mountains in this part of Africa. We used Oxygen for the first time since leaving the States. It didn't bother me and I was very relieved—that's for sure. Khartoum is on the banks of the Nile River—very picturesque. Landed around 3:00 P.M. and preparations were immediately under way to get the ship ready for take-off in the morning for Cairo, Egypt. After a relaxing dinner in the Mess Hall, saw an outside movie with Bing Crosby, "White Christmas". Certainly put the crew in a very sad mood. All of us were thinking of home and family and what the weeks ahead might have in store for us. After I walked down to the Nile and sat there for over an hour, just wondering about these weeks ahead.

TUESDAY, MARCH 9, 1943

Leaving clouds of dust behind us, we rolled down the sand runways of Khartoum and headed north for Cairo, over 1,000 miles away. We flew up the Nile which cuts like a knife through the desert. All around and near the Nile because of very crude irrigation methods, it's very green and looks beautiful. Many sailboats, almost like huge barges traveling up and down the Nile. I'd guess 95% of the land area is barren sand.

We opened our orders a little early and we're assigned to the 9th Air Base, 376th Bomb Group currently operating against the Axis forces outside Soluck, Libya. As we approached Cairo, I asked Lear to bring the ship close so some photos could be taken. The Pyramids are awesome. Masterpieces of construction. They completely dominate the area for many miles around. The Sphinx, sitting quietly nearby. You could also see in the distance the Step Pyramid of Sakara, reported to be the oldest Egyptian pyramid. Again, immediately upon landing at Cairo, the ship was readied for take-off in the morning. You could literally feel the excitement among our crew members. Also a growing feeling of apprehension—almost a fear of the unknown. Haven't heard anything regarding Fisher and Keller. Thought maybe at the base they could give us an update on them.

The crew went to bed early. Would have liked to have gone into Cairo—maybe I'll get a chance to do this later. From now on, it's mess kits, etc. Drew two extra blankets because it really cools down in the desert at night. One can't help but wonder more and more what the future holds for all of us. It's hard to believe all of this is happening to me.

WEDNESDAY, MARCH 10, 1943

Up and at 'em early, filled with great expectancy. Left Cairo early this morning and headed west to Soluck, Libya about 50 miles south of Bengasi. Headquarters of the 376th Bomb Group. Don't know yet as to which Squadron we'll be assigned. As we circled Cairo, a hugh field of wrecked planes came into view filled with both German and English planes, many smashed tanks and trucks and all sorts of field cannon—a grim testimony as to the destructiveness of war. We flew west at about 1,000 feet off the desert. As far as the eye could see was mile after mile of wrecked trucks, aircraft, tanks—all strewn over the desert and all within a few miles of the Mediterranean Sea. Fox holes and shell hoes dot the desert like huge craters on the moon. It's certainly a saga of the desert written in destruction and death. Makes one think deeper as to the future.

We landed early afternoon at Soluck and immediately were taken to the Mess Hall for lunch. The ground crew was sure eager to see what "goodies" we had brought with us. We posted a guard at the ship so nobody could walk off with our treasures— candy, cigars, etc.—some of them hadn't had a candy bar for months. Haven't even seen any magazines.

We've been assigned to the 513th Squadron. As soon as we unloaded our ship, it was taken from us and assigned to another squadron. Wonder if we'll ever see her again. You certainly become attached to that bag of bolts.

Large scorpions in the African Desert were dangerous and deadly. The G.I.'s made jokes of their size.

The officers were assigned tents in the officer's area and the enlisted men of the crew to an area nearby. It's hot—windy. They tell me the wind blows all the time. The desert is continuously moving—wind—blowing dust and sand—sand flies— fleas—lizards and scorpians—millions of flies. This has to be the jumping-off place. The only light is candle light. After getting everything unpacked, cots set up and bunks made, we all went to sleep. Our first night in the war—the Bomber front line.

The train depot, pictured above, is evidence of the battle damage of Soluck. The town, and all 40 miles of track to Bengasi, were in ruins. No trains ran for months.

THURSDAY, MARCH 11, 1943

Woke early this morning—very cold out—my hands and fingers were swollen badly due to some insect bite or a rash of some kind. Went immediately to the medical tent and they gave me several shots in the arm. Wrecked, burned out tanks from both sides are all over the area as are crashed and damaged aircraft. We're about forty miles south of Bengasi at a little town called Soluck. It's almost in ruins from attack from first the German "Afrika Corps" and then the British 8th Army retaking the area. This procedure went back and forth time and time again. The wind blows constantly and the blowing sand and dust is terrible—water for drinking and bathing is very scarce. We draw our water from a lister bag outside in the sun and heat near squadron headquarters—about a helmet a week for bathing. Most of the food at the mess tent is canned and it is not too bad. You have to eat it—there is no restaurant nearby to go to. There is no electricity for lights, etc. We use candles and get them from squadron supply. There are plenty reminders around that you are in the war zone and the comforts of home are just something you dream about. It's plenty rough and that's for sure. Terrifically hot in the daytime—wind—dust—sand—millions of flies—sand fleas—lizards and scorpions—freezing cold at night—crowded tent conditions with all five enlisted men crowded into the same tent—hardly space to move around—somehow we'll all adjust. We divided up the survival package in the aircraft. I still think the officers gave us the short end. Good canned food—great variety, etc. Spent most of the day getting acquainted with nearby tent groups...ground personnel and certainly 513th Squadron Headquarters. Will expand the area trips to familiarize myself with the whole area—Group Headquarters—the 514th—515th and the 512th areas—also what's left of the town, Soluck.

Mess tent for all of the 513th squadron. The flies really got the best deal. They never had it so good. Boxes of canned food are stored next to mess tent.

Fresh water at Soluck was very scarce to the point of being rationed—Byers bathing with helmet full of water—once a week event.

Unidentified flier taking a crap in the crudely constructed facilities outside
(good view of area) at Soluck.

FRIDAY, MARCH 12, 1943

Again, was up early. The pain in my hands and fingers is considerably worse—fingers like big hot dogs—skin stretched tight—hard to write in the diary. After breakfast went again to field hospital. Am breaking out all over the chest and back with a rash. The doctors don't have any idea at this point what's causing the swelling and the rash. They are thinking of sending me to the 15th General Field Hospital in Cairo. Hope this can all be resolved as I don't want to miss any of the phasing in of our crew to the 513th Squadron. We've been moved to a new tent today—at least they know we're here. Some of the tents nearby are sandbagged just in case the "Jerries" come over from Crete and Greece or from the boot of Italy. We are going to do likewise. They also recommend that we dig slit trenches adjacent to the tent for bombing protection. Land mines are still all around the area and Headquarters forbids any traveling around the area until all the mines can be located and defused by special British squads. Several of the British troops have already been killed by them. The word is, "don't pick up anything if you value your life!" General conditions on a day-to-day basis is tough. Talking with some of the other crews that have a few missions under their belts is, "It's plenty rough." The fighters—ME-109's—FW-190's and Machie 202's (the first two are German and the third is Italian). The fighters you can fight back, but the Ack-Ack is just plain hell to sweat out.

SATURDAY, MARCH 13, 1943

The swelling has gone down some but the rash is still there. Am still getting shots at the hospital tent. Am feeling no great pain at present, so hopefully all will pass away. A squadron of twelve B-24's left to bomb Italy at noon today. Some of the crews we've just met were in on the mission. We laid around all day—played cards and checkers. Our bombers were met at Bengasi by two squadrons from the 98th—the other group comprising the

9th Air Force. The sky over the target area was 100% overcast—all the ships returned home with their bomb loads. They reported Ack-Ack was quite heavy but not too accurate. All ships returned safely. The mission went to Naples. The bombers were after the shipping in the harbor.

SUNDAY, MARCH 14, 1943

Went again to the base hospital. Everything seems to be returning to normal. Am considerably better. We all worked around the tent today getting everything in shape. Hopefully making daily living conditions more convenient and comfortable for all of us—if that's possible. Got acquainted with a few more of the crews. Don't know what's happened to our ship, "Patches"—which squadron she's been assigned to—would like to keep track of her combat record—after all, she did bring us this far. Played a few cards—everything seems to come to a halt when the sun sets. Candles don't light up the tent area too good. So we all retired early—as do the lizards and the scorpions. They usually look for protective cover for the cold desert nights.

MONDAY, MARCH 15, 1943

General Jimmy Doolittle arrived today and things should begin in a big way directly. More combat crews arriving on a daily basis as are ground personnel. Seems to me that something big could shortly be in the making. Our crew is anxious to go through the combat training procedures. So far, nothing has been scheduled. This afternoon I was briefed on combat radio procedures during a mission—also emergency procedures if difficulties arise—ship problems with engines, etc.—dead and wounded aboard. Our crew should be scheduled for a mission very soon. The crew will be broken and fly with more experienced crews till all of us have had some combat experience. Then together to fight it out against the "Krauts" and the "Ities". Seems almost like a strange adventure story. Haven't heard anything yet as to the well being of Keller and Fisher. Hope they make it back soon so the crew can all be together again. Certainly miss my lovely wife, Anne. Seems we've been apart for months already. I hope and pray we'll all make it through this mess. Our deal seems to be if you survive 300 hours of combat (completed missions) you'll be returned to the Zone of the Interior (United States). That could be 30 to 40 missions. Seems like an impossible goal to achieve. One cannot help but ponder over how one will react under fire. The fighters trying to shoot you down—the flak bursting all around your ship—the frightfully cold temperatures—certainly nobody wants to be killed. The job has to be done. I'm confident all our crew will pass the test with flying colors—I pray to God we will.

TUESDAY, MARCH 16, 1943

There isn't much of anything cooking today. The whole group seems to be going through a complete reorganization. New crews and ships arriving daily. Several practice missions are going on daily with the newly arrived crews and P-40 fighters keep buzzing all around the formations to get the crew used to enemy fighter conditions. It gives the gunners practice on trailing the fighters with their 50-caliber machine guns and also the turrets. We should be participating soon.

WEDNESDAY, MARCH 17, 1943

Hooray! We're scheduled for a practice training session mission today. We're all excited but at the last minute, it was called off. No reason given. Also, a real mission to Italy was cancelled because of overcast, clouded conditions over the target area. The food here under the conditions is fair, but it gets damn tiresome eating the same stuff three times a day, day in and day out with no variety. Seems to be a lot of messing around and poor organization here. Hopefully things will improve. Anne and I have been married a month—seems we've been apart for a year.

THURSDAY, MARCH 18, 1943

Wind—sand—dust—almost drives a man crazy. Again nothing developing. It's almost as if we weren't here. They just seem to ignore us. We're restricted to this area because of land mines, etc. Can't walk anyplace—not even to Soluck. We laid around all day—played cards. Haven't even got any reading material. Big news—they took Soluck off limits. Holbrook, Linderman and I walked to Soluck. It's practically all in ruins. A few of the inhabitants have returned. A pathetic looking group. One cannot help but feel sorry for them—especially the small children. They certainly don't comprehend what this is all about. They all looked very hungry. They just stood there and stared at us. It started to rain. We all headed back to the tent area. I'm sure we'll be back with some food for the kids. The flies are around everything. Seems like millions of them.

The "noseless wonder of Soluch"—it was reported the Germans cut her nose off because she wouldn't leave Soluch—she apparently took care of some of the troops.

FRIDAY, MARCH 19, 1943

The rain came in cloudbursts all night long. We didn't have our tent sidings ditched to keep the water from running in and out through the tent area. We almost floated away. Had to take everything off the ground stored under the cots and place all on our beds—sleep was almost impossible—mud all over. Everything is a mess—wet and damp. It rained off and on all day. Guess it's the beginning of the rainy season. The rain bogs down the bombers. The runways are bulldozed out of the sandy rock areas and when wet, can't support the heavy bombers. Nothing to do but play cards. Thank God somebody had to foresight to bring cards! Called it a day early.

SATURDAY, MARCH 20, 1943

Early this morning the sun finally came out after a miserable night of rain and cold weather. We didn't move around too much—mud all over everything. Just went to the mess tent and that's it. Played cards most of the day. Bombers are bogged down in the dispersal areas. Ground crews are doing some maintenance whenever the rain allows them to do so. The rumor is floating around that two of the squadrons will soon be moving. Bengasi has been named as the new location on the shores of the Mediterranean. We're really catching up on our sleep. Too bad we can't store it for when we're flying missions.

SUNDAY, MARCH 21, 1943

It's Sunday, but no Mass to go to if you're of the Catholic faith. Gekas and I are the only Catholics on the crew. The priest has so many places to go to holding services and says he'll be with our group later on in the week. The sun finally broke through. Everything dries out in a hurry as the sun is very penetrating. Some of us got together and played softball. At least it's something to do. Also played cards again. The dope is we're scheduled for a midnight mission tomorrow night. Haven't been told yet where or any of the briefing information. All retired early.

MONDAY, MARCH 22, 1943

We're sweating out a midnight mission some place over Italy. Scheduled to go over target about 4:00 or 5:00 in the morning. A great many thoughts go through your mind while waiting for a mission to go—especially if it's your first go at this business of kill or be killed. We're getting together our flying clothes, boots, oxygen mask, etc. The report just reached us that a large convoy of British troops was bombed and strafed enroute to Bengasi yesterday. Must have been far to the east as we saw and heard nothing. No other details. The Krauts probably came from Crete. Our mission was finally cancelled because of bad weather over Italy. Good news—Keller finally joined us. He looks great. We all shifted our cots around and made room for him. Had a long talk, all the enlisted men, about home and combat. Squadron headquarters just advised us a mission is scheduled for early morning and we should have all our equipment ready to go on a few minutes notice. With that, we all called it a night.

TUESDAY, MARCH 23, 1943

Early this morning a squadron orderly advised us that a mission was in order and that we should be ready to leave in a hurry. Twenty-four ships from the 376th were scheduled to leave. I can't believe we're going on a mission and at this point haven't ever fired a 50-caliber machine gun. Haven't been on any practice runs. Had to rush over to a radio briefing—rushed out to the ship with all the gear and tried to clean my waist window 50-caliber gun. The whole crew was rushing around like mad. Lear and MacDonald to briefings—securing our place in the formation. Gregg to a navigational briefing and Gekas to a bombadier's session. We've been assigned an old beat-up ship called "Lorraine"—serial number 111591. Seems the new crews get the beat-up ships and the crews with the most hours of combat get the newest 24's. Maybe that's the way it should be. If you survive a few missions in the old beat-up ships, your chances for survival have to get

22

better. Makes one feel better just writing that. The ground crew wished us all good luck. Said the ship was in good condition. We're dropping nine 500-pounders—and demolition bombs. The harbor of Messina, Sicily is the target— shipping in harbor. Messina is directly across from Italy. All German Army in Sicily. We're also throwing out the waist windows thousands of leaflets telling the people to leave as we're coming back again and again. Seems to me it also tells the Germans to move in more 88-mm and 90-mm Ack-Ack guns. I guess it's also a way of clearing our consciences. At least, we've told them to leave. Many civilians are certain to be killed.

500 pounders exploding in the water near Bay of Messina, Sicily. Note the shape of the harbor. Most of German shipping from Italy was unloaded here. We were after the shipping.

We finally got the green light to start the engines and taxi into position for takeoff. We all shake hands with each other and get into position. About 9:45 A.M. we take off. Get into our specific flight and head for Messina. We began to climb immediately and at 10,000 feet, put on oxygen masks. Lear tells us to test fire our guns—one at a time—firing and reporting OK back to him. All is OK. We reach our altitude of 25,000 feet. The temperature is right at 50 degrees below zero. We're cruising about 180 miles per hour. The wind by the waist windows is frighteningly cold and the noise of the 1300 horsepower engines is deafening. We all check our intercom systems. The whole crew was sweating it out. It seems we caught them by surprise as no fighters came up to intercept us. They did fire lots of Ack-Ack shells at the formation, but it didn't seem too accurate—either too high or way too low to do any damage.

When a huge Ack-Ack shell explodes, it creates a ball of black smoke 30 yards across. When you can hear them explode over the noise of the engines, they will do damage to the ship or the personnel of the ship. We dropped our bombs, threw out the leaflets and headed for Soluck. Huge fires could be seen and great columns of black smoke rose skyward as many fires were started on the docks and rail centers. The mission lasted 7 hours. The crew learned a lot on this, our first mission. We all thanked God we had made it there and back. All ships returned safely. The 98th Group also participated in the mission. It was the 18th mission for the ship "Lorraine". The ground crew immediately started checking over the ship. We were taken to the debriefing area and also were checked over by the squadron doctors. Then the debriefing session begins. The entire crew is asked questions concerning the mission, etc. Was very tired. Went to bed and slept it all off.

WEDNESDAY, MARCH 24, 1943

The crew had a practice mission this morning at extremely low levels out over the vast wastes of the desert. Once in a while we'd see a nomad group—very crude animal skin tents—a few camels around. The engine noise would scare them half to death. Nomads and camels running in every direction. Two other aircraft were in formation with us. We were only in the air a little over an hour. Laid around—played a little catch with the crew. The big push is on in Tunisia and we probably will be involved reference to bombing the German shipping. Finally got some mail from home and it certainly was most welcome. A touch of home. They just informed us we're allowed two cans of beer a week. Some of the crew don't drink, so I'm taking their allotment. Can't get them cold, but we try. We put the cans in a slit trench and cover them over with sand. Not too good, but not bad either. We've been away from the good old U.S. a month—seems like years.

THURSDAY, MARCH 25, 1943

Had another practice session today—four ships in the diamond formation—again at low altitudes over the desert for about an hour and a half. In the afternoon, another practice mission with four ships—this time at high altitudes. Had to wear the heavy and clumsy flying suits and also used oxygen. Checked the squadron bulletin board. The real thing is scheduled for tomorrow and we're going. The dope is, we're going to raise hell with Rommel at Tunisia with low altitude formation bombing. Sounds very exciting. Could be disastrous also. Pretty difficult to maneuver a 30-ton B-24 at low altitudes. Got my first letter from Anne today—was so happy to hear from her and to know they arrived back safely in Hibbing, Minnesota. The crew is tired. It's been a busy flying day. We all turned in early as we anticipate a very busy day tomorrow.

FRIDAY, MARCH 26, 1943

Only have to survive 293 more hours of flying combat. They officially allowed us 7 hours for the last mission. The takeoff time has not been posted as yet. Have been to the radio briefing. We're on a standby alert. Did find out we're in the "Purple Heart" flight. That's the last formation of ships to go over the target. Usually the attacking fighters hit these ships first. We're flying "Lorraine" again. Ground crew says she's ready to go and we should have no mechanical problems. Sweating out these missions once they've been posted is a little on the rough side. There's some talk of it going to Naples, Italy. We'd be after shipping in the harbor. We've sweated this mission out all day and still nothing cooking. The latest is a daylight raid in the early hours of tomorrow. Played cards and catch while waiting. The doctors won't let Holbrook go on this mission. Froze his hands quite badly while on the last mission. His 50-caliber gun froze and he took his heavy gloves off trying to get the mechanism functional. Too much grease left on the moving parts. Don't think he'll lose any fingers—awfully painful, though. He was ready to go anyway. Was just told to be ready first thing in the morning. Sweating the mission out tires you out mentally. We all hit the sack early.

SATURDAY, MARCH 27. 1943

Nothing has been posted relative to the mission today. They say weather bad over target. Heavy cloud cover. Went to a lecture on escape procedures in case you get shot down over enemy territory. Berardi of squadron headquarters can speak Italian. He's a great guy—teaches the enlisted men of our crew to say in Italian, "how can we escape from here?" Also, "take me to your leader." Attended a session on aerial photography. One of the two waist gunners will use the camera when it's scheduled for our ship—very interesting.

Good news—got a quart of beer at the PX today. Also a chocolate bar and pipe tobacco, "Velvet." Have taken some good pictures around Soluck—hope they turn out OK. All of us would be very thankful if this mess was over. I keep telling myself I'll make it OK. It's the other fellow that's going to get it. Still hard to believe they're shooting real bullets at us and we likewise. Hell, I don't even know these people (enemy). Sat around and drank my warm beer and enjoyed smoking a cigar.

SUNDAY, MARCH 28, 1943

They got us out of the sack early. The notice has finally been posted on the mission. It's going to Catania, Sicily—just south of Messina. Big harbor area with lots of shipping coming and going. No definite time posted. All crews scheduled—just standby and be ready when called. They finally cancelled the mission for today. Was actually disappointed but greatly relieved. Took a bath in my helmet. Water is scarce but it sure felt good. We all went out to the ship, "Lorraine" to check over guns, etc. Squadron headquarters says the mission will go tomorrow for sure and it'll be a day raid. The group apparently likes to schedule 'dusk' missions—hit the target just as the sun goes down and return at a pre-determined altitudes. Such as our ship at 18,500 feet; another at 18,000 feet; another at 17,500 feet, etc. No mail today.

MONDAY, MARCH 29, 1943

Had breakfast and rushed around like mad getting things ready to go and at the last minute the mission was cancelled. Guess the weather over the target area was 100% clouded over. The raid was to go to Naples, Italy, the general target area right now the hottest spot in all of Italy. Heavy troop and war supply movements. Old "Lorraine" is loaded with 500-pounders. some of the new ships can handle 12 of them. In "Lorraine" we have to carry two bomb bay tanks with gas to make it there and back. Hopefully the raid will go tomorrow. Early this afternoon, three ships took off for Malta where they will spend the night. Immediately upon landing, they will be loaded with 1000-pounders. The next morning early, their bombing destination is to be Messina—the harbor docks and submarine pens. The 1000-pounders will have delayed action fuses as the three bombers will be coming in at 50 to 100 feet off the ground level. Apparently, they are to finish the job reference to the mission we were on March 23rd. The squadron called for volunteers. It's a "Purple Heart", "Distinguished Flying Cross Medal" raid. The strategy is to catch them by surprise, drop the 1000-pounders, go back into the cloud cover for protection, and head back to Malta. Major Appold of the 514th Squadron led the ships. The bombs were dropped—the mission successful and all returned to Soluck. I hope this low level bombing isn't the pattern for future missions. Your chances of survival are cut in half—or worse.

Combat crews looking over Italian maps while briefing officer pin points target—indicates flight route to and from target assigns flight formation altitudes.

TUESDAY, MARCH 30, 1943

Just returned from squadron operations and we're scheduled for a mission briefing at 11:00 A.M. Takeoff should be early afternoon. Again, everybody rushing around getting all the necessary items together. The weather is good. Hope it's that way over the target area. We've certainly sweated this raid out a long time, and that sometimes begins to wear on you. The three B-24's that bombed Messina just arrived back and received the applause and congratulations of the entire 376th group. They should all receive a medal for the achievement. Again, everybody all set to go. Again, at the last minute the mission was terminated. Sure beats the hell out of me WHY the on-again, off-again games goes on day after day. We take our weather information from the British. Also, the majority of our target selections comes from their network of spies and communications personnel placed in strategic locations in Italy and Sicily. Seems to me it could be a little more accurate. I used to think the Air Corps could win this war—save a lot of lives—but now, sometimes, I wonder.

Because it's almost impossible to properly wash and take care of your hair, we all decided to have our heads close cut— just left a little stubble there. Sat around the tent and just talked. Conversation all gets back to who is going to survive the mess. Certainly nobody thinks he will get killed. It's always the other fellow. Maybe the mission will be re-scheduled tomorrow—we hope so.

WEDNESDAY, MARCH 31, 1943

Rose early—same breakfast—pancakes, dried scrambled eggs, and terrible coffee! Went again to squadron headquarters. Again the raid is posted. Nobody gets excited anymore. A short time later, it was again postponed. No reason given. One has to assume it's the cloud cover over the target areas. You'd think some place, somewhere, these bombers could go and do some damage to the German war effort.

British Bullfighters buzzed the field again—really smooth looking aircraft. The base S-2 officers are beginning to suspect some of the Wogs (Arabs) of being German and Italian spies and steps are being taken to keep them in a concentrated area. Many of them speak excellent English, German and Italian. Bought some English tobacco at the PX but it hasn't the flavor or the taste that U.S. pipe tobacco has. I can see why the British troops prefer American tobacco.

Keller has gotten sick again. Don't know how serious it is as yet. Have just been informed we have to stand full dress retreat tonight. The whole group is pissed off. Received several letters from my mother and also from Anne. It's like a visit home—was so glad to receive them. Takes your mind off this mess. Everything is at a standstill. Nothing cooking. It's windy, dusty and cold out. The morale of the troops could be a little better. Boy, it's quite an experience to take a crap here. Long six-foot deep slit trenches. You just straddle it and hope all comes out OK. Usually there are two or three others seeking some degree of relief. So while squatting there, you discuss the weather, the war, and anything else that comes to your mind. We call it the "Palm Room."

Need to secure more candles from squadron headquarters. It really gets cold at night.

Byers with full high altitude flying gear—with parachute and oxygen mask—the outfit restricted movement but necessary to survive at extreme cold temperatures at high altitudes.

APRIL—1943

THURSDAY, APRIL 1, 1943

Sure wish I could fool myself all the way back to the good old USA. Guess there is a briefing in a few minutes, reference to the new target. Holbrook, Linderman and I are going to squadron headquarters to get the dope. Keller is going to the main group hospital located in Bengasi—for his sake, we hope it's nothing serious. Don't know at this point who will be assigned to our crew as tailgunner. The weather is awfully damp in the mornings—chilly, too. Within a few hours, the sun heats everything up and the desert heat is terrific—almost unbearable. You could fry an egg on the top wing surface of the bombers. As has been the procedure, it's all called off again. Wonder why all the delay? The ships are just sitting there collecting dust when we could be hammering away at the enemy targets. Went to Mass this afternoon which was held in the back of the squadron tent at 4:30 P.M. A person's mind is carried away and is mentally at ease from all this destruction. We sang a few hymns and the Chaplain stated that Mass would be every Thursday from now on.

Got paid today. Will send some to Anne for when, and if, we return to the U.S. after mission completion. Retired early.

FRIDAY, APRIL 2, 1943

It's the same old broken record—another mission is scheduled. Don't know where the target is as yet or any of the details. We're alerted. Had a radio briefing and lunch. We're taking off soon. Going to Palermo, Sicily. Northwest corner of the island. More on the return.

Late Friday night by candlelight. We've just returned. Had the debriefing. Heavy overcast conditions prevented us from dropping our 500-pounders. We were assigned "Lorraine" again— Number 45. Some Ack-Ack—not too accurate. Was fired through the cloud cover. The bad thing about Ack-Ack is you can't fight back—you just stand there by the window with your 50-caliber and watch—and pray. It's at least 50 degrees below zero and the sweat literally runs off your face. Dick Lipps went along as our tailgunner. Worked hard on the radio getting radio fixes. Don't know whether or not we were lost. Fisher's oxygen mask froze and he almost died too before we could get him a 'walk-away' bottle and sent him up front where it's quite warm. The mission took 8 hours. Don't know if we'll get any credit or not because we didn't drop the bombs. When we landed, the ground crew was there to check over the ship and immediately refueled her. The rumor is an early morning mission. Am very tired and most thankful we made it back. The 98th raided the harbor of Naples, Italy. All ships in the 376th returned early.

Crudely constructed tower— mission "take-off" traffic was directed from here—each ship air borne in a pre-determined flight position for the mission.

B-24 passing under our formation enroute the target.

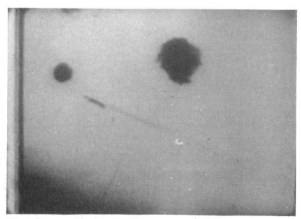

30 yards across black puffs of smoke from exploding heavy Ack Ack shells—the area soon became filled with these black balls of smoke.

They called her an "old lister bag"—"flying coffin",
"hopping grasshopper"—also "bag of bolts" to those of
us who flew in her—she was beautiful—could take
terrific punishment and also dish it out to the enemy-
she took us there (target) and brought us home (base)
there'll always be a warm spot in our hearts for the
liberator.

SATURDAY, APRIL 3, 1943

Yesterday's mission and events deserve a little more space in this diary of events. As we headed north to the boot of Italy, we passed directly over Bengasi and the many months of siege can readily be seen from the air. Practically every building is badly bomb-scarred or in ruins. The only exception is the huge church right near the harbor area—looks as if not a single bomb came even near it—almost a miracle. The great Bengasi harbor is filled with sunken ships and is rendered almost useless. Six or seven big cargo ships have been sunk in strategic places throughout the harbor area. One big one right across the front entrance, closing it off even to small craft. The 98th Group is stationed nearby. They were bombing Naples as we headed for Palermo. Also, the British have a fighter unit here comprised of the famous "Bullfighters."

As we headed out, the Mediterranean was very calm with only an occasional white cap disturbing the blue waters. Several rather large ship convoys were heading west—probably going to Malta. A lot of thoughts go through your mind as you stand by your gun scanning the skies looking for fighters. I still can't believe this is a kill or be killed proposition. It's really destruction on a gigantic scale, almost beyond belief.

A mission is scheduled but doubt if it will materialize. This morning we sweated out the beer line. Got there a little early, so didn't have to wait too long. One quickly develops a keen appreciation for the better things in life— beer, candy, a can of peaches, etc. There is some talk of the Germans beginning to evacuate what they are still holding in Africa.

Finished supper and strolled over to the orderly tent. Rumors are around and plenty of them. The general impression is that we're moving next week to Bengasi. Anything would be an improvement over this hell hole. Bengasi has asphalt hard runways. Weather (rain) would have no effect on takeoffs and landings as it does in Soluck. It's beginning to rain—very damp, penetrating cold. We just bought 30 ekas (eggs) from the Wogs (Arabs) and are boiling them. What a celebration—warm beer and hard boiled eggs. Lear, the crew pilot, is just celebrating the news—his wife just gave birth to a nine-pound baby boy. Went and got Keller's beer rations as he's in the Bengasi field hospital and I didn't want them to go to waste. Will retire early tonight. Tried writing a few letters home—not too easy by candlelight. They really censor what you write home—nothing of a military nature at all. More on censorship later.

SUNDAY, APRIL 4, 1943

Really cold and damp today. Had the same old breakfast— rubber pancakes and burnt toast. Got a can of Velvet at the PX and a can of peaches that were canned in British Malaya even before the Japs took over. Laid around all morning in the tent. No electricity. Can't even listen to a radio. I strolled over for lunch and was informed a mission was going off at 1:30 P.M. Have already missed the radio briefing held at 11:30 A.M. Ate a quick lunch and rushed over to the radio tent and got what information I felt was needed for the encounter. Rushed back to the tent and got the flying clothes—parachute, oxygen mask, etc., together. We are leaving in a few minutes for Naples, Italy—harbor installations. We're assigned "Lorraine" again, Number 11591. This will be her 20th mission. She badly needs a going over—is in terrible shape. We had her to Palermo and Messina.

I don't know quite how to finish this—so much happened on the way to the target. Eight ships of a flight of 24 turned back because of engine trouble and returned to base. You're at high altitude, using oxygen for at least six hours on the Naples run. We test fired the guns at about 15,000 feet. The 'boot' of Italy is an interesting picture. On one side, the Adriatic Sea and on the other, the Tyrrhenian Sea. The temperature was at least 50 degrees to 65 degrees below zero. Fisher's oxygen mask froze first. He took a walk-away bottle and went up to the flight deck to defrost the mask and return to his hand-operated belly

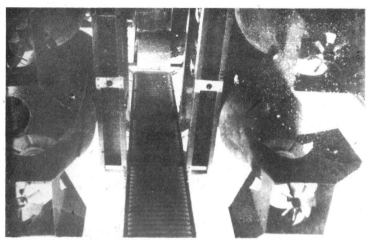

500 pounders in B-24 bomber bomb bays. Notice how narrow the "cat walk" is from flight deck to rear of ship where waist gunners are positioned.

gun. A few seconds later, Holbrook's mask froze and started him off to the flight deck with another walk-away bottle. He was to immediately fix his mask and return to man the other waist 50-caliber. Our altitude is right at 20,000 feet. The indicator on the bottle registered 'full' but it proved to be almost empty. He (Holbrook) collapsed in the catwalk and was hung up between the catwalk bracing with 500-pounders hanging on both sides. Called Lear on the intercom and advised him of the situation. Called Gekas, the Bombadier, and told him if the bomb bay doors are opened now, Holbrook would be sucked out of the ship and gone. Took several deep breaths of oxygen—tore off the mask and rushed out into the catwalk to get him. Dragged him back by the waist window and immediately began to revive him. He was already unconscious. His face was the color of purple ink and his mouth was closed so tightly on the walk-away tube, I had to tear the rubber in two to get it out. By prying open his mouth, I inserted another tube from the main line but he bit on it so hard, no oxygen would flow through. Finally forced a piece of wood in his mouth to keep it open. A few seconds later his eyes opened and he was coming around. In the freezing cold, got his mask operational and got him back in fighting shape. We were about five minutes from the target. While all this was going on, Lear peeled off and dropped to 10,000 feet and we were headed for home (Soluck).

Naples harbor could be seen in the distance even with darkening skies. Italy is very mountainous—roads wind in an About making an interesting pattern from the air. A smoking volcano could be seen from one of the many islands that surround Italy. Islands are so numerous, they are not even on the maps.

As we again were passing over the 'boot' of Italy, enemy search lights were hunting us and Ack-Ack shells were bursting so close you could hear the explosions above the noise of the engines. The shrapnel bangs into the fuselage and the expended pieces hitting the wings and fuselage like giant hailstones. It looked pretty bad for us for a while. The sweat runs off your face. You can read a newspaper at 10,000 feet from these searchlights. The Krauts try to intersect us between two lights. Then they close the big 88 MM or 90 MM Ack-Ack guns on the ship in the cross. Cloudy conditions allowed us to escape their closing in on us. We would maneuver the ship—lose 1,000 feet— then gain 2,000 feet while turning right and left. In a matter of seconds it could have all been over. You live a lifetime in a matter of a few moments.

Holbrook and I stood by the guns as we expected night fighters to come up and do battle. The searchlights are scanning the skies looking for us. The night fighters never came, but you constantly search the skies until you are beyond their reach. You almost fire a few rounds at the stars. You'll swear to one another that you saw something moving out there. Everyone is plenty nervous. Personally, the sky isn't big enough when one ship can't see the other. Our superchargers stand out like four big shit houses in the fog. Nothing we can do about that.

The weather going home was extremely rough and stormy. We still have our bombs aboard. They should have been salvoed over Italy—certainly over the Mediterranean. We finally landed with about 1/2 hour of gas left. What if we crash landed? What if the Ack-Ack flattened one of the tires? We could have crashed. Some of the ships returned salvoed theirs. Our ship was ten hours in the air and maybe they won't even give us credit for the mission 'cause we were forced to turn back just short of the target to probably save Holbrook's life. We've plenty to thank the good Lord about. Will be thankful when it's over. Win—lose—or draw. You get so damn *cold* standing by that waist window, hour after hour. Sometimes you reach a point where you really don't care one way or the other.

Another mission is posted—ground crew told us. Am dead tired. Should be ready to take off early in the morning. Went through the debriefing. It's almost 2:00 in the morning. Am writing this by candlelight. The crew is asleep already. had a successful trip as far as the radio goes. Almost froze my face, hands and feet. One ship was seen going down in flames over Naples, a ship called "Lady Be Good." Number 64 from another squadron is also reported missing. Won't have any trouble sleeping the next few hours.

MONDAY, APRIL 5, 1943

The scheduled raid today was immediately cancelled because of cloud conditions over target areas, and also because many of the ships have Ack-Ack holes in them and need repair. Am scheduled to make a flight tomorrow with Colonel Compton, Commander of the 376th. Don't know any of the details. Guess it's to Cairo. Certainly hope we stay a day or two. Got three letters from home today. They are like an oasis in the desert. Just laid around and rested. The moving to Bengasi rumor is still floating around. Everyone retired early. Very cold out.

TUESDAY, APRIL 6, 1943

This morning they posted a mission scheduled for Messina, Sicily. Colonel Compton won't be going to Cairo.

A Major Sukom is taking his place. After checking over everything, we took off about 2:00 P.M. for Heliopolis, an airport just outside of Cairo. We are taking 20 fliers that have completed their hours and missions and are on their way to the Zone of the Interior—the good old United States. Boy! Do I ever envy them! For them, it's over. They've survived the mission ordeal—lucky bastards. We're then taking the ship to Deveswal for repairs throughout and flying one back that has been repaired and ready for combat. We're staying overnight in Cairo at the Grand Hotel which has been taken over by the U.S. for R & R purposes. The main runway at Heliopolis is very rough and composed of hard desert rock. The runways are literally lined on both sides with wrecked aircraft that have been hauled in from the desert war. Nearby, we caught sight of what resembled a street car—statues of lions are all over—most apartments have balconies. It was an interesting ride into Cairo. Many horse drawn wagons in use— traffic was heavy. You'd certainly never guess there is a war going on. Checked into the Grand Hotel and rushed over to the American Bar. Joe (Flight Engineer) and I had a few cold beers— such a delightful experience—then to bed.

WEDNESDAY, APRIL 7, 1943

Early this morning, Joe and I were up early. Had a tasty breakfast. We had until noon to see all of Cairo—which is impossible. Walked around Cairo for a while and then took a cab. Also hired a guide and we were off to the pyramids and the Sphinx. Went through the temples and tombs—rode camels and horses around the pyramids which are absolutely awesome—over 400 feet high and cover over 13 acres of ground. Was in the tomb of the Prime Minister to King Faruk—saw his coffin and his mummified remains—had photos taken and took plenty myself. We hurried back to the hotel and rushed out to the Heliopolis airport. Major Sukom was waiting for us and advised that we'll be staying another day. We immediately return to the Grand Hotel and check in—go by cab to the Sheppard Hotel—it's referred to as the "Crossroads of the World"—the gathering place of diplomats and generals from the world over. Relaxed at the sidewalk cafe and watched the passing parade. Cairo is a surging mass of moving humanity. The kids are all over begging for money. You can't help but feel sorry for them. Had a great dinner with wine, then a show and back to the Grand.

THURSDAY, APRIL 8, 1943

Joe and I were at the Heliopolis airport early and met Major Sukom. We immediately took off and headed for Deversaur north of Cairo. Upon landing, we were advised that the B-24 we were to take back wasn't ready yet. They flew us back to Cairo in a DC transport. The ship was outfitted and used by generals— beautifully done inside with carpeting, swivel chairs, etc. Sukom advised us after landing that we had 3-day passes. We immediately check back in to the Grand Hotel. Borrowed $40.00 from the Major and also tapped Joe for a $20.00. Went again to the American Bar overlooking a huge square. It was most interesting to sit in the roof garden and just drink a few cold beers and watch the passing parade. We saw the King of Egypt, King Farouk, and the English Ambassador at a command performance given for the English relief (Eighth Army). Walked around Cairo for awhile. Wandered over into the old section. You could get lost there and they'd probably never find you. Finally took a cab back to the hotel.

FRIDAY, APRIL 9, 1943

Joe and I hired our own personal guide and rented a horse-drawn cab and off we three went to see Cairo and take pictures. Told the guide to take us to all the places that he would recommend we see—spare no expense. We had the Egyptian money sticking out of all our pockets.

We visited the Citadel, the Alabaster Mosque of Mohammed Ali, the Sultan Hassan Mosque, "Mousky" and visited the oriental bazaars. The guide could speak English and we became good friends. We treated him as one of us. When we ate, he ate with us and when we drank, booze or a beer, he had one with us. Again took lots of photos. The guide took us to places the average tourist wouldn't see. These mosques are fantastic structures—beautiful inside. Had to take our shoes off to get inside. After a busy, fascinating day, Joe and I had a few beers, saw a show "Billy the Kid" and also "Sun Valley Serenade." Certainly am getting very lonesome for Anne. Wish she could be here and enjoy all this with me.

SATURDAY, APRIL 10, 1943

What a spectacular day—our personal guide took us to places of interest—the Grand Palace of King of Egypt, King Farouk. Couldn't go through the palace, but did get to see his personal band perform and the changing of the Palace Guards. Such splendor in a land where the majority of the people live in utter poverty. There is no middle class—only very rich or very poor. It happens to be the King's birthday. He certainly is a fat one. Rode over to the Nile and took a boat trip down the Nile to the Delta Barrages—The Gardens and Museum. Soldiers from all of the allied world were on board—African troops, Indian troops, Australians, British—guess Joe and I were the only Americans on board. This was a YMCA sponsored trip. The Nile by Cairo is very wide and extremely picturesque. High sailing vessels that haven't changed greatly for several thousand years. A few houseboats dot her shores and many native villages dot her banks. Haven't changed much in thousands of years. Very primitive. The camel seems to be the workhorse. The natives are very friendly to the American soldier and have a lot of respect for them. We're by far the best dressed and equipped soldiers in the entire world.

For lunch we were served sandwiches and soda water—no cokes—no beer. We rented a couple of old donkeys and rode around the island looking over the Aswan Dam and beautiful gardens. Took pictures and had some taken. The wind was really blowing up a storm—white caps on the Nile and the trip back was rather rough. We had supper at the YMCA, along with our guide. Saw the movie "Always in My Heart". Got pretty lonesome for Anne and wished so that she could be here with me enjoying all the fantastic sights of Egypt. Walked around Cairo. It's got to be the greatest show on earth—just to watch the 'Wogs'. Back to the Grand and to bed.

SUNDAY, APRIL 11, 1943

Left Helpro by transport for Deversaur—stopped at Kabrit and Fayied. These two villages are also aircraft repair depots— American and British. At Devesaur bought a lot of things for the boys—a whole bushel basketfull of goodies. Our B-24 was ready so we immediately left and headed back for Helio and Cairo— seems the Major wanted to give it another go. Personally, would have preferred going direct to Soluck to see how things are going there. Besides, was anxious to get on with the war. While in Cairo, ran into Lt. Dore—he was also staying at the Grand. We had quite a chat. Told me of Lt. Marsh's death by Ack-Ack— also of Sgt. Dunsmore and Lt. Tomilson's deaths. I felt so sorry for them. This mess really kinda gets to you when people you know have already paid the supreme sacrifice.

Went to a British show. Before the movie starts, everyone stands and says, "God Save the King." They showed a short travelogue on Minnesota—another reminder of home and how far away from home we all are. Got very lonesome.

MONDAY, APRIL 12, 1943

We left the Grand Hotel in a pouring down rainstorm. After securing a flight clearance, we headed west and home (Soluck). We cruised along at 180 MPH about 500 feet above the desert. Again, mile after mile of wrecked war equipment—tanks, trucks, aircraft—hundreds of slit trenches all telling a gruesome story of life and death in the desert. After landing at Soluck, we find out the 513th Squadron has moved to Berka Number 2 outside of Bengasi near the shores of the Mediterranean. We had a fast meal at the mess tent—some of the ground troops were still there—then headed for Bengasi. Finally got all my belongings straightened out—what a mess. but was thankful the boys moved all my gear. Was glad to see Keller back from the hospital. The crew thought something had happened to me— supposed to be gone overnight and was away for six days. The boys really liked all the goodies I brought back—candy, booze, Egyptian chocolate, etc. There was a telegram from Mrs. Dunsmore wanting to know all the details of her husband's death. She just received the "Killed in Action" government telegram. Will write her a long, detailed letter. Hopefully, it will console her a little. At least for him it's over.

Building damage was extensive throughout all of Bengasi. Most of the rubble was hauled into the desert. Streets were quite clean.

Our tent is only about 100 yards from the Mediterranean. In the distance can be seen Bengasi— walking distance—war's destruction readily visible—on buildings and sunken ships in the harbor. Barrage balloons are floating over portions of the harbor. British troops man all the Ack-Ack guns around the harbor and bases. The 98th is here and now the 376th. Both groups comprise the 9th Air Force.

Fisher and Linderman cleaning inside of tent area. Notice the bleak surroundings the tent housed the 5 enlisted crew members.

Hundreds of pieces of field artillary left behind by retreating German "Afrika" corp near Bengasi.

Fisher examines wrecked tank near Bengasi.

Bengasi Harbor showing scuttled ships leaving the facility almost useless to the allies for the efficient unloading of war material—bombs, guns, transport, etc.

Snodgrass on deck of partially sunken freighter in harbor facility was almost rendered useless by the sunken freighters.

Beached freighter in Bengasi Harbor. One among many that were sunk in harbor either by shelling or on purpose.

Wrecked transport planes left throughout the Bengasi area—transports played a vital roll in bringing supplies to the front.

TUESDAY, APRIL 13, 1943

Spent most of the day working in a mess hall detail unloading truckloads of canned goods, meats, vegetables, fruits, etc. Was able to stash away a gallon can of tomato juice, canned cubed pineapple, grape juice and grapefruit juice. We lived high on the hog in our tent for several days.

Wrecked aircraft are all around. When the "Afrika Corps" finally left, they moved out in a hurry leaving behind huge ammunition dumps—large quantities of 2,000 pound bombs—they break off the fins. Bombs were still fastened to shipping sleds—stacks of 88 MM and 90 MM cannon and thousands of machine gun bullets. The British warned all of us not to go in the area or to handle any of the shells because many of them could be booby-trapped. We disregarded the warning and moved in taking pictures of crew members lying on top of the 2,000 pounders— holding up the 88 MM and 90 MM shells. British demolition crews are blowing sections of the amo dump. Guess we were lucky— several serious accidents did occur with the British from the German booby-traps.

WEDNESDAY, APRIL 14, 1943

Well, things are returning to normal here in Bengasi. Early this morning a mission was posted—shortly after, it was cancelled. The C.O. called a meeting and advised us on the situation in Tunisia. If Rommel evacuates, he guesses we'll really pound the shipping from Africa to Sicily around the clock—should accumulate a little combat time in that operation. The C.O. also informed us of new air tactics used by the "Jerrys". They now fly (fighters) above our bomber formations and drop bombs to explode on our bombers. They also employ divebombing procedures on our formations, picking out specific sections of the formations. Guess we'll now be getting it from below and above. It's plenty rough and a terrific mental strain. Have just been advised Lear (pilot) is in the hospital. He could be grounded for good. Hope not—he's a great guy and we'd all miss him greatly.

Barrage balloons up all over Bengasi—about 35 of them. We could be attacked from Italy, Crete, Greece. Every now and then the British fire their Ack-Ack guns for practice. Gives you a feeling of security that someone is looking out for you.

Linderman and I went for a swim in the Mediterranean— refreshing, but the water was really chilly. We're not getting along too good with Fisher. Guess all this is beginning to have an effect on him. You live a lifetime during every mission and sweat out another while waiting to go on the next one. No mail today—am rather lonesome.

THURSDAY, APRIL 15, 1943

The scheduled mission for today was again called off early this morning. The target was not designated. The 98th, however, was on the go. They passed over our base about 11:00 A.M. headed for Italy. Seems they were trying to tell us something. They were a beautiful sight—24 ships in two flights. They refer to them as "A" and "B" flights— usually four ships together in a diamond shape, or three together in a triangle formation.

Several of us walked around the base and also portions of nearby Bengasi. Near the base is a huge graveyard for German and Italian wrecked aircraft. Upon close examination, it's evident that the Italian Air Force equipment left a great deal to be desired. The German aircraft were a different story—ME 109's, FW 190's— great aircraft. Also a few JU 88's and several of their tri-motor transports. Took some interesting photos. Also nearby was an abandoned munitions dump. The largest collection of different caliber shells we've ever seen. German bombs of all types and sizes—hundreds of them. Usually the fins were busted off—certainly indicating that they left the area in a hurry to get away from the rapidly advancing British Army which was equipped with a great many American vehicles. Interesting.

The main roads leading out of Bengasi west and east are a continuous line of mechanized units moving slowly east toward Egypt for repairs and maintenance. A fascinating sight of men and equipment of war.

Received a telegram from Anne today and it was like a great beneficial uplift to me. Haven't heard from her for some time. It's very windy out and chilly.

The "Afrika Corp" buried their dead in style early in the desert war—two German graves in a cemetery near Bengasi, Libia

FRIDAY, APRIL 16, 1943

They woke us up early. Immediately went to breakfast and to a radio briefing. Don't know the specific target as yet. We're taking "Lorraine" again—Number 45. We should be soon graduating up to newer ships and give "Lorraine" to the newly arriving crews. Linderman is going along as top turret gunner. The target is shipping in the harbor of Catania in Sicily, south of Messina. Started taxiing out to take our place in the formation takeoff procedure when the expander tube on the left wheel broke and hydraulic fluid was running all over the taxi strip. A quick decision was made—we agreed to take off anyway but soon found out after we were airborne that we couldn't raise the wheels or close the cowl flaps or the wing flaps. We circled the field for quite some time. We watched the bombers head out over the "Med" to Catania—again, we were left behind. Advised the tower of our condition. Was advised to land shortly. Tower alerted the wrecking crews and the fire fighting trucks. We began to sweat out the landing, not knowing whether the wheels were properly locked down or not. Thank God, we did make it OK. Not only do you sweat out the missions, but also the condition of the ship taking you.

Of the twelve ships going to Catania, only nine finally made the mission. The ships have all seen better days. The blowing dust and sand has to be extremely hard on the 1300 horsepower engines—causes a lot of engine failure and ships not completing missions. My stomach is acting up—hopefully will feel better in the morning. Pete Keller went to the hospital today—has chest pains and in general, doesn't feel great. His morale has certainly cracked in the last few days. Hope he snaps out of it for his own good. We all like Pete a great deal—good member of the crew.

SATURDAY, APRIL 17, 1943

The word is 'go' again and I'm scheduled to participate. The 513th has four ships that presently are flyable. Boy, she's getting rough and that's for sure. Attended a radio briefing. Mission again to Catania. We had a quick lunch and out to aircraft. We're scheduled in "Pink Lady". Twenty-four ships will be in the formation. It's scheduled to be a dusk raid— hitting the target just as the sun goes down and returning in the darkness at pre-determined altitudes. "Pink Lady", Serial No. 124000. Targets again, are the tankers in the harbor—reportedly have enough gas to keep the Luftwaffe going for three months or more. Colonel Compton informed us we were to have fighter cover from Malta. That's a first. Certainly hope it materializes. Twenty-four battle scarred ships took off and headed north-westerly toward Catania. "Pink Lady" is in the third group of ships in "A" Flight.

As we neared the target flying about 20,000 feet, Mt. Etna presented a beautiful view—snow capped and she was belching a huge column of white smoke drifting skyward. Also, snow was falling all around her—beautiful, peaceful. As we headed for the target area, the Ack-Ack was heavy but not too accurate, although they did score severe hits on Lt. Dick Hurd's ship. Three fighters appeared on the scene but didn't make any passes. They stayed out of our gun range about 800 yards. Probably radioed our altitude as the Ack-Ack became extremely accurate. No fighters (British) from Malta came to give us protection. The 30 yard across black balls of smoke from Ack-Ack explosions sometimes got so thick they literally formed huge black clouds— menacing. As previously written, you can't fight back—just stand by the waist window watching and praying they don't explode so you can hear them over the engine noise. If you can hear them, they are going to do damage. The sweat literally runs off your face.

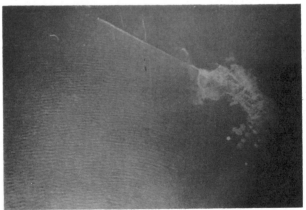

500 pounders salved from 20,000 feet exploring in the water near the Bay of Catania, Sicily—we were after tankers carrying gas to fuel the German fighters.

Number "71"—"Blue Streak" famed B-24 of the 376th group near Mount Etna in
Sicily—the ship made successfully over 100 missions was flown back to the states
for war bond rallies.

SUNDAY, APRIL 18, 1943

Cold and windy today. Just checked squadron headquarters. Another mission is scheduled for the same place, Catania. Apparently, we didn't destroy the target. Because of heavy cloud cover, the raid was again cancelled. Hurd's crew crash-landed at Malta. The ship caught fire. One of the crew burned to death and seven others are from critically to severely burned. It's the first ship from our squadron we've lost since we've been here. Ack-Ack is like driving in a heavy fog—you never know what's in store for you. When it's accurate, it's plenty rough and very damaging.

We were advised Pete will be in the hospital for an extended period of time. The doctor advised a few additional shots to be certain my fingers don't swell again. Will write a few letters and call it a day. If there is nothing brewing tomorrow, Linderman, Holbrook and I will wander into Bengasi and look around and take some photos.

Wall paintings of Mussolini were all over Bengasi—this one is above Casa Del Fascio Cafe—next to bombed out theatre—Bengasi.

Date trees dotted the area—notice tents among the trees—they provided some much desired shade from intense heat and sun.

Date and fig trees dotted the area around Bengasi—photo shows the fruit in a ripened state ready for picking.

Sanctissimo Nomine Iesu Church near harbor in Bengasi—except for minor bomb dammage remained untouched. Stood out as a beacon to the surrounding area.

MONDAY, APRIL 19, 1943

Three men have now died on Hurd's crew and a fourth is not expected to live. The horror of war hitting pretty close to home. I know all those men very well and can't make myself believe they're gone. Hurd's ship took a direct hit from Ack-Ack on the Number One engine. His Number Four engine was already feathered. With two engines, he made it to Malta. In the darkness, overshot the field on his landing approach and didn't have enough power to pull up to clear a revetment at the far end of the runway. The undercarriage caught the top of the revetment and turned the ship over, crashing it and bursting in flames.

A few of the gang went swimming in the "Med" again and generally just laid around. Got several letters from home. They really are excellent medicine from home. Would give anything to have a cold "Coke." Still no electric lights for our tents, but the rumor is soon we will have them. Would be like a touch of home.

Some of our neighbors near our tent area resting-Bengasi. There was a very special animal with the desert nomadic tribes—because of it's ability to travel days without water.

Left to right—Keller, Linderman with unidentified flyer looking after a stray donkey—the little fellow became our good friend and mascot at Bengasi.

TUESDAY, APRIL 20, 1943

A beautiful sight—early this morning a 17 ship convoy steamed as close to the Bengasi harbor as they could. Ack-Ack guns and shore batteries were periodically testing their guns just in case the fighters paid the convoy and our B-24's a visit. The barrage balloons were also all in position.

We went swimming in the "Med" again. The water is getting quite warm and the desert heat is terrible. The millions of flies are even worse than that—they are like a group of fighters—always buzzing around.

Berardi came and told us a mission was scheduled for tomorrow and we're on it. Probably going to Naples. The C.O. is going along to lead the ships. Keller is still in the hospital. Maybe he is the lucky one.

WEDNESDAY, APRIL 21, 1943

We were up and at 'em early, but the scheduled mission was cancelled because of adverse weather conditions over the target area.

Went into Bengasi and looked over the city. Every building shows signs of war—many are totally destroyed. Took some excellent photos. The natives (Wogs) are beginning to filter back into Bengasi and are managing to get much of the rubble cleared away. Much British activity going on in a military way— troop movements, etc. Part of the convoy has left. Ack-Ack guns tested again and balloons still in position.

Back at the base saw a show, "Sleepy Time Gal" in an outside amphitheatre. Sat on gas cans—not too comfortable. Retired early.

THURSDAY, APRIL 24, 1943

The doctor gave me three shots in the arm today— feeling a shade on the rough side. Rumors are floating all around the base. The latest is, no more missions to Italy and Sicily because the powers are working on a surrender agreement with the King of Italy—not Mussolini. A mission was posted, but was immediately cancelled. We had to take squadron exercises this morning and then a roll call was taken. This place is getting military. Next they say the enlisted men will have to start saluting officers.

Linderman and I went for a swim—water was a shade nippy but the wind was even colder. Received three letters from home this morning and more in the evening mail call. Great morale builder.

More ground personnel seem to be arriving daily and also a few additional flying crews and B-24's. Maybe we'll soon be up to combat strength. Big news—we got hold of a pressure stove. No more shaving in cold water. Squadron headquarters told us to dig a slit trench just adjacent to our tent in case the Krauts fly over and give us a bombing visit. Sent Anne a money order for Five Pounds.

Enlisted men's bar at Bengasi—a place to gather, talk about loved ones, home, and also your chances of survival on a mission to mission basis.

The Waldorf Astoria it was not—the "Palm Room" was a very popular spot—a place to seek relief and relax—and try not to fall in the slit trench.

SUNDAY, APRIL 25, 1943

It's Easter Sunday and there is no Easter Parade. Only parade is to the "Palm Room." Seems everybody has the 'trots'. A mission was scheduled again and everyone placed on alert, but soon was terminated. The latest information handed on down the chain of command is we're to begin bombing Rommel and his Afrika Corps as they begin evacuating Tunisia. Am feeling pretty good, but not good enough for a mission. Was glad it was terminated.

Church services were held at the Bomber Command Headquarters this afternoon. Returned from services— had supper and went immediately to a briefing for a mission to Bari, Italy. The "no more missions over Italy" didn't last too long. Target is the gas works near Bari.

Thirty-six B-24's are scheduled to make the run from the 376th Group. This will be the first time this city has been bombed and we really don't know what to expect in reference to Ack-Ack strength. We're going over the target at 19,000 feet. More ground personnel moved into the area today. They have separated the flying personnel from the ground personnel sleeping area. Should make it easier to get us up for emergency missions. All indicators point to the fact that we'll soon be moving—India and even China are mentioned.

It's windy and downright miserable out. Received six letters in the mail—very pleasant Easter surprise.

MONDAY, APRIL 26, 1943

Early this morning ships from the 376th and 98th took to the sky. Circled out over the desert until all got into specific formation in "A" or "B" Flights of the 376th. Thirty-six ships from the 376th were airborne. We were in "Pink Lady', Number 124000, carrying nine 500-pounders of demolition, incinerary and fragmentation bombs. When all were in place, we buzzed the field, tipped our wings and headed for Bari, Italy on the Adriatic sea, the southeast corner of Italy. The formation flew between the heel and toe of the Italian "boot." A few large ships could be seen as we headed over mountainous country that surrounds the shore all along the Italian coast—a beautiful sight from about 20,000 feet. All the Italian 'boot' can be seen. Adriatic Sea on the east and the Tyrrhenian Sea on the west. Interesting roads wind their way through and around the mountainous ridges. Very picturesque and colorful. The cities seem to be crowded into a little space and look so peaceful. That soon will change.

As we approach the target, Ack-Ack was extremely heavy but not too accurate. Seems hours go by from the time we meet the Ack-Ack till we fly out of it's range. We encountered no fighters—this was a pleasant surprise. As we left the target area and headed for home, huge columns of smoke could be seen rising thousands of feet into the sky. All ships in the 376th returned safely. In the harbor at Bari, we counted eight ships. Another mission might be scheduled to go after them. Rommel is being pushed further into the "Med" and we should get a few missions bombing the ships taking them to Sicily.

The ground crew was there to greet us and immediately get the ship ready for another flight. Went through the debriefing. Had supper and to bed. Very tired but thanked God we completed another mission safely. We were 9 hours and 15 minutes in the air.

TUESDAY, APRIL 26, 2943

Holbrook, Keller, Linderman and I went into Bengasi—hitchhiked. Looked over the ruins again—took some good pictures—and in general, just relaxed. Purchased a pair of sandals for the beach.

Was called into S-2 Intelligence about some of the negatives I was sending to my wife—photos of war equipment, wrecked aircraft, demolished buildings, etc. They finally gave them back to me. Will have to try another method of getting them back to the U.S. Mac, our co-pilot, is currently squadron censor. I really didn't think he'd turn me in. You might say I was testing him to see how far I could go. He was just doing his job.

A mission is posted and the crews have been briefed. It's headed for Naples and we're not scheduled. Thank God. Takeoff is for early morning—could be a rough one if German fighters attack the formation from their big base at Foggia, Italy.

Bought some canned goods at the PX and we had a little lunch in the tent and called it a day.

WEDNESDAY, APRIL 28, 1943

Early this morning ships from the 376th and 98th took off and headed for Naples—shipping in harbor the target. About two hours out, a ship from the 512th squadron crashed into the "Med." The first reports were that Captain Mayfield and crew went down. Later, the report came through and the war really hit home that Benderitis' crew crashed and four of the crew could be seen floating around on a raft after the ship sank. B-24's sink in a matter of seconds. We've heard nothing official reference to the crash as yet—just rumors. The target was the German and Italian subs in the harbor. A person really gets fed up on this damn war. It all seems so foolish—such a waste of human life and equipment. The equipment can be replaced but the life is lost forever. Nobody really wins. Poor Mrs. Benderitis if he's lost.

Wandered over to the club but it was closed. Good thing— probably would have gotten drunk if it would have been open. Am awfully tired and rather down in the dumps. Keller and I walked over to the 512th area and it was Benderitis' crew all right. Three men were saved— don't know who as yet. They figure he (Benderitis) was hedge-hopping a few feet above the "Med" and got just a little too low. Speed probably in excess of 180 MPH. The ship hit the water and the "Med" literally pulled the bomber into it. What a price to pay for a little so-called 'fun' buzzing a B-24. A mental picture keeps forming in my mind. All of them were swell fellows. Already they are picking up their belongings—personal things to be sent home. Another crew will soon occupy the tent. Here today, gone tomorrow. That's war, I guess. There really isn't any tomorrow for a lot of the flyers in the 376th. For them time is running out—maybe also for me.

THURSDAY, APRIL 29, 1943

Another huge convoy of 18 to 20 ships steamed into Bengasi escorted by about 10 destroyers. Very interesting to watch them approach as they appear over the horizon. The official word on the Benderitis crash—three saved— six lost. Benderitis lost a good part of his left leg. Reynolds was safe without a scratch. The fellow who took Thelman's place is in the hospital, but will be OK. Smith got out of the ship OK, but drowned swimming for a raft.

Chris, Keely, Strepo, Giesler and Finneron also went down with the ship. The cause of the crash is not official yet, but the consensus is "buzzing." Benderitis will be in the hospital for some time and then my guess is he'll be sent home. Maybe he's lucky at that.

A mission is posted and is going out in the morning. Huge 2,000 pounders are being loaded into the ships. Mac and I went to church this afternoon. Always glad to get a chance to go. Everything seems so peaceful while there. Believe me, there are no non-believers in combat. Got several letters from home—very welcome. So far, Marsh, Dinsmore, Tomilson, Chris, Stepo, Giesler, Finnerman, Smith, Hoover, Cook, Sectenback, Cota and Steiner have been killed out of our group. We were all together at Salina, Kansas before picking up our ships—combat is rough and the above proves it. Nobody wants to die. Thank God our crew is still intact.

FRIDAY, APRIL 30, 1943

This morning 24 ships from the 376th took off and headed for the harbor of Messina, Sicily. We're in "Tangerine" again—Number 111916. This is the 31st raid for the ship and the 6th for the crew. Carrying three 2,000 pounders and will be tossing out leaflets informing the people of Messina to get out of the harbor and city area as we're coming back again and again. As usual, we're in the "Purple Heart" flight. The last ships over the target. The cloud cover was about 80% overcast but not enough to ruin the bombing mission. These 2,000 pounders are huge bombs and their destructive capacity must be tremendous.

We passed over a seven ship convoy heading east—probably to Egypt. As we approached the target area—about 20,000 feet—the Ack-Ack fire began and immediately increased in its frequency. The shells were exploding all around and amongst the formations. They were accurate. By the time we leveled off for the bomb run when the Bombadier actually controls the ship, the skies were black from the smoke of the 88 MM and 90 MM shells exploding. One of our aircraft was shot down from the exploding shells from the 512th Squadron. It was rough as hell and that's stating it mildly.

When we salvoed the 2,000 pounders, you could follow them all the way to the target area and then all hell broke loose. Gigantic explosions just tore the area apart. Dust—smoke and fire immediately filled the area. As we headed home out of the Ack-Ack range, enemy fighters attack us—FW 190's—ME 109's. Large columns of smoke could be seen rising skyward. The fighters made three or four passes at us. Our guns were blazing away at them. Every fifth shell from our 50-caliber gun is a tracer, so you have some measure of checking your shooting pattern at the approaching fighter or fighters. The fighters soon left us as we headed out over the "Med" back home, losing altitude rapidly so we can get off the oxygen. From extremely cold temperatures—50 to 60 degrees below zero to the desert hear is quite a change for the body.

Ground crew again was there to welcome us. Also to prepare ship for another mission scheduled for morning. We accumulated 7 hours 30 minutes flying time, placing me at only 255 hours of combat to finish this damn mess. We're scheduled for tomorrow's raid. Went through the debriefing. This being on oxygen for hours really tires you out. Am very tired. Returned to the tent and slept the clock around.

 # MAY—1943

SATURDAY, MAY 1ST

As the sun was coming up over the desert, all the crews scheduled for the mission were busy with last minute details. We rushed out to the aircraft and the mission was cancelled. By mid-morning, it was "go" and we went through the process again—new radio briefing—gathering together all the flying gear, etc. we were again in the "Purple Heart" section of the 376th. Rolled out for takeoff and started down the runway. Had to back away and return because of generator problems. The target was Reggio-di-Calabria, Italy, near the water straights between Sicily and Italy. The target was reported completely overcast and no bombs were dropped. Would have been a damn good mission to add hours to your total accumulated time and we have to stay on the ground because of ship problems. We seem to be in on only the rough ones.

Some of the guys went swimming and in general just laid around. The weather front seems to be moving this way as it is clouding over heavily. Sent Anne another $25.00 and got four letters in the mail—a touch of home. Went to the club and got pretty drunk, along with about 15 other fliers. Am tired and will soon retire. The caution siren is blowing and all lights go out. From the distance, huge flashes can been seen—looks like a terrific sea battle is taking place just off Bengasi harbor. The din of the big guns can be heard plainly from our tent area. We're also sweating out an air attack. Everything is set and ready in case they do pay us a visit. Much later everything quieted down, although everything is in darkness. Am writing this by flashlight. Nearby, the Ack-Ack gun crews are still standing by—what a day this has been!

SUNDAY, MAY 2ND

Reference to the raid that was to go to Reggio but turned back because of a solid cloud cover over the target. The 98th had two ships crash and go down. That's rough. Probably will never know if any of the crews survived. The sky isn't big enough when two bombers can't see where the other is and what direction they're traveling. Just something else to sweat when in heavy cloud cover. The usual procedure is to maintain same height and direction, only spread farther apart. Then, when through the cloud cover, again draw up in tight formation.

The desert heat is really getting terrifically hot and the insects are a constant distraction. One can't help but wonder what it will be like in July and August if we're still lucky enough to be alive.

Another convoy steamed into Bengasi and several hours later, pulled out to sea for the night, just in case the Krauts fly by. Looks like the German bombers would come from the island of Crete.

The squadron had an open-air movie in our little outdoor theatre. "King's Row"—one of the best I've ever seen. Am very tired. After sharing a can of peaches with the other four tent members, we all turned in as nothing is in the mill because of bad weather over all of Sicily and Italy.

MONDAY, MAY 3RD

The German attack on the British convoy last night, it is reported, that three Heinkel bombers were shot down by Ack-Ack from the ships and the English "Bull Fighters" that went to intercept shot down five of them. As far as we can find out, all of the ships in the convoy had little or no damage.

The heat is almost unbearable and the damn flies don't help the situation any. Seems the air is literally filled with flying insects. A group of combat men went to the beach this afternoon. Also, early in the evening to try to escape from the heat. Combat in Africa isn't all bad when you consider the luxury of swimming in the "Med". It's not cooling off at night as it did several weeks ago, which indicates the real desert heat can't be too far off. I feel sorry for the ground crews working on the ships all day long in this unbearable heat. One quickly develops a health respect for the desert. We'll all sleep on top of the blankets tonight.

TUESDAY, MAY 4TH

With an overcast sky and a front moving in, with the wind and the dust and sand blowing, our B-24's rolled down the runway of Berka Number 2 and headed towards Italy. The target was to be Reggio-di-Calabria. We all had a gut feeling we shouldn't be making this mission. It always seems to happen to our crew. About an hour out climbing to altitude, Lear got very sick and we were forced to return to base. Another zero. All of us went swimming and sweated out the others making the run. All the ships eventually returned safely and everyone was feeling better until Fogels crew came in for a crash landing. Fighters ME 109's and FW 190's had really worked the ship over. Among other damage, one of the landing tires were shot out. Fortunately, they all got out OK, but Lipps, the tail gunner, had a few close calls from exploding shells from the fighters' guns. From their report, the German fighters really raked them over with 30-caliber and 20 MM shells. From the condition of the ship, they were lucky to make it back to the base. Charles was shot up badly in his left leg and heel. Combat seems to be getting rougher as the Germans become more determined. Everyone is so thankful when you complete a mission with no dead and wounded aboard. It's almost a relief to get up in the sky where the air is crisp, clear and clean with no bugs, flies or insects—but not at the price that some have to pay— crippled or dead. Personally, I don't think I could take it on the ground day in and day out—would drive a person crazy. Hopefully, Fogel's crew will all be OK shortly. Took good pictures of the crashed ship.

The crew by "53"—"Pink Lady" just before mission "take off". Notice the 50 calibers sticking out in front.

The Dean Lear crew having a cup of coffee during the mission de-briefing process—Lear is at the extreme left, then Fisher, Byers, and MacDonald.

The British Ground troops protected our base—they built around Bengasi many dummy Ack Ack installation even went to the trouble of sand bagging 'em.

WEDNESDAY, MAY 5TH

The official report on the raid to Bari, Italy, April 26, 1943 proved to be the most successful ever run by the 376th and the 98th groups which comprise the 9th Air Force. The bombers really knocked out the target as shown from the recon photos that were just given us. A raid was posted and we're on it, but was shortly cancelled because of weather over the target. The briefing for another mission is for early in the morning. Think maybe it will go to Reggio. Am scheduled to fly with another crew as radio operator—waist gunner. Lear, our pilot, it still in the hospital and is grounded. Hope it's only temporary.

Went swimming and generally laid around and took a few pictures. The boys that survived the last B-24 crash at the Berka 2 base are making excellent progress. Think maybe I'll see the show tonight, "The Westerner". It really gripes me that the officers get all the front cans and we, the enlisted men, get what's left. That's a bunch of shit. They take their pants off the same way we do. When we shoot a ship down, they can't walk away—they go down with us. This lying around between missions tends to get you out of shape. have got about 50 hours of combat in. It's a slow process of accumulating combat hours, especially when the odds of achieving the goal are becoming very slim. But one can hope and pray—and we all do.

Drinking water is still kinda scarce—not yet rationed, but they are thinking about it.

THURSDAY, MAY 6TH

Early this morning they got us out of bed, briefed, and immediately headed for Italy. The target again was Reggio. We're dropping nine 500-pounders and tossing out the waist windows thousands of leaflets telling the "Ities" to get out of the city. We're in ship "Let's Go" Number 124032 with 24 ships in the 376th formation. The 98th group also has 24 ships on the mission. Demolition type bombs are being dropped. As we approached the target area, huge columns of smoke could be seen rising skyward. Observed two flights of 12 each B-24's heading for home. The 98th got there before we did. The 24's make a beautiful sight in formation, leaving long streams of vapor trails behind them. The 98th hit first and we rolled in for the kill. As usual, "Let's Go" was in the "Purple Heart" flight. One of these days hope to graduate out of this formation.

The Ack-Ack was extremely heavy as we made our bomb run, but not too accurate. Our ship had a camera aboard and we took some good photos for S-2. Certainly hope they turn out showing extensive target damage. The entire harbor area and surrounding buildings were a gigantic blaze of fire, explosions and smoke. Four ME 109's attacked the "Purple Heart" flight and my 50-caliber unloaded 250 to 300 rounds of bullets at them. The intercom was busy. "3 o'clock high—6 o'clock low—4 o'clock low—9 o'clock high." The voices kept coming over the intercom giving positions of the attacking fighters. Seems as though no damage was done on either side. As the ME 109's attack, they present an awesome picture—

three guns on each side of the wings blazing away. All you see is balls of fire and smoke as the shells leave the cannon barrels. They could have moved in closer reference to their passes. Enroute back, passed over a huge Italian hospital ship—very well marked. Suppose if the tables were turned the "Ities" would have sunk us. The huge ship certainly was a perfect target.

Immediately after landing—were seven hours in the air— another mission is posted. The ground crew informed us that Lear was back and combat ready and am flying with him. Good news— this time we're scheduled to lead an element instead of trail one. Thank God for that! Am very tired and immediately after the debriefing had a fast supper and to bed as soon as we'll be flying again.

FRIDAY, MAY 7TH

Huge 2,000 pounders have been loaded into the ships and a mission has been posted. We're scheduled. Target not yet announced. Everything is 'stand-by.' Be ready in a moment's notice. As many times before, all was called off because of heavy cloud cover over all of Sicily and Italy.

Spent most of the day relaxing and reading. Played some poker. The news from Tunisia is very encouraging. Prisoners taken state they've had no food for three or four days. Water very scarce. Supplies are extremely short. Doesn't look good for the "Afrika Corp." Our pounding of Italian and German shipping in their harbors is beginning to show results as they report receiving very little necessary supplies. It's doubtful if they'll attempt a full scale evacuation with our apparent air superiority. Our troops are within 6 miles of the huge Tunis harbor. The next several days should finish them off. We've had some heavy casualties on both sides. This will be the first major defeat for the Axis forces—Africa will belong to the Allies.

Tri-motored air transports were extensively used by Rommels "africa" corp bringing war material—food from Italy. This one left behind in perfect condition.

Many of the transports were shot down as the British gained control of the air ways from Italy to Africa. This one almost made it to Bengasi.

Byers (front) and Linderman (at controls) of wrecked Italian aircraft. The British began hauling them to Bengasi area from nearby crash sights.

Keller, Holbrook and author looking over Italian wing insignia of crashed Machie 200 near Bengasi.

SATURDAY, MAY 8TH

Early this morning, Bizerti and Tunis fell into Allied hands. What a morale builder for all British and American forces. Fierce fighting is continuous in the peninsula of Tunis. both the 376th and the 98th standing by on a scheduled mission in case they evacuate. They report JU 88's are evacuating some of the Afrika Corps. It's doubtful if they'll attempt a full scale evacuation to Sicily. Would be almost suicide on their part.

Rumors around here now we'll be moving into the far east. Turkey is also being mentioned as the talk is she is ready to declare war on Germany. Time will tell. Guess you might say, "Never a dull moment in daily living of a combat flier."

SUNDAY, MAY 9TH

Our mission is scheduled but will go out early Monday. Guess the weather is still a factor. The news from Tunis is scarce but the next few days should close a chapter in this gigantic Book of Death and Destruction. The mission target has not been announced. Laid around all day. Went for a brief swim in the "Med" and saw a movie, "Tale of Two Cities." We all went to bed early.

MONDAY, MAY 10TH

Early this morning under sunny desert skies, a 28-ship formation from the 376th took off—each bomber in specific formation and flight—"A" or "B" Flights—and headed out over the "Med" for Messina, harbor installations and shipping. We have three 2,000 pounders in the bomb bays and old "Tangerine" Number 45 is taking us. It's her 32nd raid. Wish it were my 32nd raid! We're at about 21,000 feet and making our approach to the target area. Bomb doors are opened— Ack-Ack is heavy and accurate. The B-24 is most vulnerable during the bomb run because the ship has to maintain a steady course and altitude. A 90 MM Ack-Ack shell burst close enough to the ship we could hear the explosion over the noise of the engines. It actually rocked the bomber and the Ack-Ack shrapnel tore into the ship all over. It took out our electrical system and the only guns we could use were the hand-operated 50-calibers. The gun turrets couldn't be operated. The huge 30-yard across black puffs of smoke from the Ack-Ack is a scary sight. The sky gets black from them.

As we salvoed our 2,000 pounders and headed for home, the fighters attack—both German and Italian. The "Ities" would stay out of our range in the Mackie 202's but the Germans come to fight and literally ripped through our formations. We were really sweating this out because of our inability to fight back. If they (Germans) had singled us out, there is no way we'd have made it. Thank God they didn't. The formation was close together. This gave us greater protection as guns from other ships were assisting our efforts. We shot down none of theirs and they failed to down any of ours. It's sort of a game with real bullets. This certainly proves there is strength in numbers and why close formation is vital to survival in combat.

We were very thankful when the wheels touched the ground. Had to hand-crank the wheels down. Enroute home we passed over Mt. Etna—a beautiful sight from the air. She was belching huge columns of white smoke. Ground crew informed us another mission is scheduled for early morning. They immediately set upon repairing the electrical system. Went through the debriefing and a fast supper and to bed.

Time in the air—7 hours and 15 minutes—have accumulated 61 hours and 40 minutes of combat to date. Seems that 300 hours is almost an impossible goal.

TUESDAY, MAY 11TH

Last night a terrific explosion literally tore the area apart. It occurred over in the German and Italian ammunitions dumps. Apparently the British are demolishing as many of the shells and bombs as possible. The rumor is again around that Turkey is about to enter the war on our side. We'll probably move there if she goes to war. Am certain we'll soon move somewhere, but can't say where. Hope it's not England. The fighting in Tunisia is about over—isolated pockets of resistance. Also, what few naval ships Italy has don't amount to anything. She really has taken a beating in shipping losses. S-2 has a report that Germany is moving most of its aircraft from Italy. We'll find that out tomorrow as I think we're heading for Naples. A briefing has been set for early morning and we're heading the second element of the formations—Flight "B". all of the officers of the crew have made First Lieutenant and are they proud. Clouding over rather heavy—might rain. More when the mission is over.

As we prepared to take off, the target was changed to Catania, Sicily. The information is the harbor is filled with ships. We're in "Tangerine" again carrying nine 500-pounders. The 98th and, for the first time, the 178th from the Royal Air Force are participating with us. Approximately 72 aircraft on the mission.

After takeoff we immediately climb to the designated altitude and ahead in the distance, Mt. Etna again makes an impressive sight.

Another first—a rather large British fighter escort from Malta pulls up along side. We almost fired on them, thinking they were enemy planes. Suddenly, our Number 4 engine was leaking gas and oil and smoking heavily. We had to feather the engine, peel off from the formation and head for home on three engines. Catania could be seen in the distance. We'll be given no credit for this flight. The damn ships are in bad shape. No fault of the ground crew—they just don't have the replacement engines, etc. It certainly gets one 'pissed off.' Guess we've been lucky after all. No crew member to date has been wounded and we've always made it back home.

The 12th Air Force, B-17's, pounded Palermo and left it practically in ruins. Reported that Ack-Ack shot down a ship from the 98th and it landed in the water and skidded up on the beach near Catania. Hope the boys all made it OK. Probably prisoners of the Germans. Ack-Ack gun implacements seem to be getting heavier and heavier all over Italy.

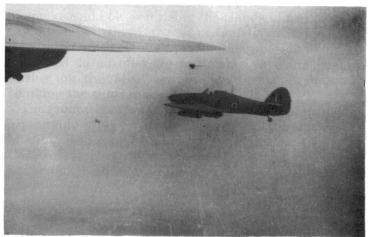

British "Spitfires" giving the big one fighter protection over Sicily and southern Italy. They were based on the island of Malta.

Snodgrass and unidentified flier holding 88mm Ack Ack shells Germans left behind, Bengasi. Eventually the British blew up entire ammo dump.

WEDNESDAY, MAY 12TH

Rumors are really thick around here as to what's to happen to us and where we'll be assigned. What theatre of war? Narrows down to about three or four places—Turkey, if they declare war on the Axis, Palestine or Syria, or maybe take the group home and reassign from there. The latter seems impossible.

A mission has been posted—no briefing time or target assigned—probably a standby situation, just be ready at a moment's notice. Wind is blowing in off the "Med" and it's a biting cold—lousy day. Here's a good one—the stations are saying in their propaganda radio broadcasts that we are dropping pens, pencils and other gadgets containing high explosives that when they are picked up will blow up and injure or kill whoever handled them. Seems they'll (leaders) go to any lengths to instill hatred in the minds of their people so as to make them fight and resist with more determination. Sometimes we think the cities should be deliberately bombed to show them how terrible war really could be come if we wanted it that way. To date, our objectives have always been military targets. Certainly some of the bombs dropped missed the target areas.

We're again leading a flight. It's a good feeling rather than trailing. Rumor is we'll be going to Naples. Here's a good one—a few days ago while the 98th was on a raid, one of their ships got lost and it started to land at a base in Sicily— approaching the runway, its wheels and flaps down about 1,000 feet off the ground, every gun in the area opened fire at them and practically blew them off the universe. The hydraulic systems were shot out—the wheels couldn't be retracted and two engines were shot out and feathered, the other two badly smoking. The ship looked like a sieve but finally got out of their range and headed for Malta on two rough running engines, constantly losing altitude. The badly shot up B-24 finally crashed into the sea. Of the ten aboard, all got out but one. They were lucky any survived the ordeal. Malta sent out a rescue fast-moving boat and picked them up almost immediately. They were in contact with Malta by radio before the crash. The radio operator and the navigator were certainly at fault. It's bad enough to fly these missions—makes an impossible situation when you get lost on the return home.

Saw the show "Vivacious Lady" and then to bed. Nothing cooking on the mission as yet.

Linderman, author and Holbrook looking over crashed JU-88 German aircraft near Bengasi. Many crashed aircraft dotted the area.

Front view of crashed German JU-88. Linderman, Byers and Holbrook looking over aircraft near Bengasi.

Crashed German bomber stripped down to wing and pencil-like fuselage twin engine, near Bengasi.

THURSDAY, MAY 13TH

They woke us up even before the desert sun rose in the east. Had breakfast and a fast briefing and we'll be taking off in a few minutes for Augusta, Sicily. As we make a sweeping turn to make the bomb run, numerous ships can be seen in the harbor. We're at about 20,000 feet and the temperature is about 45 degrees to 50 degrees below. The Ack-Ack never disappoints us— it's heavy, accurate, and our ship had many pieces of shrapnel bang into the fuselage, tearing rathe large jagged holes. Many of the exploding shells could be heard over the engine noise. The explosion concussion, in many cases, actually rocks the ship. The Spitfires stay out of the Ack-Ack circle. Certainly don't blame them. No enemy fighters come to intercept us and them. The sky is black from the smoke of the exploding shells. The Spitfires join after we leave the Ack-Ack area and head out to sea. They put on quite a show for us—buzzing all around and doing barrel rolls and finally a salute of tipping of the wings and back to Malta they go. Malta could be seen clearly in the distance.

We were given six hours and forty-five minutes for the mission. We were lucky none of the Ack-Ack injured the crew— just the ship. All ships returned safely and that's always a comforting situation. Ground crews immediately prepared the ships for another mission.

FRIDAY, MAY 14TH

The scheduled mission for today was called off because of lack of oxygen. Seems the source of supply has experienced a delay in getting it to the 9th Air Force. Shouldn't delay the missions only a day or two. Went into Bengasi and more and more of the city's old inhabitants are returning and rebuilding. Will be a long process. Little Arab children all around. The poor kids are begging for food and money. Really saddens your heart to see all this poverty and misery. We always have plenty of piasters in our pockets—nickles—dimes—quarters in Egyptian money for them. Many of the shops in the bazaar are open and business activity seems to be progressing in a normal manner in spite of shortage of materials and supplies.

Headlines from Egyptian Gazette, the English version printed especially for the British Eighth Army. We secured a copy from one of the Ack-Ack gunners. The headlines across the front page were *"Every Man for Himself As Axis Makes Last Stand"*. *"Tunisia Prisoners May Exceed Over 100,000"*. *"Island of Pontellaria Out Of Action"*. *"Germans Feverishly Cementing Defenses."* *"Germany Demands Italian Cooperation."* *"Captured Generals Enjoy U.S. Food."* *"Goering In Rome Fears Russia."* *"Nazis Fear Bulgarian Uprising."* Headlines from the American Publication *STARS AND STRIPES* edition for the Middle East were as follows: "Axis Resistance In Africa Ends," "Allied Victory Staggers Axis—400,000 Total Prisoners," "Tunisia Victory Opens Way For Invasion Drive," "Guerillas Are Ready To Hit Hitler's Rear," "Ninth Dropped Plenty on Axis In April."

Since we started bombing Italy and Sicily, over 13,000,000 pounds of bombs have been dropped and it looks like that is just the beginning. Bought some tobacco at the PX and called it a day.

SATURDAY, MAY 15TH

Although the fighting has ended in Africa, the battle scars will remain for years as constant reminders of man's inhumanity to man. Huge bomb craters—wrecked tanks and trucks— crashed aircraft—and certainly the thousands of graves that dot the desert from El Alamein to North Africa. Convoys have been coming into the Bengasi harbor all day—protected by destroyers and a few heavy cruisers. A mission is going out in the morning but we're not scheduled. Photos taken during the August raid to Sicily proved highly successful—considerable damage was done to the harbor itself—the docks and surrounding warehouses. What a way to spend Saturday night—cold and windy in a tent wondering what tomorrow will bring. One develops a keen appreciation for life and the good things that surround it when you're in a combat crew.

Information has reached us that the 98th on the August raid lost two ships—one going down over the target hit by Ack-Ack shells, and the other damaged to the point that the ship couldn't make it back to Bengasi and headed for Malta, crashing during landing procedures. Don't know about the casualties as yet, but pray most of them make it. There's no sense worrying about the missions in the future as there isn't much you can do about it. Some of the boys thought of quitting, but my guess is they'll fly on one way or the other.

SUNDAY, MAY 16TH

The 9th Bomber Command reports that so far this month, the 376th and the 98th have dropped more than 300 tons of 500 and 2,000 pounders on Sicily and Italy. This does not include the 750,000 pounds of bombs dropped at Messina, Catania and Augusta in only 3 days.

What a great surprise! Captain Eddie Rickenbacker paid us a surprise visit this morning and gave us an amazing, inspiring talk concerning the war effort both in America and the war zones. Also related his experiences in the Far East to us. A couple of Generals and several Full Birds were with him and related to us the new type of pursuit and bomber planes that would soon be rolling off production lines. He also predicted that Italy would capitulate—unconditional surrender—in the next 90 days. To us, this means bombing continually Italian and Sicilian cities and ruining them. An invasion of Sicily might not be far off. With all the convoys sailing in the "Med" something is in the military planning. Italy could be bombed out of the war and that would leave us closer to Germany. Certainly would put us within range of a great many German cities—time will tell.

It's cloudy and chilly out. The raid was cancelled because of heavy cloud conditions over target areas. Saw the show "Hunchback of Notre Dame." Tired and to the sack.

MONDAY, MAY 17TH

This business of having your mail censored is getting to be quite a contest. Nobody argues against the need for the security. The enemy certainly knows where we are. Their recon planes are over the bases every day and every day the British send up intercepts. We eagerly watch the vapor trails but neither shoots the other down. It's getting so all you can write home about is, "Hello—we're fine. Hope you are all OK too, etc." This poem appeared on the Bulletin Board as a message to the Censor. It's titled, "A Combat Soldier's Writing Dilemma."

> Couldn't write a thing—the Censor's to blame!
> Just say we're well and sign our name.
> Can't tell where we flew from,
> Can't even mention the dates.
> We can't even number the meals we've ate!
> Can't say where we're going,
> Don't know where we'll finally land.
> Couldn't inform you if met by the enemy,
> Can't even mention the weather—hot or cold.
> Can't even say if it's wet or dry.
> All military secrets must secrets remain.
> Can't keep a diary, for such is a sin.
> Can't keep the envelope your letter came in.
> Can't say for sure what I can write,
> So I'll call this my letter—
> And close with "Good Night."

The author of course remains anonymous. Hope the censors get the message. Have been married for seven months—seems like yesterday on one hand, and on the other, we've been gone for years. Early this morning a British sea-going plane crashed in to the sea within sight of shore. A British speedboat came to assist—to see if the crew were wounded and safe. A two-engine "Wimpy" circled overhead for some time. Seems as though they all went down with the aircraft seconds after she crashed.

Another raid is scheduled for early morning and we're flying the good old "Purple Heart" element again. Think it may be a new target for us. Was to be Sergeant of the

Guard tonight, but the mission took preference and got out of that distasteful task. Went over to a nearby British field and took some good pictures. Also wandered over to the Italian and German graveyards. Hundreds and hundreds of graves dot the area. One could say, I guess, for them it's all over. No more sweating it out.

Got a short haircut again and then went to the weekly show— Ida Lupino in "The Hard Way." During the show the Ack-Ack batteries surrounding the area let go and really laid a barrage up around a cloud. The sky was ablaze with shell bursts and the huge balls of smoke from the explosions soon looked like giant menacing rain and storm clouds. The boys were just testing their big guns. Nice to know somebody is looking out for you. Guess an all-out effort to get as many bombers combat ready for tomorrow's mission is in order. Ground crews working almost the clock around. Could be the beginning of the invasion of Sicily. Am physically and mentally tired but my hopes are high and faith in Christ.

British four engine "Lancaster" bomber crashed near shore line of the Mediterranean and floated ashore. Was returning from night mission over Italy.

"Lancaster" bomber was pulled ashore and taken to a British repair depot near Bengasi.

TUESDAY, MAY 18TH

Due to a very heavy cloud cover over the target area, the mission was called off. It's scheduled to go in the morning—weather permitting. It's supposed to be the final knockout blow of Messina—fragmentation and incinerary bombs are loaded in all aircraft scheduled. Played a little cards with the boys. Went over to the 'Club' (big old tent—no chairs or tables—sand floor—bar made of 55 gallon cans and old lumber floating in the harbor) and had a few "nips." Very chilly out tonight. Visited some of the boys in the hospital.

WEDNESDAY, MAY 19TH

What a beautiful full moon high in the sky and the ceaseless noise of the surf pounding the shore near our tent and penatrating the stillness of the desert night. They woke us up and told us to be at a briefing as quickly as possible because takeoff has been changed. The mission is to Messina and it's an all-out effort. Damn it! They called it off again because of weather conditions being very adverse. All of us were really pissed off. It's getting so that sweating them out is worse than going on them. The more you think about them, the worse they seem to be and at best, it's a pretty tough deal. Chilly out. Wind blowing in off the "Med." Received three more letters from home.

THURSDAY, MAY 20TH

Because of weather conditions, we were put on stand-by alert and ready to move with an hours notice. However, nothing came of it. Holbrook and the writer really got into an argument and an actual fist fight. Have been riding him pretty regularly and guess it got to him. Other members of the crew had to separate us. Both of us finally calmed down. Think maybe the exceptionally close quarters the five of us live in could be getting on everyone's nerves. Also, the constant mission scheduling—the stand-by—and the final cancelling of the raid has got to have a negative effect. Everybody is on edge.

The Chaplain of the 9th Bomber Command is here and will be here until Sunday. He's announced sort of a religious retreat during those days and has invited all who desire to attend. He delivered a wonderful opening speech—gave one a warm feeling that Someone above cares for all of us in this war mess. Saw the show "Casablanca". What a great movie—a real winner! Right at the close of the show, Colonel Compton announced an early morning mission was scheduled and all crews participating were to be up at 4:00 A.M. Good grief! At the last minutes, all ships making up the last ship of the formation diamond were not to make the mission. That's us. All ships were tossing out incinerary sticks and the prop wash from the other three ships of the diamond could carry the sticks against our ship and that would be all she wrote. The incinerary sticks weigh only about 15 to 20 pounds and certainly would get picked up in the prop wash. Laid around all day.

FRIDAY, MAY 21ST

The mission today, which we missed because we were the diamond ship, was not the all-out raid anticipated. The 376th and the 98th went to a small coast city directly across from Messina called Reggio-di-Calabria. All aircraft returned safely and ran into very little Ack-Ack. These are the missions to go on. We call them "Milk Runs." They add nicely to your total hours. Went again to the Chaplain's retreat service. Crowded— certainly gives one a peaceful feeling. A mission is again posted. No definite takeoff time as yet. Called it a day.

SATURDAY, MAY 22ND

Nothing much of anything cooking today. Everybody (air crews) just kinda lying around, resting, relaxing. Rumors are all over the place again reference to our moving. My guess, we'll stay here quite a while and bomb Sicily, Italy, Greece an other middle east targets affecting the German war effort. When we do move, it could be to Tunisia joining the 12th Air Force. They operate B-17's. A raid is posted and briefing is set for 7:00 A.M. Means an early breakfast again. With all the German shipping in the Italian-Sicilian straits, guess we'll be heading in that direction—probably Messina.

SUNDAY, MAY 23RD

Last night we wandered over to the 'Club' for a couple of relaxers and ended up tending the bar. What a night! A couple of us really got drunk and fought the war over again. Seems like every drink sold, there was one for me. A real bash. When we finally closed the Club, all of us went for a midnight swim in the Mediterranean with all our clothes on. Berardi walking back to the tent area fell into a slit trench. All of a sudden he was gone—not a sound. A phrase was coined that lasted for months—"Don't hear you talking, Berardi."

We were up and at 'em early. Breakfast and briefing and we all felt like a truck had run over us. Thank God, as we headed out to the aircraft, the mission was scrubbed. All of us were grateful beyond words. We're looking forward, however, to taking off tomorrow. They report good weather still over prime target. Field rations are being unloaded almost daily. Could indicate a move is not far away. Really, when you think about it, Bengasi is not the worst place we could be located. The good old "Med" is a fantastic plus.

Went to church and that was the end of the retreat. Gives one a good feeling. This was the first retreat or mission ever conducted by a Catholic Chaplain to overseas service personnel. The Chaplain is on his way to Tripoli. Have just been advised the British have fixed up a theater in Bengasi. A truck load of us went in tonight and saw "Eagle Squadron." Upon return, learned that an early morning raid is going to Reggio. We're scheduled to lead an element. Am awfully tired.

MONDAY, MAY 24TH

At the crack of dawn, rushed out to the aircraft "Let's Go," Serial Number 124032. She's loaded with six 2,000 pounders. There will be 24 ships in two elements. We're in "A" Flight. We're also tossing out incinerary sticks by only the last ships in the diamond so the prop wash can't pick them up and smash them into trailing ships. We're also tossing out of the waist windows thousands of leaflets again telling the Italians to leave their military installations and also leave their cities as we'll be back again and again. We hope.

We immediately crank up the engines and taxi out into a specific position ready for takeoff. Holbrook and I always stand by the waist window and wave goodbye as we head down the runway. Out over the desert to give all the ships a chance to slip into their specific locations and we roar over the base at about 100 feet above the desert—tip our wings in salute—and head out over the "Med," climbing to altitude for Reggio, Italy. We're in tight formation as we make our approach—bomb bays open—it's colder than hell. We're again right at 20,000 feet—no fighters in view—Ack-Ack extremely heavy and accurate. All one does is watch these giant explosions and pray. You can't fight back. Drives you crazy. Now come the fighters. Many ships are taking flak holes—wings and fuselage. The fighters are buzzing all around us—6 o'clock high, 4 o'clock low, 9 o'clock high. Keller's tail turret is really blazing and he's credited with shooting down an ME 109—good show. These 50-caliber barrels get plenty hot. You could fire up to 250 rounds a minute, every fifth one a tracer. The fighters follow us quite a way out over the "Med" before peeling off and tipping their wings "goodbye." Friendly fellows, those Krauts.

All ships landed safely and as of this writing, no deaths or injuries. We were 7 hours and 20 minutes in the air. Have now accumulated 85 hours and 45 minutes. Mayhew is being returned to the Zone of the Interior—the good old USA—and is taking with him a lot of negatives, photos and other material to send to Anne. I'll be sweating out hoping she receives everything. They've scheduled another mission for early morning.

Went through debriefing. Keller officially got credit for the downing of the ME 109. We're all piling up a few combat hours and that's what counts. We're all very tired—so to bed.

Number 51 "Let's Go!" off our right wing enroute to target. Photo taken from waist window.

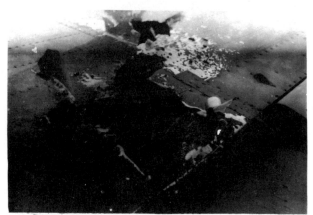

Ground crew members in the process of examining and evaluating flak damage after a mission. The B-24 could take a terrific flak pounding and make it back to base.

(More pictures on following page.)

(Caption on previous page.)

TUESDAY, MAY 25TH

Attended an early morning briefing—mission is to Messina again, after shipping in the harbor. Am flying in "Wild Wolf", Serial Number 240209. This will be the 11th mission for this ship. Carrying six 1,000 pounders and are throwing out incinerary sticks. Ships are flying in the triangle formation because of the incinerary sticks. Immediately after takeoff, and all went well, and 24 ships from the 376th formed into position over the desert and headed for Messina. Started to immediately climb to altitude. Check fired our guns, reporting to the pilot all "OK." Weather clear and the "Med" presented a beautiful sight. Not even a white cap. The constant roar of the 1300 horsepower engine is deafening to your ears. You never quite get used to it. Holbrook and I are back to searching the skies for fighters. It's always freezing cold by the waist windows. From 100 degrees to 110 degrees heat to 50 degrees below zero or more in a matter of minutes is quite an adjustment to make. The 98th also is on the mission and is scheduled to hit the target area first—then the 376th and behind us come the 12th Air Force with their B-17's. Should be a knockout blow to Messina.

As we climbed to our designated altitude, we flew over a German sub surfaced and charging it's batteries. It immediately crash-dived, gracefully slipping under the water in a matter of seconds.

As the 376th approached the target area, already huge columns of fire and smoke were darkening the skies around Messina. The 98th could be seen leaving the target in close combat formation. Ack-Ack was heavy and 30-yard across black puffs were appearing all around us. The Ack-Ack was heavy and accurate. We had a dozen or more pieces of shrapnel explode through the fuselage—no injuries. The B-24 is most vulnerable when flying a straight course getting ready to salvo the bombs or toggle them off separately. The ship can't be maneuvered up or down or sideways. The Ack-Ack gunners certainly know this and concentrate extremely heavy fire in those few minutes. We salvoed our bombs and immediately began to drop altitude, out of the Ack-Ack range. No dead or wounded aboard—just a great many Ack-Ack holes. Was greatly relieved to be home again with your feet on good old solid ground. Seems so funny to call this place home. It's really heaven compared to flying through Ack-Ack and doing battle with the enemy fighters. Was allowed 7 hours and 10 minutes on the mission. Mayhew left the base with all my negatives and photos. Hopefully he can get them through all the way. Ground crew again immediately started work on the ship as they were advised that another raid is scheduled for in the morning. We were immediately trucked to the debriefing area. Was advised that I would be radio operator on Fogel's crew. Lear and the rest of the crew were not scheduled. There seems to be a shortage of radio operators in the 376th presently. Am really exhausted. It's been a long, hard day mentally and physically.

WEDNESDAY, MAY 26TH

This has to be the roughest day I've ever put in. Spent most of the day in the "Palm Room" straddling the old crapper slit trench. Acquired the "G.I. Craps." Couldn't eat a thing all day and it's left me very weak. If things are no better in the morning, will check into the base hospital. The combat fliers refer to it as "Honey Bucket" time. The doctors took me off the scheduled mission because of my condition. Gave me some pills to take. Between the "Palm Room" and the tent, I got my share of exercise today. Am really tired.

THURSDAY, MAY 27TH

At daybreak this morning, a large transport ship convoy steamed into view on the horizon with destroyers and cruisers circling the transport ships. The cargo was German and Italian prisoners being taken to the various internment camps throughout the area. Heavily armed guards were all over the harbor area. It was interesting to observe the Germans were guarded heavily but relatively few guards looked after the Italians.

A new mission has been posted. All of Lear's crew scheduled. Briefing time is 6:00 A.M. Means getting up at 4:00 A.M., getting things ready, quick breakfast then to the briefing. Rumor is it's a brand new target. Takeoff immediately following the briefing. Have just received the final report on the last mission to Messina. Three ships from the 98th landed at Malta with seriously injured men on board from the Ack-Ack. Lt. Dore's ship was one of them. The 12th Air Force B-17's lost eight ships from the heavy Ack-Ack. Am still extremely weak but feel considerably better. The missions are getting rougher and rougher. Seems the Ack-Ack gun implacements have increased considerably over the target areas. Everyone really sweats these missions out more and more. You keep thinking, 'I've only 200 more hours to go—can we make it?" That thought prevails almost constantly.

A colonel from headquarters visited with us and speculated on upcoming events. Looks like we'll keep bombing Italy regardless of whether she surrenders or not. The Germans will still be there. In the months to come, Italy will take a hell of a pounding from our bombers. The mail situation seems screwed up—none received here in a week. The weather here took a turn for the worse—high winds and threatening rain. To bed.

FRIDAY, MAY 28TH

Last night the desert really blew up a storm. Wind was so strong it almost blew the tent down. We had to go out in the driving rain and re-tie the tent ropes. Several had pulled loose. Early this morning we rolled down the runway in "Wild Wolf," the ship's 11th mission. Twenty-four ships from the 376th headed for Italy—a new target—Foggia, a giant German airbase. We're carrying 12 500-pounders. Bomb bays are really stuffed full with them. 98th was also on the mission. They were to hit the target first. By the time we arrive, the Ack-Ack will really be

97

tuned in. The lead navigator really got things screwed up and before we knew it, we were practically flying over Greece. Made a sweeping turn in a northwesterly direction and headed for the Adriatic Sea—Italy on the left—Albania and Yugoslavia on the right. Foggia is near the Gulf of Manfredonia on the east side of Italy near the spur on the Italian boot. The cloud cover was solid and the formations flew around for what seemed an hour looking for an opening giving us an opportunity to drop our bombs. Our objective was a huge aircraft assembly plant adjacent to the big air base. The Ack-Ack was very inaccurate but looked menacing and dangerous. The formations finally headed for home with our entire bomb load. We had plenty of opportunities to drop them on the cities below as periodic openings in the cloud cover gave us the chance to do so. We didn't, because our objective was the aircraft assembly plant and the nearby airbase. Our policy at this point was not to indiscriminately bomb Italian cities and kill civilians. The Germans are bringing in more and more heavy Ack-Ack guns and increasing their aircraft fighter strength. We landed with our bomb bays filled with 500-pounders. It was a long and very tiresome mission. All ships in the 376th returned safely. We were 9 hours and 10 minutes in the air. Immediately after debriefing, we all hit the sack.

SATURDAY, MAY 29TH

The crew laid around most of the day relaxing and resting. The long missions like yesterday's really tire you out. You're at high altitude for six or seven hours in sub-zero temperatures and on oxygen. They've scheduled another mission for tomorrow. No briefing time as yet. No doubt if the cloud cover clears, we'll go back to Foggia. Colonel Compton, 376th Commander, and two other Majors are flying with us. Good Show. Mac, Gekas, and Gregg of our crew are not making the run. With all this rank on board, it's fairly obvious that we'll be leading the 376th formations. If Lear does a super job of managing the flights, we could be in a position of leading them in the future. Keller just informed us the briefing is for very early in the morning. Tomorrow's raid will be four of 'em in seven days. The combat hours are adding up. The crew seems to be holding together in great form. Nobody visibly is cracking up under the mission stress and strain. Went over to the club and had a few warm beers. Am again very tired.

SUNDAY, MAY 30TH

As the desert sun began to rise in the east, we taxied from our dispersal area maneuvering into position for takeoff. Twenty-six ships in the 376th flight—the 98th also in on the raid—target Foggia. Circled out over the desert waiting for the ships to get into specific formations and then roared over the base. The traditional tip of the wings and we're off for the Adriatic Sea. We'll pass just west of the Island of Corfu. On board our aircraft "Wild Wolf," her 12th mission, Colonel Keith Compton, Commanding the 376th, Colonel Kelleorn of the 9th Bomber Command, Major Doyle and Captain Hagen. We're carrying the 'Brass' today. We're also carrying the 12 500-pounders and fragmentation bombs. The 376th will be dropping approximately 260,000 pounds of bombs. That's a lot of explosions. The officers on board were a grand group. Very easy to get along with them. No problems encountered enroute to the target area. Our altitude about 21,000 feet. Skies partly overcast to heavy. We went up the Adriatic, turned westward over land and then headed south to Foggia.

The 98th hit the target first and were well on their way home when we arrived on the scene. Ack-Ack rather light and off range. No fighters attack us. As we headed south on our bomb run, we expected the worst to happen. Nothing. A perfect bomb run but the bombardies did a lousy job. Salvoed the bombs and followed them all the way to the ground. The hangers remained intact but the aircraft in the dispersal area really got it. Most of them were blown-up—ruined. All the time we were over enemy territory, not one fighter came to intercept us. Really had a successful radio mission. All the 376th ships returned safely.

Had a debriefing and were allotted 8 hours and 50 minutes combat time. This places my total at 103 hours and 50 minutes. Only 200 to go. The crew is dead tired. Got very well acquainted with Compton. Not a bad fellow after all.

Another mission is posted—don't know who is scheduled as yet. Retired early.

MONDAY, MAY 31ST

Not much of anything is cooking so far today. Looks like a good day just to relax—maybe take a swim. More and more the Wogs come around looking for food, going through out garbage cans. Also, they offer to take your dirty clothes and wash them—the price is not too bad. You still have to feel sorry for the kids. They just can't comprehend all this—the big airplanes—Ack-Ack guns— etc. Rumor is we'll get paid today. Interesting—they are taking the bomb bay tanks out of the ships which could mean shorter missions and bigger bomb loads. Maybe Crete and Greece will get the nod. We can still hit Sicily— southern Italy. The newer bombers have a greater gas capacity without the bomb bay tanks than the older ships.

We all went to the movie, "Grand Central Murder". Lear is leading the 513th Squadron on the next mission. No target has been posted yet or briefing time. Seems we spend half our time checking the Squadron Bulletin board reference to briefing times, mission info, etc. We all hit the sack.

JUNE—1943

TUESDAY, JUNE 1ST

Before we even got out of the sack they cancelled the mission for today. Scheduled briefing time for early Wednesday morning. We all went in to Bengasi and bought a lot of food at the British PX. Also took some good photos of the British hauling in wrecked tanks from the desert. Went back to Bengasi at night to see the show, "Rio Rita." Very good, but left most of us in a saddened mood.

It's quite cool out and we're sitting around in the tent eating a can of peaches and beans. Received a letter from my old boss, Murphy, Coca Cola Company, St. Cloud, Minnesota telling me of the death of his son. Hard to believe this young boy is dead. Death over here becomes a grim reality and one comes to accept it as a way of life. As a crew, we're thankful all of us are still in one piece—not so for a lot of the crews since we joined the 513th in February.

Group of 513th squadron inside and out of wrecked English tank hundreds were wrecked and left to the desert through out Bengasi area.

Remains of English sailor washed up on shore near Bengasi. The sharks were not too kind to this sailor. The horror of war.

WEDNESDAY, JUNE 2ND

At the briefing this morning, they told us the target was the Catania airdrome and about 250 German and Italian fighters are in the vicinity and that we could expect fighter cover to protect us from Malta.

Before we could leave to gather our flying equipment, they called us back into briefing and informed us a new target was to be hit—Brindisi—located on the eastern portion of the heel of Italy on the Adriatic Sea. We didn't even have all our gear together and the word was passed on that the mission is cancelled because of heavy cloud cover moving in over southern Italy.

A badly mangled body of an English sailor washed up on the beach this morning near our tent area. Grim evidence of the struggle to get supplies through to the troops.

A G.I. from the 512th Squadron had his hand blown off while playing around with a German 20 MM shell, which he no doubt picked up while searching for souvenirs over at the big German ammunitions dump. The area should be fenced in and sealed off.

The heat is getting terrific. We all went swimming in the "Med" to cool off a little. Thank God we are near enough to do that. It must be unbearable in Soluck. Mission is 'go' for in the morning and we are still scheduled. Went over to the hospital to visit some of the wounded fliers. They are so eager to talk and so thankful of the time we spend with them.

THURSDAY, JUNE 3RD

Bad weather over the assigned target kept the 'Big Ones' on the ground again. The heat is getting terrifically hot—flies are around by the millions. Finally got some netting to put over the tent entrance to keep the damn flies out. Laid around most of the day. A group of us wandered down to the "Med" for a swim. Rumors as to where we'll be moving are again floating around the tent area. Personally, I think we'll be here for some time.

Saw the show at our open air theater, "Syncopation." Nights seem to be getting warmer. The desert just doesn't retain the sun's heat and the nights are always cool.

FRIDAY, JUNE 4TH

The weatherman finally gave us the green light for the mission scheduled to go to Taranto, Italy located on the upper portion of the inside heel of Italy. We're assigned ship "Fertile Myrtle" Number 240236. It's the ship's 13th mission. We're carrying 12 500-pounders and the 376th is flying 24 ships. The 98th is also participating in the mission. The actual target is Grottaglie, directly west of Taranto. We're using Taranto as a navigation point enabling the ships to better pinpoint the military targets surrounding Grottaglie. No problems enroute.

We climbed to about 20,000 feet. All guns were fired. Colder than hell by the waist windows. Headed into the bay of Taranto. The waters between the heel and toe of Italy and then in an easterly direction toward Taranto and the target area. The harbor of Taranto was filled with ships of all descriptions. Would have made a beautiful target. Chances are we'll be going after that shipping on another mission.

The Italians set off smoke pots all around the harbor to try and conceal the ships from bombing, thinking maybe we were after them. Quite effective. On the bomb run the Ack-Ack was quite heavy—not too accurate. We salvoed our 12 500-pounders and the ship immediately gained about 500 feet in altitude.

As we headed for home, the fighters could be seen in the distance. Vapor trails all over the sky from their engines. Called Lear on the intercom to draw close to "B" Flight as the fighters will be upon us in a few seconds. Soon over the intercom, "Fighters 3 o'clock high." "Fighters 6 o'clock low," "Fighters 11 o'clock." The formations seemed to draw closer together. Gives us more heavily concentrated 50-caliber firepower. All the guns were blazing away. As always, these Germans come to fight. ME-109's, FW-109's. They were all over our formations—around 'em—through 'em—a person will never get used to looking into the barrel of a 20MM cannon. Three on each wing spitting fire at you as the ME-109 closes in on your ship hoping to knock it out of the sky.

Seems like the battle will never end. Fighters—you can fight back—no time to be scared—that comes later—you battle back for survival—kill or be killed—survival of the fittest. All of the ships were receiving some damage. Several of them were heavily damaged. After about a half hour, the attackers left us and we commenced losing altitude, heading for home. It was a great feeling to touch ground again and have another mission under your belt. Went through the debriefing. All the crew was very tired. We were credited 8 hours 40 minutes for the mission. The raid was successful and many huge fires could be seen as we battled back to Bengasi. Columns of smoke could be seen for over 100 miles. All ships in the 376th returned safely—many had wounded on board.

Snodgrass and Byers sitting on stacks of German shells. Notice rows of them in background. Thousands were left at Bengasi.

Fisher, Berardi, Charles, and Linderman, mortor shells in hand and packaged by German ammo dump near Bengasi.

Byers, Fisher, Charles and Linderman sitting on German "Block Buster". Fins are broken off, shipping frame is still attached.

Author and Snodgrass with belts of German 20mm shells around their necks. In background—hundreds of huge German shells left behind as they retreated west.

Snodgrass and Byers leaning on German sea mines. Hundreds were left behind at Bengasi as they retreated west.

Author lying on German "Block Buster" with several 20mm shells in left hand. Notice the fins are broken off. Hundreds of the "Block Busters" were left behind at Bengasi.

SATURDAY, JUNE 5

Really don't feel any older today—just tired, even after a good night's sleep. This business of air combat seems to get to you a little at a time. Am 25 years old today—feel more like 46, to say the truth, and know I'm a lot lazier. Several of us went into Bengasi. Again, took some good photos of wrecked tanks the British are hauling in from the desert. By late afternoon another mission was posted. Lear was resting, but I'm flying radio waist gunner with Fogel's crew. Received some welcome mail from home. Also a telegram from Anne wishing me a happy birthday. The crew gathered together to help celebrate the birthday.

Ack-Ack crews surrounding the base and harbor had a practice drill shooting out to sea. This place is lousy with Ack-Ack gun batteries. We all went to a lecture on "booby traps" of German and Italian make. Practically every one of us had stashed away shells from the nearby munitions dump the Germans left. Most of the shells were 20 Mm cannon—souvenirs. Many of the G.I.'s have been wounded from these "Booby Traps" and headquarters was finally doing something about it. After listening to the munitions expert, practically all of the souvenir shells were disposed of. Bad enough to get killed in combat—but certainly not from a "Booby Trap". They were really fiendish in their methods of catching the souvenir hunter and noisy soldiers. After the lecture, nobody picked up anything.

SUNDAY, JUNE 6TH

Shortly after this morning's briefing, Fogel was ordered to fly to Malta with Colonels Kilborn, Zukerman and Hagen, Major Nesbitt and Captain Carter Glass III, the grandson of Senator Glass. Put through several QDM's—position bearings. We hit Malta right on the nose. Landed at a nearby airfield outside of Veletta. The British immediately placed a truck and driver at our disposal and we headed for Veletta and through several of the nearby suburbs. Buildings are all out of rock and show the scars of years of aerial bombardment. It's truly the world's most bombed spot. The people have their chins out and their spirits are up. Food is very scarce—rationed. The island is very picturesque. Will be even more so when they have rebuilt it. Our scheduled stop on Malta is about five hours. Took some excellent photos. Handed out a few chocolate bars to the kids. You'd think they got a $1,000 dollar bill. Secured two more QDM's on the way back to the base. Landed without any problems. Don't know what the big conference was all about— probably never will.

British "Mosquito" two engine bomber in special revetment on island of Malta—these revetments gave ships protection from German air attacks from Sicily and Italy.

MONDAY, JUNE 7TH

Was scheduled to fly tomorrow on a special flight to Alexandria, Egypt and then on to Tel Aviv, Palestine for overnight, returning to Bengasi the next day. Later was informed from Squadron Headquarters that the special flight was temporarily cancelled. Got the letter back sent to my wife from the censor because had stated I'd been to Malta on a special mission. Couldn't even mention Malta. Period. Makes corresponding very difficult, but certainly can see the need for the restrictions if it will save some lives. We all went into Bengasi to the cinema but it was filled to capacity with British soldiers. Nothing cooking, mission-wise.

TUESDAY, JUNE 8TH

Not much of anything happening today. A mission is scheduled for tomorrow, but as yet no briefing or takeoff time, and no target has been designated. Most of us laid around all day. Played some cards and read what old magazines we could get our hands on. Again, wandered over to the hospital to visit some of the boys. Hope they'll do the same if I'm ever in this place. Can think of a lot of places I'd rather be. Not much activity in Squadron headquarters either. Berardi just told us that briefing time is for early morning. We'll gather most of our flying gear tonight so it's not such a mad rush in the morning rushing around—shoving—dashing to the "Palm Room" and then to breakfast. All of us retired early and I've certainly dreamed about tomorrow and prayed silently that we make it back safely.

WEDNESDAY, JUNE 9

The squadron orderly has to be the most hated soldier in the 376th Bomb Group. Woke us up at 4:00 A.M. stating that a briefing was scheduled for 5:00 A.M. in the briefing tent. Bring all flying equipment with you. Heavy flying clothes— oxygen mask—parachute etc. as trucks will take us out to the assigned ships immediately after briefing. Shaving in cold water is not the most comfortable, but it's the lesser of the problem a beard can cause at high altitude with your oxygen mask on and rubbing back and forth. After a quick breakfast of dehydrated eggs and rubber pancakes and terrible coffee, we rushed to the briefings. The target is Garbini Airdrome near Catania, Sicily. We're in B-24 "Wild Wolf"—the ship's 13th raid.

We're dropping hundreds of fragmentation bombs hoping to destroy all the Italian and German fighters on the ground. Twenty-four ships from the 376th are on the mission. We're in "A" Flight. Briefing informed us that a British fighter cover from Malta would give us air support. Gives you a good safe feeling enroute to the target area and returning. The 'Spitfires' keep the ME-109's and the FW-190's busy. Trucks rushed us out to the ship. Ground crew stated "Wild Wolf" is in great shape. As always, we shook hands with the ground crew and then with each other crew member. Started engines and got the green flare for taxing out to runway. Each ship, as always, in a pre-determined position in "A" or "B" Flights.

A combat flyer is always filled with deep apprehension as the b-24 rolls down the runway as to whether or not in seven or eight hours we'll be landing back at the base. Once in a while fliers refer to a mission as a 'milk run'— little or no Ack-Ack and few, if any, enemy fighters. If one 90 MM Ack-Ack is fired and only one German fighter intercepts, it's far from a milk run.

Our fighter escort never showed. Skies over the target clear. Ack-Ack was not too heavy or accurate. Hundreds of fragmentation bombs were salvoed over the Garbini Airdrome and believe it or not, not one fighter came up to intercept us. We couldn't believe this could happen as many, many fighters were observed in revetments surrounding the airdrome. A good mission.

Landed back at the base after seven hours and fifteen minutes in the air. Was very tired and went to bed immediately after the debriefing and dinner.

THURSDAY, JUNE 10TH

Not a damn thing cooking today. Not even a good rumor is floating around. Some of us wandered over the Squadron Headquarters to kill time. Suggested to Bererdi and Pauza that they start some rumors. Heat was terrific again and the sun really beat down. Some of the fliers are beginning to stew and worry about the missions. Wondering if they'll make it or not. some of them have even thought of inflicting self-made wounds, making them look like accidents. Sweating out the missions just seems to make the situation worse, but certainly can understand the situation. Nobody wants to be killed and nobody wants to appear cowardly. Went to the base outdoor theater and saw the show "The Next Time I Marry." Received our flying pay today. Nothing is scheduled for tomorrow.

Wrecked B-24's served faithfully as they provided much needed spare parts for the operational bombers. Fisher on the left, Keller on the right, center two ground crew personel.

Old B-24's never died—they just lost their parts, as did old Number 50. Crashed 24's became a valuable source of parts for operational bombers.

FRIDAY, JUNE 11TH

Am scheduled to fly tomorrow with Beck. Lear is resting. The group seems to have lost its priorities on everything. We desperately need new engines for the ships—dust and blowing sand takes its toll. We can't seem to secure any of them. Can't even get spark plugs. The ground crews are having a very difficult time keeping the 24's flyable. The squadron can't pull off many more missions unless the supply situation changes. To make matters worse, the boys have to smoke English cigarettes and we can't even get our hands on a few warm beers. Saw the show "Life Begins At Eight-Thirty." A person gets very lonesome for home.

SATURDAY, JUNE 12TH

Long before the sun was above the horizon, preparations for mission takeoff were under way. We had breakfast and immediately briefed. Trucks took us to our aircraft and ground crews were generally busy making last minute checks on the aircraft. These ground crew personnel seem to work 24 hours a day. They are always by the ships. Seconds before the signal to start engines, the word came that the mission was scrapped— target was to be the airdrome again at Gerbini. Disappointment registered on all our faces as we made our way back, walking to the tent area. It probably would have been an easy mission if, considering everything, one can make that statement.

Have been informed I'm to be Company Orderly tonight and probably will have to pull it. Had the mission been carried out, I'd have gotten out of the damn thing. We should leave Tuesday or Wednesday for a week's rest and relaxation. That probably will be cancelled by then— everything else seems to be. all of us will be thankful to get away from the war for a few days. Here, one develops an attitude, "There is no tomorrow." You seem to get more jumpy and nervous around the base everyday. Another mission is scheduled but I'm not on it. Looks like I'll have to get the boys up early in the morning.

SUNDAY, JUNE 13TH

There is no question about it—the company orderly has to be the most hated man in the group! Early this morning—4:00 A.M.—got the boys out of their cots and told them to immediately eat breakfast and then go to a briefing. The mission got underway on schedule—target was the airdrome at Gerbini.

Watched the ships take off and form into Flights "A" and "B" and head out over the "Med." A beautiful sight to see— the 24's in diamond formations. The 376th had 24 ships in the air. You also get a lonesome feeling, seeing the big ones go. You almost wish you were with them.

Several of us went for an early morning swim in the "Med." What would we do without the sea being so near our tent area? Water to bathe in is still very scarce. The sea was absolutely motionless and cast an almost perfect reflection. Great relaxation. Went to church—tent was full of soldiers. Don't seem to be too many non-believers in combat. Went to Bengasi to a show—there wasn't any. No mail again. Seems something is holding it up. The "V" mail seems to come through with no problems. Maybe that has preference.

Looks like a couple more B-24 groups are soon to join us as preparations are under way to complete two more airstrips and taxi availability adjacent to our area. Rumors are flying around again as to what Italy will do reference to their continued participation in the Axis war effort. With the soon-to-be increased bomber strength. Italy will certainly take a brutal beating from the air. Hopefully, the next several months will give me the required 300 hours of combat. Have about 120 hours in as of this writing.

There still is the feeling among the fliers, "There is no tomorrow"—rather depressing. Our crew is scheduled to go on 'R & R' Tuesday or Wednesday to Tel Aviv or Alexandria or Cairo. Will be great to be around new surroundings for a few days—away from the combat atmosphere.

MONDAY, JUNE 14TH

All hell broke loose this morning. Early this morning, near Soluck, some German paratroopers were captured and a few of them killed. The majority of them are still at-large. Special British and American troops are searching the entire area around Bengasi and Soluck. The base has been sealed off and all Wogs have been rounded up around the base and questioned. The bombers seem to be their targets. All personnel have been ordered to carry '45' pistols, rifles and even some carry machine guns. Also, we've been ordered to carry our gas masks and to wear our helmets at all times. Special guards are being placed all along the beaches and other strategic places where attempts may be made to get to the bomber dispersal area. The crews have been alerted to fly the bombers out in a moment's notice if the situation warrants it. We're scheduled to go on 'R & R'—Alexandria now is our destination. Some of us will go to Cairo and see more of ancient Egypt. We thought also of travelling by train to Tel Aviv but could not get clearance to this from Bomber Command. Maybe later we'll have a chance to visit the Holy Land.

This is the first major enemy alert we've had and it certainly brings the war even closer to home. No mail again tonight. The base is in darkness. All crews in their tents waiting for the word to fly the the ships out. Armored cars and half-tracks are patrolling the entire area. Special machine gun nests have been set up around the area. Ack-Ack gun crews have been practicing for some time in readiness for an air attack from Crete, Greece or Italy. The belief is if an air attack comes, it'll be from Crete. Our (British) recon plan photos show many German aircraft on Crete. Everybody is nervous. Nobody dares to wander outside. You could accidentally get yourself shot. The night is clear but the moon isn't too bright. Most of us are too high strung to sleep. We're just sorta resting on our cots with guns beside us.

The enlisted men of the Lear Crew. Standing from left to right—Linderman and Holbrook, kneeling from left to right—Fisher, Keller and Byers.

TUESDAY, JUNE 15TH

At midnight, the orderly awoke us and we were told to dress and sleep with our clothes on to be ready to go at a moment's notice if the need to move the bombers arose. However, the night passed without further incident.

About 8:30 A.M., Lear and crew, along with twenty-five other ground personnel, got under way for our long awaited R & R. The old B-24 was plenty crowded. Must say, we were pleased to get away from the alert atmosphere that surrounds the Bengasi base. Our destination is Cairo for a week of sightseeing and good food to help push the war completely out of our minds. We landed at Heliopolis, outside of Cairo. Pauza, Berardi and I got off at 'Helio' and the ship went on to Alexandria with the rest of the group. We'll spend three or four days in Cairo and then travel to Alexandria for the trip back to the base. With piasters (money) sticking our of our pockets and believing almost in the phrase "There is no tomorrow" we took a cab to the Grand Hotel. Checked in and immediately headed for a street cafe and a few cold beers. What a treat! Just the fact that they were *cold*! Proceeded to the YMCA to make arrangements for a couple of tours around Cairo and surrounding area. We sauntered over to the local Bazaar and looked around. Very crowded. Saw how many of the jewelry items were made, stick pins, etc.—all by hand and with child labor. Nobody pays the suggested price. You argue and argue for a better deal and usually get it.

We went through the Blue Mosque. Had to take our shoes off. Very beautiful inside. Then went over to the American Bar which overlooks a big square in the center of Cairo, and watched the passing parade. All of a sudden, the war seemed like a bad dream—thousands of miles away. We couldn't help but wonder how the troops were getting along. Wandered around the city over into the old section and we got lost. We took our knives out, just in case. You could disappear in this old section and they'd never find you. The Arabs respect our uniforms and we finally got back to civilized Cairo.

Our room is on the top floor of the Grand Hotel overlooking all of Cairo—a beautiful sight. About 2:00 A.M. the streets began to quiet donw and you can finally get some sleep. Hot and cold running water—clean bedsheets and a very much appreciated sit-down toilet. We took turns sitting on the damn thing. this was real living! We left a call for 5:00 A.M.

WEDNESDAY, JUNE 16TH

Early this morning, Berardi, Pauza and I, along with two British soldiers from Bengazi, hired a guide and a cab for the day (big spenders) and travelled to nearby cities of Memphis and Sakkara. Memphis is the oldest capital of Egypt. There we saw the Colossi of Ramses II, the giant alabaster sphinx, the step pyramid (oldest pyramid, said to be over 4,000 years old), the Mastaba tomb of TI, tombs of Pitah Hatep, Tombs of the Sacred Bulls, more statues of Ramses II, one of alabaster and another of stone. The one of stone is 26 feet long and weighs 120 tons. The carvings are very detailed and complete in every way. On one side between his legs carved in relief is the image of his daughter Bononet. On the other side of his legs is the carving of his wife with the royal crown carved on her head. Very beautiful. Carved over 3,000 years ago. The other statue is 42 feet long and weighs over 150 tons. Ramses II ruled in Egypt in 1300 B.C.

Nearby are many other statues of Ramses and other rulers of Egypt but they have been practically destroyed by invading armies of that time. The Step Pyramid was built by King Zorers in about 3,000 B.C. and is the oldest stone building in the world. The Alabaster Sphinx weighs 80 or more tons and is 14 feet high and 26 feet long. One solid piece of carved alabaster. Fantastic. This was also built by Ramses II. The other alabaster sphinx, as of this writing, is still buried underground. The alabaster sphinx statues were discovered in 1912 by a Frenchman.

King TI ruled about 2500 B.C. and was a great landowner and overseer. He was buried in his tomb with jewels and silks with Egyptian carvings on the walls all over the tomb. The coloring of the relief carvings are still very vivid—outstanding when you consider how long ago they were carved and painted. The wall carvings tell the story of his life and his tremendous power. His wife was also buried with him. Rock statues of King TI can be seen by looking through a hole in the wall inside his burial tomb. His remains were robbed, as were jewels, gold and other valuables—all taken by the grave thieves. TI had 366 statues made of himself. Most of them, today, are in museums in Egypt. The tombs were carved out of solid rock. One of the underground tunnels is 1200 feet long and has 24 separate rooms off the main tunnel where the sacred bulls were buried. The Bulls were buried standing up, wrapped in silks and jewels. The coffins were made of granite and weighed over 75 tons apiece. Paintings are all over the coffins. The 24 coffins are still there, but all the remains, etc., were taken years ago by grave robbers. How the Egyptians ever maneuvered the huge 75-ton caskets and the 2 ton lids is quite a mystery. A person feels very humble in the presence of the past.

Our guide was extremely helpful. His name is Mohammed Mohammed. Enroute back to Cairo we saw many of the sacred birds of Egypt. The 'Shis' looks like a crane. In the afternoon we went back to the giant pyramids and the Sphinx. We were escorted through the tombs of the Sphinx and also into the interior of the giant pyramid 'Cheops.' It covers 13 acres at the base and has over 2,000,000 2-ton stone blocks in its structure. Hundreds of feet tall. Arabs are all over the place looking for handouts, begging for money (Piasters). You have to pay them for allowing you to take their pictures.

The pyramids are awesome. Beside the pyramids are smaller structures where the 'High Priests' were buried. Took many good photos. Arrived back in Cairo about dinner time. Told our guide to be at the Grand Hotel at 6:00 A.M. with the horse drawn cab for another day of sightseeing. We all went over to the American Bar and toasted many times our blessings. Then we called it a day. Don't believe we thought about Bengasi once today!

This was a popular way of transporting food stuffs around Cairo—many flat loaves of bread going to the market place.

Looking down a busy street n the heart of Cairo. Photo taken from Grand Hotel. Notice how all the buildings are balconated. They use them early morning and late at night.

Looking down on a busy intersection in downtown Cairo from our room at the Grand Hotel. Notice the types of transportation.

A typical street scene in Cairo. Note the wearing of the "Fezz" and Moslem dress. Cairo was a dirty city sanitation conditions left much to be desired.

The most common way to deliver beverages in Cairo, horse and wagon. Trucks were very scarce. Most taxies were horse drawn.

Street entertainers were a common sight throughout Cairo. Here they are with dog, monkey and goat, good show!

Two aerial photos of Cairo. Top photo showing the Nile running through the center of the huge city. Bottom photo showing the large mosques and at far right the citadel—old Cairo and the new city were fascinating contracts in buildings and life.

124

The "step pyramid" of Sakkara near Cairo. Oldest pyramid, over 4,000 years old. Really humbles a person just to stand near it.

Aerial view of one of the great pyramids outside Cairo. Note the three smaller structures, they were the high priests. The pyramids are an awesome sight.

On the left—Pauza, 513th headquarters, extreme right—Berardi, 513th in between British soldiers and native Arabs. Huge statue of Sphinx carved in alabaster.

Pyramid of Cheops in background—Sphinx in center (note reinforced chin for protection in case of bombings). Entrance to tombs of Sphinx at left.

Left to right— our special guide Mohammad Mohammad, Jim Berardi, Ed Pausa and three unidentified soldiers by fallen colassus of Ramses II near Cairo.

The pyramid of Choeps—largest of the Egyptian pyramids. 13 acres at it's base, 435 feet high. Took over 2,000,000,000 stones to build and each weighed over 2 tons. Notice the stone erosion.

127

Side view of head of the Sphinx—notice how the Egyptians reinforced chin and face of Sphinx to protect it in case of bombings by "Afrika" corp.

Statues by the hundreds guard the entrance to tombs throughout the area around Sphinx and pyramids—near Cairo.

Sailing vessels were numerous all up and down the Nile. Almost as they were 2000 years ago, very picturesque.

THURSDAY, JUNE 17TH

We invited our guide to breakfast with us. He was most honored. Pauza, Berardi and I, along with Mohammed, took off in our horse drawn cab for another fabulous day of sightseeing in and around Cairo. First stop, the Zoological Gardens. Lots of animals gathered here from all over Africa. You name it—they had it. Most interesting. Next, a fascinating trip into old Cairo and the "City of the Living Dead". For years, the inhabitants of this old section buried their dead by digging a very shallow grave in the sand right in their lot—mostly in front of their meager shacks. The shifting sands from the winds would uncover the graves and the skeletal remains, of course, would be visible. Very weird—thus, the "City of the Living Dead."

Went through the Captik Churches, an old synagogue, the Hanging Church Mosque of Amr. Also toured the Citadel. Cannon shot from Napoleon's guns are still embedded in the walls. The Alabaster Mosque of Mohammed Ali—absolutely fantastic—he is enshrined inside in a gold plated casket. No picture taking allowed inside of the mosques.

The last mosque we went through was "The Sultan Hassen Mosque." We took our shoes off, followed the guide and said nothing. When the Arabs knelt to pray, we did too. Most interesting. We plan to go to Alexandria in the morning by train—that should be an experience.

The guide told us to go to "Grappie's Bar & Cafe", the place in Cairo. While there eating and toasting a few, in came King Faruk and his entourage of about 30 beautiful Egyptian women. The King has to weigh 300 pounds. Tried to go over and visit with the gals but the guards warned us to stay away. Faruk couldn't handle one of 'em, let alone all thirty.

Bought a few things at the bazaar. Later we took in a movie. Before the movie starts, all stand and say, 'God Save the King." It's extremely hot in Cairo and an odor that hangs over the city is lousy.

FRIDAY, JUNE 18TH

Had a leisurely breakfast at a sidewalk cafe and watched the passing parade. Scheduled to go to Alex on the 12:30 train. Arrived at the station and what a mad house! Wogs all over the place—beggars—peddlers—very noisy place. We got first class tickets which at its best is none too good. Seems the leaving of the train from Cairo to Alex is a major production. People rushing around everywhere. Second and third class travel is absolutely the pits. Our cattle cars provide better facilities, almost. Much confusion surrounds the departure, but we finally get under way. The miles of shacks on both sides of the tracks is depressing as we leave Cairo. Enroute we passed through many villages. Conditions are unbelievably filthy. Women, as well as men, relieve themselves right in the street. Some sight. People seem to be laying around all over. Nobody is in a hurry. Heat terrific. They live almost as they did a thousand years ago. The old method of thrashing grain is still used, where the bull pulls a sled over the cut grain. Many of the small villages had beautifully constructed mosques.

Arrived in Alexandria about 5:00 P.M. Went immediately to the Red Cross. Met the rest of the gang. Checked in. Had a few drinks—talked about many things—watched the passing parade—ate a good dinner and took in a show and to bed.

SATURDAY, JUNE 19TH

We enjoyed all the comforts of home—just relaxing and lying around in bed. had a leisurely breakfast with all the troops. Not too many American soldiers in this area. A few on R & R. The big attraction seems to be the race tracks just outside Alex. The boys agreed we should have stayed in Cairo. We all took in an evening show. Returning to the Red Cross Hotel, several Scottish and English sailors were really fighting it out. Guess there's not too much love lost between these two services.

SUNDAY, JUNE 20TH

We all rose early and went to church at St. Catherines—a beautiful structure. Again, we mostly laid around at the Red Cross Center. Later wandered over to the Anglo-American bar and had quite a few relaxers. We know this would all end in a day or so as we return to Bengasi and the grim reality of combat missions. Generally speaking, most of us would just as soon go back now and get with it. One can't help but wonder what's happening with all the gang. Most of us would welcome some news from our wives and family. We're certainly in a different world. We tried calling home (the U.S.) but soon found out only military calls were accepted.

Spent most of the day at the Red Cross Center visiting with some of the British 8th Army soldiers. Those ground troops really had it rough against Rommel and his Afrika troops. They fought two enemies—the desert and the Afrika Corps. Some of the troops advised us that the British had legalized houses of prostitution and that the 8th Army troops stood in line, according to their rank. That's pretty crude, but they told me the lines were as long or longer than the chow lines. Well, to each his own. Maybe if I were in the desert for 12 months or longer like they were, maybe it wouldn't be such a bad deal. We should go over to the place and take some pictures—they'd probably bust the cameras.

TUESDAY, JUNE 22ND

Lear called me and told Fisher and I to be ready by 11:00 A.M. to fly to Tel Aviv. We'll be picked up at the Red Cross Center. The crew that's going on R & R is going to Tel Aviv and Lear, MacDonald, Fisher and I will fly them there. The 24 that's bringing them to Cairo s going on the Fazid for general repairs. We'll spend the n ght in Tel Aviv and return to Alex early in the morning, pick up the rest of the crew and the remaining R & R's and imn ediately head for Bengasi. We'll be anxious to be home aga in. Would have enjoyed all this much more if my lovely w. fe Anne could have shared it with me. I'm sure lear and Mac felt the same way.

Upon arriving at the air field just outside of Alex, we immediately got clearance for takeoff and headed out over the Sinai Arabian Desert. As we approached the Suez Canal, proper identification had to be established or the Ack-Ack gun crews would shoot you down. We fired several colored flares. The color identification changed every hour. The Suez was filled with ships unloading or ready to unload as far as the eye could see. A spectacular sight. We're flying at about 3,000 feet. Tanks, guns, trucks, ammunition being unloaded. The Sinai is a very desolate place. good for nothing but flies and lizards. Landed at Lydda Airdrome about 4:00 P.M. Trucks took Fisher and I to the Red Cross for a check-in. The officers went to a special officers' hotel and club. By the time we got through the red tape, identification, etc., it was getting dark. We did get a chance to walk around the city. It's probably the most modern in the Middle East. The Jewish people seem to dominate the area. Many refugees from Balkan countries rushed here to escape Hitler's troops as they ran over Greece. Was hoping we'd have an opportunity to see the Holy Land while here. That would be equally as exciting as seeing Cairo—probably even more so as it's the beginning of religion as we know it today. Sat around a sidewalk cafe with several other soldiers and had a few cold beers. Turned in early as we're leaving around nine o'clock in the morning.

WEDNESDAY, JUNE 23RD

Fisher and I had a leisurely breakfast. Lear and Mac picked us up and we headed for Lydda Airdrome. Made immediate preparation for takeoff. We circled Tel Aviv looking over the countryside and then buzzed the beach, flying about 40 feet off the ground. The beach was already filled with bathers. They waved as we roared over their heads and headed for Alex.

We again identified ourselves as we passed the Suez. Landed shortly thereafter at a field called LG 90, a British base. the group was ready and boarded as soon as we stopped at the ramp. Secured a clearance' and headed for Bengasi. Didn't take long for us to get back to the grim reality of war. The desert was still littered with wrecked tanks, trucks, aircraft, slit trenches all along the route. We set down at Berka Number 2 about 4:30 P.M. and a giant dust storm was in progress. All our showers seemed now for naught as the blowing sand and dust literally covers everything. Got things organized in the tent. All of a sudden, you wished you were back at the Grand Hotel or the Red Cross facilities. A dramatic change. Had supper and immediately knew we were back in the war zone. A far cry from meals in Cairo and Alex. Received 12 letters from home.

The invasion scare is still on and they (German paratroopers) have done plenty of damage to aircraft in the surrounding area. At a nearby "whimpy" field (British), eight of their ships were sabotaged and blew up on takeoff, killing two complete crews. Over at the 98th Group, two B-24's were damaged and two soldiers killed by the paratroopers. Many of them have been rounded up, but Intelligence tells us that many are still at large in the area dressed as Wogs and as British soldiers. The heavy guard is still on throughout the area and everybody takes turns pulling it. Retired early and was actually glad to be back.

THURSDAY, JUNE 24TH

Squadron Headquarters sorta gave us a day off to get reacclimated. A mission did go to Salonika/Sedes, Greece. Would certainly have liked to be a part of it as it was the raid of U.S. Bombers over Greece. All of the enlisted men of our crew are scheduled to pull guard duty tonight on one of the planes. We'll have four guards to a plane, just in case any Germans wander near. Relaxed and wrote a few letters home. We have to be at Squadron Headquarters at 5:45 P.M. with pistols, rifles, and also a few machine guns. This is the crew's first guard duty in the service.

We placed ourselves in strategic places around the aircraft—one in front—one in back—and one by each of THE landing wheels. While it was still daylight, nobody got too nervous. but as the sun disappeared in the west, the tension got greater. The desert is incredibly still. One could almost hear the lizards crawl. We decided to check in with each other at short intervals and every now and then walk around the ship and change locations. There was no conversation between the ships and if anybody approached and didn't have the proper signal, that bastard was shot immediately. No questions asked. I never knew the night could be so long. We were never so glad to see the sun come up as it meant the ordeal was over. A change of the guard. The ships were never left alone.

FRIDAY, JUNE 25TH

Most of us tried to catch up on our sleep today but the damn flies wouldn't leave us alone. There are so damn many of them, they darn near darken the sky. The whole field seems to be a parade ground for guards, especially when the sun goes down. Once in awhile we used to go for a fast dip in the "Med." That would almost be like signing your death certificate. Would make the guards patrolling the "Med" shoreline very nervous. Several of the Wogs have been arrested and are going through intensive questioning.

SATURDAY, JUNE 26TH

Here's one for the books! All of the squadrons have been practicing low altitude flying—wingtip to wingtip—instead of the usual diamond formation. The ships are from 20 to 50 feet off the ground. This is a most unusual procedure and my guess is that something big is in the making. Could be a low level strike as a prelude to an invasion force to Sicily, Italy, or Greece. If this materializes, it'll be plenty rough on us. It's difficult to maneuver a B-24 at high altitude—almost impossible at low altitude. We'll no doubt be dropping delayed action bombs to keep the ships behind us from being blown up. Everything points to an invasion soon. Ground troops and aircraft build-up—mostly aircraft—American and British. The harbor area is filled with huge barges and tanks, trucks of all sizes are being loaded aboard them. A mission is scheduled for in the morning. Lear and crew are scheduled as a spare crew in case some crew can't make the run for one reason or another. My guess is it's to Greece again.

Had a few with the boys at the Non-Com Club—quite a few.

Low flying B-24's over squadron tent area—practicing for 'Ploesti' low level mission of sunday August 1, 1943.

SUNDAY, JUNE 27TH

We were up at 4:00 A.M. Breakfast and to the briefing. We didn't have to standby for long. Was assigned ship No. 111779, "Lil Abner", her 29th raid. Maybe this is a lucky ship.

We are dropping 12 500-pounders and the 376th has 24 ships in two formations, Flights "A" and "B". The target is Kalamaki airdrome just outside of Athens, Greece. After takeoff, we immediately headed for altitude as Crete is not too far away and had a good quantity of ME-109's and FW-190's. We passed west of Crete and just east of Marea, a large island adjacent to southeastern Greece. We leveled off at about 20,000 feet. Very cold by the waist windows as Holbrook and I scanned the skies for fighters. Picturesque snow-capped mountainous Greece presented a most beautiful sight from the air. Even more so than Italy. The country is surrounded by hundreds of little islands. A fantastic picture. Our vapor trails also presented a beautiful picture— for the enemy. They certainly knew we were coming and probably, no question, the target. As we headed for the target preparing for the bomb run, one could see the Acropolis—beautiful. The Ack-Ack was relatively heavy but not too accurate. You almost began to get used to the damn shells exploding around the formations. The sweat still runs off your face. You can't fight back.

As we approached the airdrome, we toggled off the 500 pounders and headed back out to sea. The fighters could be seen approaching our formations and, as always, they came to fight. Buzzing in and around our "A" and "B" Flights. The intercom was in use constantly—"Fighters at 3:00 o'clock low"— "Fighters at 9:00 o'clock high"— "Fighters at 6:00 o'clock." Seems as though they stayed with us for hours, but in reality, was about 25 minutes. Looked as though the airdrome was destroyed and the mission successful. Several of the ships got shot up pretty badly. Some had wounded on board. Thank God all returned to Bengasi safely. We were 6 hours and 30 minutes in the air. Was debriefed, ate, and went to bed.

Author lying on 1000 pounder with practice bomb in vertical position.

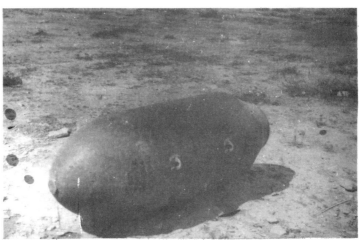

500 pounder waiting for assembly process—tail fins and fuse.

MONDAY, JUNE 28TH

The crew laid around most of the day trying to catch up on much needed rest. The hours in the air, oxygen, standing by the waist windows, the heavy noise of the 1300 horsepower engines grinding away in your ears, all seems to take its toll. The enlisted men of the crew are scheduled again to pull the plane guard tonight. Rumors are again flying around the squadron area. This time, that an invasion has started in Sicily, Sardinia, or Crete. Nothing really definite. Nobody seems to know how and where these rumors start. Something has to be in the making. The 93rd bomb Group came in today and landed at their new base a few miles from here. The group had a long trip from England. The first thing they said is, "We've got nothing but milk runs down here compared to what they have to go through in Europe." A real friendly group. Also, a group of "Lancasters" (British bombers) have also been transferred here from England. Looks like the Middle East Theatre is getting ready for something and that's for sure. Some place soon is going to get the hell bombed out of it—invasion or no invasion.

Very windy and dusty again today. Needless to say, "It's hotter than hell."

TUESDAY, JUNE 29TH

The heat and dust is again terrific. Hard on the aircraft engines. This desert really tries a man's ability to remain sane. Certainly have nothing but admiration for the ground crews. Armament personnel seem to labor endless hours in this wind, dust and heat.

Another low level practice mission was scheduled for the afternoon. Seems incredible to be cruising along 180 to 200 mph only a few feet above the ground. Took some good photos. The nomadic Arab tribes deep in this desert don't quite know what to make of all the low level flying. The camels and goats just about go crazy from the penatrating engine noise. They run off in all directions, as do the Wogs. Lately, the ships have been flying directly over the

140

nomadic skin tents and then immediately pulling up. The prop wash would immediately blow the tent down and all over the area. Upon landing, we were informed to check Squadron Headquarters as a mission was posted for early morning. We've finally arrived—were assigned a new ship, Serial Number 240660. The 24 doesn't even have a name yet. Laid around—had a few at the Club and to bed.

WEDNESDAY, JUNE 30TH

The company orderly again got the crew up at 4:00 A.M. Briefing at 5:00 A.M. and as we left for the ships in trucks, the weatherman blew the bugle on the mission because of heavy cloud cover over the target area. We also were informed that another mission is scheduled for early morning. Same crews involved. It's going to be an airdrome somewhere. We just laid around most of the day. Weather hot and windy. One develops a healthy respect for this desert heat and wind. Your survival in it is very brief without water and protection from the sun.

We got paid our flying pay today—also base pay. Two pounds and a couple of Piasters. The rest allotted out to mother and wife.

Attacking the enemy airdromes seems to be a good go. They don't seem, at least at this writing, as heavily guarded with Ack-Ack guns as are the harbors and military factories. Went for a swim in the "Med." Guards still all around the shoreline. Took in the show at our outdoor theatre, "Sweater Girl." Gave one a lonesome feeling for home and the good old U.S.A. Several of the group have been stung by the scorpion. Could be fatal. arms and or legs swell up like double their size—very painful. They like to move into the tents to get out of the heat.

Capt. Dickhurd, Squadron operations,
T/Sgt. Byers leaving briefing tent. Col.
Compton, commanding 376th just
before a mission take-off.

B-25 medium bomber—twin engines being gased up Berka 2 at
Bengasi—the bomber was referred to as a "Hot Ship".

JULY—1943

THURSDAY, JULY 1ST

Due again to bad weather over the target area, they let us sleep as the mission was again postponed. Stout, Linderman and I wandered into Bengasi and to a show. Couldn't get in as it was crowded with British sailors. On the way back to the base, we bought a watermelon. We were like a couple of kids. What a prize! We sat down and ate the whole melon like kids with an all day sucker.

Immediately after dinner, the word came down to be at a briefing at 7:00 P.M. for an early morning mission. the 98th, 93rd, and 178th, along with the 376th will be goint to different targets in Sicily and Italy. This has got to be the largest bomber effort to date by the American Air Force in the Middle East. What a pounding the enemy will take. We're going to hit the sack early as 4:00 A.M. rolls around plenty early. Our target is Taranto/Grottaglie airdrome near by. One cannot help but wonder when your time and your luck will run out—and a person keeps praying.

FRIDAY, JULY 2ND

The most beautiful time of the day in this desert is when the sun comes up in the east—a giant red ball of fire. The desert again begins to move—flies—sand fleas—lizards and scorpions become active after seeking shelter from the bitter cold nights. It's about 5:00 A.M. Ground crews and armament personnel have been busy most of the night getting the ships ready for the mission. The bombers look like huge grasshoppers silhouetted against the rising sun. We're assigned the newest ship, Number 240660—her first raid. No name given her as yet.

Beautiful ship. We're carrying fragmentation bombs and six 500-pounders. Twenty-four ships from the 376th in the mission. We're in "B" Flight. It's quite a temperature change from 110 degrees to -30 degrees to -40 degrees in a matter of several hours. Takeoff was routine and when all ships were in their proper location, we headed over the base and out to sea to Taranto. We're at about 22,000 feet. The "Med" was quiet. Looked like a gigantic mirror. The 93rd Group, a new one to join us from England, flew close to us as their target was just south of ours. We met with little opposition. Ack-Ack was light and not too accurate, but the formations got screwed up and some of the fragmentation bombs Gekas (our bombadier) salvoed fell on and through the other element flying below us. Fortunately, none of the ships were damaged. No fighters came to intercept us. What a blessing. The trip home was uneventful.

The 93rd and the 98th each lost a ship. Brownley, Evans and Hout were in the 98th ship. The first thing to hit in landing was the heat. Unbearable. You almost wish you were back at high altitude—clean, crisp, cold air. At the debriefing nothing special. Targets were hit. The topic of conversation was invasion—where and when and what will the 376th's part be. Another group of B-24's has moved into the area—the 43rd. We think they are from India. This makes six heavy bomb groups in the Middle East area to pound Sicily, Italy, Crete and Greece. One cannot help but feel sorry for the civilians—especially the kids.

SATURDAY, JULY 3RD

We laid around most of the day. Went to the doctor. He finally took the tapes off my chest. It's still pretty sore but coming along nicely. Another mission, the usual Sunday one, is scheduled for tomorrow but Lear and crew are not to participate. A couple of new crews have joined the squadron. Gakas and Gregg of our crew were censors this week. Sent to Anne a great many negatives and they passed them though. However, they said "no more" in a very friendly way. We all went to the show after dinner, "Mister V". Was pretty good. The desert night sky is clear and blue. Shows what seems like millions and millions of stars. Very peaceful. The British fire a few rounds of Ack-Ack shells and scare the hell out of everyone. Had a few drinks at the bar and to bed.

SUNDAY, JULY 4TH

Because of heavy cloud conditions again over Sicily and southern Italy, a quiet Fourth of July was celebrated here. A mission was to go out, but we were resting. Don't really know which is worse—to go or to sit them out. Seems that's all we do is take things easy and rest. Another heavy bomber group moved into the area—the 44th—and it's from England. All around the clock, bombing throughout the Middle East could be under way soon. The destruction has got to be beyond your imagination and the death toll staggering. I guess it boils down to you or them. With all this big bomber buildup, our crew could get its 300 hours completed in a couple more months. I've accumulated right at 134 hours to date.

MONDAY, JULY 5TH

The mission today went to the harbor of Messina. What a pounding Messina and the harbor area has taken so far. All returned safely although the Ack-Ack was heavy and accurate, according to the debriefing reports. Some of the ships had Ack-Ack holes in the fuselage and wing sections. Another mission is on the docket for tomorrow—early morning. Lear and crew is leading the 376th. Seems to make things a little easier when leading instead of trailing the "Purple Heart" flight.

It's extremely windy today and when there's wind in the desert, there is miserable dust all over—even had to wear our dust masks. Looks like we really have a couple of dust and sand dunes in our tent—layers of dust all over the G.I.

blankets. Nothing escapes this desert dust. The ground crews hate it because it causes serious problems with the engines and greatly affects their efficiency. Also causes great problems reference to smoothly operating 50-caliber guns. The cleaning of the guns becomes a major operation. In trying to get things in the tent somewhat livable, we found and killed several scorpions. How they found their way inside the tent is a mystery. Almost had to come through the front, as sides and back are sand covered. Everybody fears them. We almost tie our hands together at night to keep arms from hanging down over the sides of the cot within easy reach of the scorpion sting. Everyone going to bed early among dusty sheets as all are pretty tired. For the life of me, I can't figure out why. Guess maybe it's just being here that makes one tired.

TUESDAY, JULY 6TH

After several unsuccessful attempts at mission briefings because of cloud cover over Sicily, they finally got things organized. Much rushing around back and forth from the tent area to briefing headquarters—carrying heavy flying equipment—oxygen masks—parachute, etc. Everything was 'go.' We were assigned the new ship—240660—carrying 12 500-pounders. Garbini airdrome is the assigned target. The 376th had 24 bombers in the air and the 98th was with us. Takeoff time was scheduled for about 3:30 P.M.—sort of a daylight-dusk over target—return at night type of mission. Not the best kind.

With all ships in formation, we immediately gained altitude and headed for the Garbini airdrome. As we neared the target area at about 19,500 feet, British Spitfires could be seen off in the distance from Malta, giving us air cover. The fighters stay away from the target area because of Ack-Ack and this time it was exceptionally heavy and accurate. The sky around us in a matter of seconds became one big black cloud from bursting 90 MM shells. We would gain altitude, about 500 feet, and then lose 300 feet to throw the gunners off who were taking their shelling altitudes from German aircraft off our left wing about 1,000 yards. Seems the Ack-Ack was with us for almost 15 to 20 minutes. We just stared out of the waist windows looking at the gigantic explosions that make a black ball of smoke over 30 yards across. Some of the ships have to have been damaged severely.

We salvoed our 500-pounders and watched them plunge earthward towards the huge airdrome. ME-109's and FW-190's were coming to attack as we left the circle of Ack-Ack. Thank God for the Spitfires as they kept them from concentrating heavily on our formations. The British came to fight. It was interesting to see them attack each other for a change. Sort of a great sideshow. One of our bombers was heavily damaged and couldn't make it back to Bengasi, so our ship escorted the B-24 to Malta. As of this entry into the diary, don't know if any dead or wounded were aboard. After the ship successfully landed, we headed south into the "Med" at deck level and then East towards Bengasi. Darkness was settling over the area. Gregg is a great navigator and directed the ship to Berka II, our base at Bengasi.

Sicily is taking a terrific pounding. The invasion has to be directed there and in the near future. The other bomber groups hit other targets throughout Sicily. This business of landing at night is risky. German fighters could slide into our flight pattern and go undetected and literally raise hell with the landing ships. Those JW-88's could come from Crete. The mission time allotted our crew was 6 hours and 45 minutes. The debriefing revealed many of the ships had heavy Ack-Ack damage. We called it a day and thanked the good Lord we made another successful mission.

WEDNESDAY, JULY 7TH

The 98th and the 93rd are going out today. Beautiful sight to see the 30-ton 24's maneuver into a specific flight position over the desert and then head out over the base, tipping their wings in a salute. An exciting sight. The sad part of it is that human lives are involved. The 376th rested today. Ground crews got the ships airworthy again. We're scheduled to go some place tomorrow. Looks like a continuous round-the-clock bombing of Axis targets. No doubt has to be a prelude to an invasion.

The daytime heat continues to be unbearable. The military dress of the day is to be comfortable. There just is no escape from the heat. The flies seem to multiply by the millions. The desert doesn't hold the heat and the nights are biting cold. Everything that moves seeks shelter from the cold. Received a birthday present from my wife, a month late, but came through in good condition—cigars and cookies. The crew really enjoyed them. Took in a Bob Hope show and to bed as we're getting up about 4:00 A.M. Another mission.

THURSDAY, JULY 8TH

They allowed us to sleep. Apparently it's an afternoon mission. As each day passes, invasion fever becomes stronger and stronger. The bombing tempo of the bomber blitz has increased considerably over Sicily. Last three raids to Sicily targets added up to 750,000 pounds of bombs dropped. That's a lot of explosions. The invasion blow has to be struck at Sicily.

The afternoon mission to Catania is definitely on. Rail centers and communications installations are the specific targets. Twenty-four ships from the 376th scheduled and the 44th group will be with us. Immediately after lunch briefings were scheduled and everything is 'go.' Crew is in a good positive mood. Takeoff was uneventful and we headed for Sicily immediately climbing for altitude, putting the masks on at about 10,000 feet, firing the 50-calibers and reporting to the pilot that all is OK. Again, as we approached the target, Ack-Ack fire was extremely heavy and most accurate. The expanded schrapnel sounded like hail stones on a tin roof as it hit the top of the bomber falling to earth. You never get to the point where Ack-Ack doesn't bother you or affect your nerves or attitude. It's brutal.

The whole city of Catania was completely engulfed in smoke immediately after the ships salvoed their 500-pounders. We were carrying 12 of them. A devastating sight. Many of the ships again have to have been damaged by the Ack-Ack. The black balls from exploding shells again filled the sky. Ship Number 99 from the 515th Squadron received a direct hit from a German fighter that was buzzing around and through the formations. No assist from the British Spitfires. The gas tanks caught fire and blew up. Five parachutes were floating toward the sea as the flaming bomber circled and plunged to the sea and its death. These die fighting, as do the crews that man them. Lucky five of them got out. It's only a few seconds between life and death when the bomber has been hit.

Landed after 6 hours and 30 minutes in the air. The debriefing brought out the fact that another ship, other than 99, was lost on the mission. None, thank God, from the 513th Squadron.

FRIDAY, JULY 9TH

Again today the bombers were in the air. the 376th is resting. The target this time was the headquarters of the German General Staff in Sicily. The staff headquarters is located in a resort city just at the bottom portion of Mt. Etna. Certainly would have liked to be in on the raid. Invasion talk again has reached a high pitch and, according to the dope, it's to commence tomorrow night someplace in southern Sicily. The heat again as usual is terrific as are the damn flies and sand fleas. All of us will be so thankful when it's over and of course we hope and pray we'll survive it all. Get very lonesome for my lovely wife. Seems we've been apart forever.

All the ships returned safely from the Mt. Etna headquarters mission and report the target area completely destroyed. An invasion fleet is massing together in the center of the Mediterranean south of Sicily and hundreds of ships of all types could be seen maneuvering into position with destroyers and cruisers patrolling the entire area. The returning crews stated that the ships stretched for miles. An incredible sight to behold.

Another mission is scheduled for tomorrow. Don't know at this time who is scheduled. Rumored to be a fifty-footer with delayed action 500 pounders. Hope we're scheduled to participate. Bombers of the 513th flew again out over the desert at altitudes of 15 to 50 feet off the ground at 180 to 200 mph, wing tip to wing tip. Fantastic sight. We flew around the desert attacking simulated targets, dropping 100-pounders filled with flour. Huge crosses (X's) were placed in specific locations and the 100-pounders with flour dramatically showed the bombadiers whether or not they were hitting the targets. Very dramatic. Smuggled Berardi aboard. Really got my ass chewed out for bringing unauthorized flying personnel aboard. Berardi really enjoyed the low altitude flight. Had a few at the club.

SATURDAY, JULY 10TH

We were all called together early this morning and S-2 informed us that the invasion of Sicily has begun and in a big way—involving hundreds of ships, landing craft and thousands and thousands of soldiers. The landings are on the west coast of Sicily. Units of the Allied Navy have been shelling coastal positions of the enemy and also coastal cities. So far, very little resistance has been encountered by the landing forces. News beyond that is very scarce. Sure would like to see the headlines in the States. Although we're fighting this damn war, we know little of what to expect and damn little as to what goes on in the 9th Air Force. British Intelligence is not too accurate—especially when it comes to weather over the target and the enemy resistance we could expect—Ack-Ack guns in the target area and fighters (numbers) to intercept us. A low altitude mission was posted but shortly after announcing same, they postponed it. A regular high altitude raid is scheduled for tomorrow. Hope we're on it as we'd like to see first-hand the invasion forces and all the activity surrounding it.

SUNDAY, JULY 11TH

We used to think of Sunday as a day of rest and relaxation. Now it's another scheduled mission—a kill or be killed proposition. Seems bomber command thinks the enemy is resting and relaxing on Sundays. Maybe so, but we always run into heavy opposition. We're scheduled to bomb Reggio di Calabria airdrome just outside of the city. Reggio is located right at the west end of the toe of Italy. The Strait of Messina separates Reggio from Messina in Sicily. Ack-Ack should be extremely heavy. The 376th and the 389th are together on the mission and again we've been assigned ship Number 240660. It'll be her fifth raid and nobody yet has named this B-24. We're carrying fragmentation bombs and six 500-pounders. The bomb bays are absolutely filled with them. All ships quickly got into position and we headed for altitude immediately, travelling in a northwesterly direction. Ships are at about 19,000 feet. About 30 degrees below zero. As we headed for the target, heavy shipping could be observed in the Strait of Messina. Ack-Ack was surprisingly light and very inaccurate—probably because no fighters at all came to intercept us.

Leaving the target area, huge fires with columns of black smoke covered the entire area. Returning to Bengasi, losing altitude, we observed huge Allied convoys heading for Sicily. Battleships and aircraft carriers supported by cruisers and destroyers comprised the convoy. An almost unbelievable sight. Fighters from the carriers came up to look us over—did a few barrel rols—tipped their wings and headed back to the carrier. all ships landed safely. We were 6 hours and 30 minutes in the air. Have accumulated about 162 hours of combat. Another mission is scheduled for tomorrow. Ground crews and armament personnel immediately began refueling, rearming and checking over the ship in general. Somebody should inform the brass how important home family mail is to a combat flyer. It's the greatest medicine. It's very cool out tonight.

Many of the bombs dropped were personalized to "Hitler" or "Mussolini". This was the author's gift to Hitler.

Crashed, burning B-24 after attempted landing at Bengasi. Ground personel excavating dead and wounded still aboard the ill-fated ship.

The left landing gear collapsed on landing. This battle weary 24 had successfully completed 34 missions. Several crew members were injured.

MONDAY, JULY 12TH

The Sicily invasion seems to be progressing satisfactorily in all areas. News is very scarce here reference to the battle. Almost as if they wanted to isolate it from us. Squadron Headquarters has just advised us of a mission tomorrow. The other groups are in the air today. Lear is not scheduled. Mac, our Co-Pilot, is checking out as a First Pilot and will be leaving the crew to take over and form another of his own. Don't know who will replace him as yet. We all hate to see him go as we've been together for many months. We all wish him the best in his new responsibility. Hope this doesn't bust up the crew where we all become fill-in spares.

The Ninth Air Force has been complimented on their

great contribution to the Allied war effort. Axis fighter planes haven't as yet made their appearance in the Battle of Sicily— attesting to the accuracy of our bombing raids to the airdromes of Gerbini, Messina, Catania, Grottaglie, etc.

Rumors are again floating around that things are progressing so well in Sicily, that it could soon fall into Allied hands. Although we can't tell yet where the main battle is to be fought. Seems Montgomery and Patton are not the best of friends. Saw the show, "Mexican Spitfire". Here's our tent's great morale builder—our tent has finally been connected to electricity— after all these months of writing in this diary by candlelight, now beautiful, bright electricity. The generator they secured will just handle so many tents and ours happened to be located in just the right area. Hooray! What a gift of luck. Over here in the desert, one appreciates many of the little things we take for granted in the United States. The crew is most elated. In fact, we take turns turning the light on and off. We've been advised of a mission tomorrow and Lear and crew are participating. The tent all turned in early.

TUESDAY, JULY 13TH

Rushed around like mad early this morning. Boy did we ever appreciate the convenience of good old electricity. Seemed to have made everything much easier. Especially when you're looking for something. Immediately after briefing, we were trucked to the ships. We're again in B-24 No. 240660. It's the bomber's 7th raid and believe we've been in every one of them. Somebody should give her a name. Mission is to Crotone in Italy and we're dropping 12 500-pounders again. Twenty-four ships of the 376th on the run. This is an all-out effort as every available bomber, both heavy (4-engine) and light (2-engine) in the Middle East and North Africa are scheduled to hit Messina and harbor sometime during the day. Also Crotone to knock out shipping in the harbor. Crotone is located in the southern foot of the boot of Italy near the Ionian Sea. The

93rd group is with us and a ship roared off the end of the runway and overturned. It blew up, killing all nine men aboard. The giant explosion could easily be heard at our base, even above the noise of our engines. Over the target area, very little opposition in Ack-Ack and also fighters. This is as close to a 'milk run' as one could ever hope for. We were allotted 7 hours combat time. Upon landing, was informed that another mission is scheduled for tomorrow and we're heading the flight.

Colonel Compton is in Algiers and, as usual, rumors are again flying around the base. Some say when Italy surrenders, the 376th will be sent home. Somehow that doesn't seem feasible. Am to be awarded the Soldiers Good Conduct Medal (Good Heavens! What would the pool hall gang say??). They should give everybody here a Good Conduct Medal—there's no place to get into any trouble. Also, am to be awarded the Air Medal and two Oak Leaf Clusters. Have about 161 hours of combat time.

WEDNESDAY, JULY 14TH

As per yesterday, again every available heavy and medium bomber in the Middle East and North Africa hit Messina and the general area surrounding the Bay of Messina. B-24's, B-17's, B-26's, B-25's. Seemed strange to see the two-engine boys on the same mission with the heavies. We're dropping 500-pounders and the 376th has again 24 ships in formation. Bombers of all types seemed to fill the skies as we approached the target area. As we neared Catania, enroute we circled waiting for the smoke and dust from exploding shells to clear somewhat away from the target area and flights of bombers could be seen leaving the general area after dropping their bomb loads. The front lines of battle could be seen through the haze on the ground.

As we approached the target, Ack-Ack was extremely heavy and damn accurate. 90-MM's were exploding all around the formations. A large piece of shrapnel burst through the bottom of the fuselage and rammed into the bottom of (my) chest chute. Almost knocked me down. Thank God I had the chute on or it could have ripped into my face.

All 376th ships come through the Ack-Ack but many of them had severe flak damage. Black smoke from the exploding Ack-Ack shells formed a big cloud cover over the target area. We were allotted 7 hours combat. I turned my chute over to briefing personnel. Was issued another and informed that another raid was scheduled for early morning. No definite departure hour as yet. Dead tired. Had a couple at the club to settle the nerves and to bed.

THURSDAY, JULY 15TH

Bombers again were out over the desert flying at exceptionally low altitudes—deck level, 15 to 35 feet off the desert. The high command has authorized this type of flying indicating something big is in the making. It's not only the 376th that is flying low altitudes, but all the other groups as well. There are only two targets in the Middle East worth that kind of suicide mission, and that's the oil fields of Ploesti in Romania, or the Brenner Pass in northern Italy where 95% of German war material passes into Italy. An all out mission to Bari, Italy is scheduled but we're not included. Bari is located on the top eastern side of the heel of Italy, on the Adriatic Sea. Mac is flying with another crew as Co-Pilot. Looks like our crew could be splitting up and used as fill-ins for other crews. Don't like the prospects at all. Neither do the rest of the crew. The mission has been scrapped for today.

Went over to the hospital to visit some of the boys. It's really very sad. Facilities aren't the best, but it's the best available. The wind and dust is blowing heavily again— really miserable out. Just laid around.

FRIDAY, JULY 16TH

Watched the ships take off for Bari, Italy and was by the runway watching them come back. Noticed some were missing. Went over to the debriefing and this is one entry I hate to enter into the diary. Today's mission, by all standards, was supposed to be an easy one—a milk run. But it turned our to be one of the roughest since we've been in combat. The 376th lost two ships from the 513th Squadron and one from another. Hinson and Smith's crews went down. All were seen to bail out of Smith's ship before she blew up and that's only a matter of seconds. Three parachutes were seen opening out of Hinson's ship. None were observed bailing out of the third ship shot down from another squadron. Apparently they were all pinned to the walls by the centrifical force caused by the spin-out as the ship circled into the sea. FW-190's and ME-109's shot them down.

B-24's returning from mission pealing off preparing for landing—ships with dead and wounded aboard had landing preference also those with mechanical problems.

B-24 crashed on landing at Bengasi from a mission—Germans had shot out the tire causing the landing gear to collapse has seriously wounded aboard.

Debriefing reports say the fighters were extremely aggressive and eager, flying into the formations to within three to four hundred yards and closer. Many of the ships had seriously wounded on board and shot red flares when coming in to land for landing priority and ambulance service. Looks like from now on the going could get rougher and rougher. Every one of the combat fliers with over 150 hours is beginning to show the strain. It shows up in conversations and in individual attitudes. Looks like it's now or never for Italy and she's out to do or die. Maybe we are too.

Received a package from my old boss, Murphy, and one from my mother and lovely wife. Am really supplied with cookies and cigars. The crew in the tent were delighted too. Hope we all live long enough to enjoy it all. Looks like the usual Sunday raid will be on schedule. Nothing posted as yet. Wish we could look into the crystal ball and see the future. Maybe what we could see would depress us beyond our endurance.

SATURDAY, JULY 17TH

In yesterday's mission, the 513th Squadron lost 19 men—missing or dead. We'll probably never know for some time who is alive and who is dead. Most of the ships have holes in them from 20 MM shells and from Ack-Ack. A couple of them came in with feathered props because of engine damage. Ground crews are working practically around the clock to keep the 24's in shape. Would hate to go out with less than 24 ships in formation. There is some degree of safety in numbers. Not from the flak—just the fighters.

Several of the other groups went out. Some of the 513th ships were again out over the desert practicing low level flying. A fascinating sight to see the giant B-24's only a few feet above the tents. The engine roar as they fly by could almost bust your eardrums.

Anne and I have been married eight months today. Seems we've been apart for years and living in a world of no tomorrow. Dashed into Bengasi and to a show. Hot and windy today.

SUNDAY, JULY 18TH

Not much of anything cooking today. Not even the usual Sunday mission. Squadron Headquarters informed us that an all-out mission of all North African bomber aircraft and Middle East forces is being scheduled for early morning and all crews are to stay close by for further announcements and instructions. The inside info is the raid is to go to Rome, the Eternal City, and Lear is leading the flight. Thank God we're away from the "Purple Heart" element and that's an accomplishment. We're still alive. Laid arourd and went for a cooling dip in the "Med." Base security is still tight. Guess you just get used to all the guards arcund and armored trucks moving through the area. Believe it or not, we still sit around and look at our 60-watt light. After months of candlelight this is a great improvement and it delights all of us. To bed early as 4:00 A.M. rolls around in a hurry and that's usually the magic hour.

Mount Etna, Sicily smoking. Etna served faithfully as a
navigation check for targets in Sicily and southern Italy.

22-B-17's enroute to target Monte Cassenio, Italy in an all out
attempt to destroy the abby as a German observation post. 17's
were from 12th Air Force based in Tunisia.

160

MONDAY, JULY 19TH

We've just finally returned from the mission—10 hours and 55 minutes in the air. The all-out effort of medium and heavy bombers was to the historic city of Rome. Bombers from the 12th Air force, B-17's, participated and all British ships also. We were on oxygen for over 7 hours and stood by the waist windows scanning the skies for fighters for over 8 hours. It was colder than hell even with two sets of heavy long underwear on.

Briefings were held even before sunrise and the ships got under way about 7:00 A.M. We're ship No. 240660. It's her tenth raid and think we've made all of them with her. This was a great day. The crew finally decided to give her a name. Being the oldest member of the crew, I was honored and flattered when they decided to call her "Little Richard". We're dropping 12 500-pounders. Target was the huge railroad yards just west of Rome. Intelligence reports 95% of German war material funnels through these yards for distribution to German troops in southern Italy and Sicily. Intelligence further reports Ack-Ack could be extremely heavy over the target area. The rail yards are 500 yards wide and 3 miles long and over 3,000 truckloads of goods pass through the complex daily. The briefings were very specific. Military targets only. Intelligence showed numerous photos of the Vatican, St. Peter's Square, etc. In fact, Catholic members of the crews were given the option of refusing to go on the mission if they felt guilty about any stray bombs falling into Rome other than military targets. A few declined to participate.

The 376th took the route up the Adriatic Sea to a point about 40 to 50 miles north of Rome, turned west across the middle section of Italy to the Tyrrhenian Sea and south directly into the main marshalling yards. We're at 21,000 feet and as we approached the target area, medium and heavy bombers could be seen leaving the target areas. Rome is a beautiful city and visibility was perfect. It's unlike any city we've seen from the air so far on any mission. The Vatican is in the center of the city—stands out like a back house in a fog. St. Peter's Square—

outstanding—and of course you couldn't miss the Coliseum. If Mussolini is standing on the deck of his villa in rome, he certainly is getting his eyes full today. A format of things to come. The people of Rome were warned of our coming by pamphlets that were tossed out a few days ago by ships from Malta and by our radio broadcasts. Opposition from Ack-Ack over the target was ineffective and not heavy. After the bomb run, we headed south towards Sicily and the toe of Italy. One of our bombers headed for Malta but crashed in the sea before arriving there. Don't know the status of the crew. Most of our ships headed for Tunisia as they didn't have the gas capacity to fly back to Bengasi. The "Little Richard" made it back to Berka II with very little gas reserve in the main tanks. The Rome mission should have a tremendous effect on the Italian people as a whole, and might even add up to their demanding Mussolini and his generals surrender.

We flew very low over Sicily (which was foolish) and witnessed much of the ground fighting near Catania. American and British troops are closing the trap for the final battle of Sicily which will be Messina. Allied shipping seemed to be everywhere around the island. Hundreds and hundreds of ships. A huge blanket of smoke hung over the area indicating the tremendous intensity of the struggle below.

Upon landing, trucks took us immediately to debriefing. Everyone in the crew was dead tired after 10 hours and 55 minutes in the air. The hours on oxygen—hours standing by the waist window—hours of noise from the 1300 horsepower Pratt and Whitney engines grinding in your ears—hours of being so cold you almost don't care what happens to you—the general strain of the mission. Sleep was certainly most welcome. The crew was yelling for the light to be turned out. Nothing scheduled for in the morning. Thank God.

TUESDAY, JULY 20TH

There's nothing moving today. We're kinda licking our wounds before striking again. Generally, the ships are in pretty bad shape all around and require a lot of maintenance. Many of the crews are still in Tunisia and should be returning this afternoon. Some, also, are in Malta. From all reports, the mission to Rome was highly successful. No religious targets were hit. Rumors are again floating around about a low altitude attack. The wind and dust is almost unbearable.

Have just received a paper, "Air Force News—July 20th," issued by Command Public Relations (HOME) Headquarters, Middle East, regarding the Rome raid and information about Sicily. Headlines—*"Day Raid On Rome Targets" "HEAVY ATTACK ON VAST RAIL DISTRIBUTION CENTER"*. It was the last of the great communications centers of Italy to receive the weight of Allied assault. Over 750,000 pounds of bombs were dropped. The paper further stated that Mussolini, over the years, had made Rome a vast weapons manufacturing center, figuring it (Rome) would be safe from air attack. Other headlines—*"SICILY ISOLATED BY NON-STOP AIR BLOWS"*. Axis resistance is practically nil and the whole island seems alive with scattered fires from fragmentation and 500 pounders. We have complete air supremacy over Sicily. One article stated for the seven days ending last Friday, the Axis has lost 175 aircraft and the Allied forces only 71. This has to be aircraft of all types from all our Allied flying forces. Prisoners so far captured in Sicily total over 30,000 including three complete Italian divisions. Seems the Italian soldiers from those questioned really hate the Germans. This certainly is understandable. Look what destruction is taking place in Italian cities. Land in general is all but destroyed by war. Mr. Anthony Eden, British Foreign Secretary, stated in the House of Commons, "We would not hesitate to bomb Rome to the best of our ability and as heavily as possible if the course of the war should render such an action." Leaflets are being dropped over Rome urging the Italians to lay down their arms as they have witnessed the beginning of unbelievable property destruction and loss of human lives.

WEDNESDAY, JULY 21ST

German recon planes from Crete are almost constantly over the bases. The vapor trail is about all that is visible. Interesting to see Spitfires flying to intercept. So far, they haven't caught the high flying German aircraft. The Germans must have a feeling that something big is in the making. A mass of low level flying practice missions is scheduled for mid-morning. Lear is leading the formations. The inside dope is that the real thing will go in the next few days. Ground troops seem to be working around the clock on the ships to have them in the best possible shape. Most of the crews in conversation are really sweating out the next 4 or 5 days. Most feel it's a suicide run—kill or be killed proposition—a medal raid. It's practically impossible to effectively maneuver a 30-ton plus B-24 25 to 50 feet off the ground. The dust is making work of any type almost impossible. Security s around the base seems to be tightening up again, even to the point where ground and flying personnel could be separated. Something is up.

THURSDAY, JULY 22ND

In this morning's practice low altitude flying, General Ent, Commanding the 9th Air Force, was along as the B-24's buzzed the desert, wingtip to wingtip, 15 to 25 feet off the desert. Formations were very close. Again, camels and sheep literally ran in every direction from the nomadic camps deep in the desert. The giant ships seem to skim directly over their heads. Many times the great ships would be indicating well over 200 mph. A beautiful sight, yet a grim reminder of what's to come with the enemy firing back with everything but the old kitchen sink.

After landing, the General stated that the terrain was very similar to that which was to be our target. There's no question now—it's confirmed. We'll be flying a low altitude mission in a few days. This statement rules out the Brenner Pass. The target has to be Ploesti.

Ground crews are putting in most of the bombers

"Bomb Bay" gas tanks for extra distance. Every mechanical part of the ships is being carefully checked over every spare moment they are on the ground. It's obvious that when the raid finally comes, it's going to be a long one. Much longer than Rome because we're going at low altitude. The tensions among the crews is reaching a fever pitch—especially among old combat veterans with 20 or more missions. More practice raids are scheduled for in the morning and afternoon. The joke going around is, we won't have to take oxygen masks, heavy flying clothes and parachutes. Very funny.

Left to right—two unidentified officers, Col. Compton; commanding 376th group, Gen. Ent; commanding 9th Air Force, Bengasi.

FRIDAY, JULY 23RD

Ground crews and ground personnel in general are becoming very inquisitive about all this extremely low altitude flying. They certainly know this has the approval of the high command, otherwise it would be stopped. It's against good flying regulations. Looks like the low level practice runs last for another 6 or 7 days when the real thing should go. It's a most fascinating sight to see formations of bombers, well over 100 of them, skimming along the desert floor at speeds exceeding 225 mph. The ground around you is just a blur. The nomads are really concerned as we keep blowing down their tents with our prop wash. Animals are going crazy from the roar of the engines. practice has got to make perfect for this most important mission. The formations have to be almost wingtip to wingtip—four abreast. Any slip-ups could mean great disaster to many ships and crews. Delayed action bombs to be used, but don't know as yet what weights, 500 or 1,000 pounders or both. Rumors are heavily flying around the base. It's a constant topic of heavy discussion as to where the raid will finally go. For the record, it's got to be Ploesti. The Romanian oil and gas refineries. Only target worth this kind of sacrifice, both in lives and ships. It'll be an historic mission as never before and probably again will heavy bombers raid in great numbers at such a low target altitude.

Number "61" passes directly over us enroute target—"A" and "B" flights usually flew at different altitudes to and from targets.

Low flying B-24's out over the desert—the "Med."—practicing for the historic low level Ploesti mission of August 1st, 1943.

All crews are sorta keeping their fingers crossed. We gather in tents and discuss the future, etc. It's not compulsory that you go, but all the crew is sticking together and if we go down, we'll go down together. That's the way we want it. What great spirit. We're certainly sweating it out. Think we're all getting a few gray hairs over this big one. It's bad enough at high altitude. At least you can bail out. But at low altitude, when you can almost reach out and touch the ground, that makes it a shade rough. Can think of a thousand places I'd rather be. One of them is home with my lovely wife. Again, windy— dusty— and very hot.

SATURDAY, JULY 24TH

A heavy fog rolled in off the "Med" and made our practice flying extremely difficult at times as the planes off our wings would just disappear from our sight. The low flying bombers moved deeper and deeper into the desert to get away from the fog. The sun would soon burn it all away.

They informed us that a week from today we're supposed to be briefed on the mission. Base security is of the utmost importance and they warned us not to discuss the mission even amongst ourselves. Our nerves are really getting a little edgy about the whole affair. We were told to stay amongst ourselves— flying personnel. All we can do at this stage is hope and pray. Terrifically hot and the flies are terrible.

SUNDAY, JULY 25TH

Again, a very heavy fog rolled in and nothing was moving. Very cold and damp. Went to church and the tent was filled—mostly with fliers. There are no non-believers going on this mission. Had a fast lunch and out to the bombers for several hours of low altitude flying. We made our bombing runs using the shore line as the target area, dropping 100-pound flour bombs. Some British soldiers happened to be swimming in the area. Hopefully we missed them. They scampered in every which direction, especially after they observed our bomb bay doors open. Upon landing, we got the rumor that Mussolini has resigned and a new Italian government is being formed. Sicily should soon be completely in Allied hands. We sat around in the tent until midnight. Had a snack and called it a day. No mail has come into the area for a couple of weeks.

MONDAY, JULY 26TH

It's official that Mussolini has resigned and that martial law has been declared throughout all of Italy. Captain Huntley, S-2 officer, and I had a session on the subject and he predicted that Italy would completely surrender and be out of the war within ten days. That makes Germany and Italy enemies. What a situation. Rumor factory is working overtime. The change in events could have an effect on us. Some are of the opinion that we will move into Sicily and bomb Germany and France. Also could mean heavier bombing attacks on Greece and Crete. There also is speculation now that heavier bombing raids on Germany maybe could force a surrender decision from her.

About 48 bombers were over the base flying at low altitude and in extremely close formation. The engine noise is deafening. The 376th was part of the formation. All precautions are being taken to safeguard the crews making this mission from a security standpoint. Apparently, the high command believes this could be a surprise attack on the enemy. I wouldn't bet odds on it with German recon planes over the base every day. There is no question this will be a history making mission as never before have heavy bombers in such numbers dropped their "eggs" at such an altitude. Much ground strafing will be in order as three extra guns are being fitting into the nose of the bomber. Five heavy groups are to be on this historic run with maximum participation from every group. Any plane that's flyable will go. Again—hot and windy.

Low flying B-24's on practice bomb run—bomb bay doors are
open and 100 pound practice bombs filled with flour are to be
dropped on a little island out in the "Med."—notice the bomb
explosions of flour on the little island—speed of the bombers is in
excess of 200 miles an hour.

Low flying B-24's approaching observation tower—practice runs for "Ploesti" mission. Notice ambulance is handy just in case, desert, Bengasi.

TUESDAY, JULY 27TH

About 175 bombers were in the sky today and in close low altitude formation, simulated a bombing run to Soluck and in general practiced close wing to wing flying. Row after row—four abreast going over the target. God! What a sight to behold. Just to say you've been here will be some story to tell. Immediately upon landing, ground crews check and re-check the entire ship. Many of the ships are to receive new engines. That tells us this has become a Number One priority mission as far as the war effort is concerned. The tension among the crews increases almost by the minute as the big day approaches. My guess is for Sunday, August 1st. Ground crews are being instructed not to engage the crews in conversation. Time has to be close. Maybe a couple of days. One cannot help but wonder, who'll get killed? Who'll survive? One always feels he will survive and the other fellows will get it. One thing for certain—if the flies don't get us, this mission will.

WEDNESDAY, JULY 28TH

One little item we've completely forgotten about is how in hell are we to get through the barrage balloons if any are floating around the area? We'll be coming in below the floating balloons. As a person thinks of all these incidents, the mission more and more grates on your nerves and mind. You wonder if your luck will finally run out. A few days should answer that question.

Rumors as to where we're going are flying around as the main topic of discussion, in spite of all that's being done to eliminate all unnecessary conversation regarding the mission. The best guesses are—Coast of France—Northern Italy to the Brenner Pass—the Ploesti oil fields of Romania. Some are even betting it could be up the Adriatic Sea to southern Germany. Aircraft factories as the prime target. Time will tell, but here's one citizen that will thank God when it's all over and we're back again running those good old high altitude missions.

The club is open tonight and it's crowded with crews probably getting drunk and sleeping it off for the last time before the mission takes off. It's an amazing situation. No one is scared or showing signs of cowardice. All are full of expectations, feelings of great adventure, and pride.

THURSDAY, JULY 29TH

Busy—busy—busy. We've had two briefings as to regards to the targets to be bombed. The first briefing dealt with the specific target to be bombed and the detailed covering of the route over and back. Gasoline is still going to be a crucial factor for many of the ships. Moving pictures were shown giving every detail possible. Not a solitary item has been left to chance. The second briefing dealt with escape if we were still lucky enough to be alive after crashing the bomber in a field and in enemy territory. Every possible aid will be given us with regards to successfully escaping. An escape package consisting of Romanian money, American money, several gold pieces, a compass, maps of the area, etc.

One can readily see that months and months of preparation have gone into advance planning of this historic event. Without question it will be the greatest mission in the history of military bombing aviation. Effects on the enemies ability to wage war should be felt almost immediately. If the targets are all hit and the mission is completely successful, it could shorten the war considerably. Five heavy B-24 groups are participating, about 175 to 180 bombers. We'll be hitting five different specific targets in one general area. Certainly it'll be a big factor in the old hat of the 24 over the overrated flying fortress, the 17. Secrecy is still the word around the base and guards now more than ever are all over the area. It's a court martial offence to openly discuss the events of the last several days with anyone. Another important briefing session is called for early in the morning in the group S-2 war room. Captain Huntley stated that the mission has a priority second only to the invasion of Sicily from a materials procurement standpoint. Pretty important war effort. New engines have been arriving daily for the ships and ground crews are working around the clock on the ships. Everyone is getting so excited that sleep is almost impossible.

FRIDAY, JULY 30TH

So important is this mission that I'll not record the target until we return. There's always a chance someone may read the diary or steal it. Officials kinda frown on the keeping of a diary. They say it could be helpful to the enemy if they ever got a hold of one.

The group war room showed conclusively the months and months of preparation that has gone into the mission. Guards with machine guns were strategically placed outside and in the room. Replicas of the targets (exact) made and placed in specific locations relative to the general target area. Huge maps and photos of the targets were all over the walls, leaving not a single item to chance. The RAF built the target replicas and has done most of the advance intelligence work reference to the mission. Again, the need for complete secrecy was stressed as the mission's success depends so very much on the complete element of enemy surprise. The whole area is alive with activity. Trucks seem to be dashing all over the place. The combat crews have been isolated from all other base personnel and no conversations between the two groups will be tolerated. We even eat in separate parts of the mess hall. A person's thoughts cannot help but reflect of home and how life would be without this mess of a war. You get pretty lonesome. One also begins to think seriously if time is running out. My guess is we'll have at least a 50% loss of ships on the raid—maybe more. Final briefings are in effect for tomorrow. Attack Day, Minus One. It's difficult to sleep but we're trying.

SATURDAY, JULY 31ST

The ships are being thoroughly checked over and over. Special delayed action bombs are being installed in the bomb bays. Some are 500-pounders and a few of the newer ships are carrying 1,000-pounders. Also, boxes of spring activated incinerary sticks are being placed by the waist windows. They weigh about 20 pounds apiece. Pick 'em up, the spring snaps to go, and she blows in about 30 seconds. The delayed action bombs are from one to six hours. The last ships over the target area are dropping bombs to explode on impact. This is cutting it pretty close.

Last minute briefings on all aspects of the mission have been going on all day. The combat crews are isolated totally from all non-flying personnel. Guards are all over. You'd think it was a prisoner of war camp. General Bereaton, commanding the Middle East Bomber Forces, spoke to us on the importance of the mission and why it must not fail under any circumstances. Thousands of lives will be saved and the war could be shorted by six to twelve months. It's effect on the enemy war machine will be felt immediately. General Ent, commanding the 9th Air Force, also addressed the group. He is making the mission with us. Colonel Compton, commanding the 376th also spoke. Later in the day, the head of the British Air Forces, Air Marshal Tedder, addressed the group. Eddie Rickenbacker told us of his Pacific experiences and wished us "God Speed" on this greatest of historic bombing missions. To top it off, General Bereaton closed by saying, "If not one bomber returns and the target is totally destroyed, it will be worth the sacrifice in men and bombers." A great morale builder for all the combat crews.

Most of us have already determined we'll lose at least 50% of the striking force. The groups coming down from England to assist us no longer refer to this theater of war as "Bombing Milk Runs." After the mission, they will be returning to England. The long-range B-24 will make this mission one for the history books and fliers for years to come will discuss this controversial raid. In a few hours from now we'll be on our way. We'll be flying "Little Richard", Number 240660, and Colonel Compton's ship, "Teggie Ann," carrying General Ent will be just off our left wing.

The 513th is leading the 376th and the 376th is leading the other four groups participating. The 98th will be directly back of us. Our ship will be the number five ship to take off and there will be only four ships directly in front of us. There will be no sleep tonight. The crews participating are gathering together the items they want to send home. These are placed at the head of the bed. At the foot of the cot are the items the survivors can take and share with the thought that it could make this day-to-day living a little more convenient. Also, the Security Officer told us we could write one letter home, seal it, give it to him, and if we didn't make it back, he would mail the letters uncensored. The letter was addressed to my mother and inside was another addressed to my wife for my mother to mail.

Tension is at it's highest level as the countdown seems to be under way. God willing, I'll be here tomorrow night to record the historic events of Sunday, August 1, 1943.

It's an honor to be a small part of this historic undertaking that could change the course of history and the war. Our crew, I'm proud to say, all stepped forward to volunteer. There was no question in anyone's mind. If we don't make it back, this diary will be given to Captain Huntley and he has been requested to send it to Mrs. R. G. Byers, 2705 3rd Avenue East, Hibbing, Minnesota.

It's 3:00 A.M., Sunday morning, August 1st. We've stuffed our pockets with candy, gum, cigars, cigarettes. If we're going to crash, we want some of the comforts. Even took a few beers along. No parachutes. They have given us "Flak Protectors" made of woven steel. Should stop bullets and flak. Looks like a baseball umpires protective front. Very heavy and restricts movement. My guess is we won't wear them and take our chances with bullets and flak. Breakfast is at 3:30 A.M. Sorta like the condemned man's last breakfast. Best we've had since February.

Everyone had an opportunity to go to a brief religious service of his choice. Believe me, there are no non-believers going on this mission. We all made our final peace with God. The expressions on the faces of these young men told a great deal. Your life seemed to pass by. Thoughts were of home and loved ones and also of the grim task ahead. No one spoke. Just silent reflection.

The trucks immediately took the crews to the ships. Upon arriving, the ground crew personnel stood in front of the ship. We passed by, shaking hands. Nobody spoke. They could see the determined expressions on our faces. They knew nothing concerning the targets to be bombed. They immediately left in the truck. We grimly shook hands with the crews adjacent to our ship. Then we shook hands with each other and boarded the "Little Richard."

In a few minutes we'd start engines and taxi out into position. The moment has arrived. Our weeks of training and preparation. The success of this mission will largely depend on whether or not we can take the enemy by some degree of surprise— get in and get out. Hopefully, we'll be back to record the events of this historic day.

God willing, we will.

Captain Eddie Rickenbacker speaking to "Ploesti" crews July 31st. Gen. Ent seated directly behind Rickenbacker.

General Ent—9th Air Force Commander wishing the crews "Ploesti" bound God speed—Saturday, July 31st—General Ent was on the ill-fated mission.

General Doolittle speaking to Ploesti crews on Saturday July 31st—"If not one bomber returns and the target destroyed it'll be worth the sacrifice," he said.

'Ploesti' crews stand at attention as Gen. Doolittle—Gen. Bereaton —Gen. Ent—British air marshall, Tedder—Capt. Eddie Rickenbacker. Col. Compton and others approach the stage to talk to the crews—wish them well.

Warren Gregg, of our crew having Captain Eddie Rickenbacker sign his "Short Snorter" bill, Bengasi.

Left to right—Col Compton commanding 376th group, unidentified officer in center, British General Bernard Montgomery, better known as "Monty", Bengasi, July 31st, 1943.

Byers wearing jacket issued to waist gunners for low level "Ploesti" mission—protect the gunner from ground firing machine guns and 88mm shells.

AUGUST—1943

SUNDAY, AUGUST 1ST

The target was Ploesti. Five major refineries in and surrounding the Ploesti area. Almost 14 hours in the air. The historic events of the day are almost beyond imagination and belief. If the story was fiction, the reader would say, "A fantastic imagination in story-telling—beyond belief." But it's all true. The mission to Ploesti was written in sacrifice, blood and death from the beginning.

As the sun began to rise in the east, 177 bombers built to bomb at high altitude began taking off from airstrips surrounding Bengasi. The 376th and 98th had asphalt runways. the Other three airstrips we just bulldozed out of the desert and blowing dust from bombers taking off presented a serious delay in the takeoff. The "Little Richard" was the number five ship off from Berka Number II strip. Ships immediately flew out over the desert and into specific locations as quickly as possible. the 513th Squadron lead the 376th Group and the 376th in turn lead the other four bomber groups into the hell of Ploesti. The ships were overloaded with over 3,200 gallons of high octane gasoline and at least 4,400 pounds of bombs, plus a huge quantity of 20-pound incinerary sticks, spring activated. All ships were carrying extra belts of 50-caliber bullets, armor piercing, incinerary and tracer shells. The "Liberandos" had 28 ships headed by Colonel Compton. Thirty-nine ships from the "Traveling Circus" group headed by Addison Baker. The 98th headed by 'Killer' Kane. The "Pyramiders" had 47 ships in formation. Leon Johnson's group, the "Eight Balls" had 37 ships in the air. the "Sky Scorpions" headed by Jack Wood sent up 26 ships—177 bombers.

The target, Ploesti, is about 1,300 miles distant and deep in enemy territory. We're going unescorted as fighters haven't the gas capacity. The Russians could have given us air cover as Ploesti can't be over half an hour from Russia. None came and we couldn't under any circumstances fly a crippled bomber to Russia, the high command instructed the crews. If you are forced to crash-land, do so in enemy territory—not Russia. We could have carried twice the bomb load and half the gas if we could have proceeded to land in Russia after bombing Ploesti. Strange, as Russia supposedly is our ally.

The 98th had an overloaded bomber roar off the end of the runway, overturned and exploded. No survivors. A huge column of smoke rose into the sky—a warning of events to come. Time could be running out for over 50% of the striking force. About an hour into the mission, the ship carrying the lead navigator flying about 10 feet off the "Med" crashed, broke into two pieces, sank immediately—no survivors. The group circled, looking for swimmers, but none surfaced. Shortly after, we flew directly over a German surfaced U-Boat charging its batteries. Most of the crew was diving off the sub and swimming. We should have bombed and sank her as she no doubt sent an urgent radio message, something reference to huge bomber formations heading northeast direction.

The Island of Corfu near Albania just south of the Strait of Otranto was our first navigation check point. The Mediterranean was still, like a huge mirror—no white caps—very peaceful. I'm sure most of us wished we could have been elsewhere. As we headed through the mountains of southern Yugoslavia, heavy cloud cover caused the formations to spread out and become separated. The 98th was behind us, the other three groups are about 45 minutes behind us. Had problems getting off because of blowing sand and dust.

After literally going through the mountains, we came into the flat terrain of southern Romania. Crossed the blue Danube— better described as the 'muddy' Danube. Circled again, waiting for all elements of the formations of the 376th and 98th to again get into formation. The Danube was an important navigational aid. Navigation in a strange land at high altitude is difficult—at altitudes of 35 to 50 feet off the ground, and speeds exceeding 200 mph, navigation is almost impossible. Everything goes by blurred. The countryside completely changes every few seconds or so.

The bombers hit the critical navigation point, the city of Tirgoviste and should be headed straight for the final navigational check, the city of Floereste and then turn southeasterly directly into the city of Ploesti and the five major refineries. The group erred and the ships turned southeasterly at Tirgoviste and we were headed for Bucharest about 50 miles south of Ploesti! Bucharest was headquarters for the German Luftwaffe. By now, what little surprise was left, was gone. There can be no question about the targets as far as the enemy is concerned. Every fighter within flying distance of Ploesti had to be alerted. The battle was soon to commence.

By the time we got reorganized, turned around in a south to north direction, heading up the valley to Ploesti, all hell broke loose. We were approaching Ploesti from it's heaviest guarded area. Seems tracer shells of all types were coming from every direction. The battle of Ploesti has begun and it looks like a "kill or be killed" proposition. A survival of the fittest.

Haystacks spread open revealing dual purpose heavy guns— machine gun nests—heavy Ack-Ack guns. We were flying just above the tree and house tops. The lower to the ground the ships could fly, the safer they seemed to be from the heavy fire. Bomber formations became disorganized, dodging barrage balloons, and many times hitting their anchor cables. If hit with the propeller, it would snap the cable probably unbalance the prop so the engine would have to be feathered. The ship was forced to drop out of the formation as it couldn't keep up with only three engines. The German fighters attack it in numbers and in a few moments would shoot the bomber down. The great ground-air battle had begun. Some ships hit the cable with a section of the wing. Bomber would climb the cable, stall out, crash or the cable would spin the bomber around causing the ship to crash. Poor devils never had a chance. Straddled a freight train heading north— turned out to be an Ack-Ack flak train—tops and sides of cars opened revealing light and heavy guns. Before bombers could get below levels of gun fire or distance between bomber and flak train, we would lose about 20 bombers. Many bombers were 10 to 20 feet off the ground in speeds excess of 200 mph.

The "Little Richard" cut two balloon cables with the props. Fortunately we didn't have to feather the engines. The good Lord was on our side. General Ent and Colonel Compton in "Teggie Ann" were directly off our left wing. The din from the gun fire was like a thousand cannons going off at one time. Machine guns firing constantly. They shot at us with everything—pistols, rifles, machine guns, 20 MM and 30 MM cannon and the big Ack-Ack guns. Fighters were cruising just outside the ground fire perimeter waiting for their chance to finish us off. By now, some of the ships were dropping their delayed action bombs. We were tossing out the incinerary sticks and shooting the 50-calibers at storage tanks and anything that moved. Terrific explosions could be seen and heard in many sections of the oil fields.

All of a sudden, all of Ploesti became a mass of fire and smoke. Because of the extremely low altitude of the bombers, many were caught in the concussion and flames of the gigantic gas explosions. Bombers had to tip their wings to keep from hitting the numerous smoke stacks that dotted the area. In just a few seconds, bombers were all over the sky flying every which way, trying to escape the murderous gun fire and gigantic explosions. Bombers were crashing all over the area. Many were flying on only two and three engines. Many were smoking heavily. The 376th was circling around looking for our specific target. Approaching from south to north instead of west to east complicated matters. The three groups way behind us were now approaching Ploesti from west to east—we were on a collision course with them and that complicated the bomber airflow over Ploesti. Everyone is too busy to be scared—time for that later if you survive. We're getting the shit shot out of us. Machine guns and flak. Seems we've been at this for hours. We dropped our 45-second delayed action 500-pounders on a power house. We couldn't find the specific assigned target. Blew up many storage tanks.

Just north of Ploesti bombers were regrouping for the long run home. Gas is critical. The fighters attack us from all angles. They tried to dive at the bomber, blazing away with their guns and dive underneath us. Several of them hit the ground and explode. We got down to deck level and fought off the fighters as we headed west. We were practically wingtip to wingtip. There's only one word for this—disaster! We've probably lost 70 to 80 planes over the general target area. All of a sudden, the great ground-air battle of Ploesti was over. The critical problem now was gas. One of our bomb bay tanks was never filled which left us about 400 gallons short. We discussed bailing out before we hit the Adriatic Sea but decided to take our chances with the ship. Even to the point of bellying it into the "Med". The immediate problem was to lighten the ship. We tossed out everything that wasn't fastened down. Even tossed out some unused 50-caliber belts but kept enough to battle the fighters that could intercept us when we reached the Adriatic. We even began to toss out some of our clothes. The engine mixture was leaned out. Fortunately, when we hit the Adriatic and headed south, we had an extremely heavy tail wind.

We were not intercepted by German fighters from Italian bases. Observed 30 or more large aircraft on an airdrome about 20 miles from Corfu, northeast. The trip south across the "Med" was uneventful. We landed about 8:00 P.M. almost 14 hours in the air. Had very little gas left in the tanks. The ground personnel was told the target at 12:00 noon—our estimated time of arrival over Ploesti. The ground crew was there to congratulate us. Bombers were crashing in the sea—running out of gas. Almost every one fired a red flare indicating landing priority—dead or wounded aboard, or mechanical problems. We've got to have lost 80 to 100 bombers, give or take.

185

The crew all knelt down and kissed the good old solid ground. We had survived Ploesti! The question is, why were we selected to survive? Bombers were being lost all around us. I remember walking back to the debriefing area and looking up in the sky—millions of blinking stars—and asking the good Lord, "Why me? Why was I selected to survive?"

At the medical tent where we were examined, they gave us several ounces of bourbon. Most of the crew didn't drink, so the writer drank theirs. Those who survived Ploesti will never, never forget it. It was the ultimate in human adventure. After the debriefing, the crew hit the sack. Everyone's nerves have about had it.

Sunday, August 1st—the great bomber disaster of World War II—low level mission to the oil fields of Ploesti, Romania.

Author along with Linderman standing by
ship "Little Richard".

Artists conception of B-24's over "Ploesti" ship 100—"Teggie
Ann" carried Gen. Ent, Col. Compton. Notice bombs dropping out
of bomb bays—incendiary sticks out of waist window.

Low flying B-24's enroute to "Ploesti" Sunday, August 1st, 1943. Notice the shadows of the ships on the ground.

B-24 on take off Sunday, August 1st—target Ploesti—heavily bomb loaded—500 pounders incendiary sticks and bomb bay gas tanks.

9th AIR FORCE GIVES PLOESTI HELL

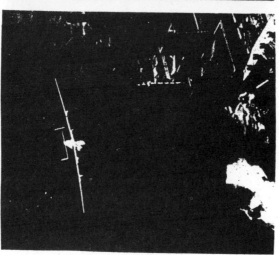

Just how close the U.S. Liberator bombers came to the refinery smokestacks is shown in these photographs. This congested portion of Rumania is a main nazi source of oil, and its loss would be one of the worst nightmares Hitler could experience. Only the Nazis themselves know how much the attack—one of the longest mass bombardment raids in history—had hurt them, but returning forces believed it had hurt plenty. They reported direct hits on installations, plants, fractionating columns, tank farms, and power houses. (All photos by 9th U.S. Air Force — Passed by U.S. Military Censor)

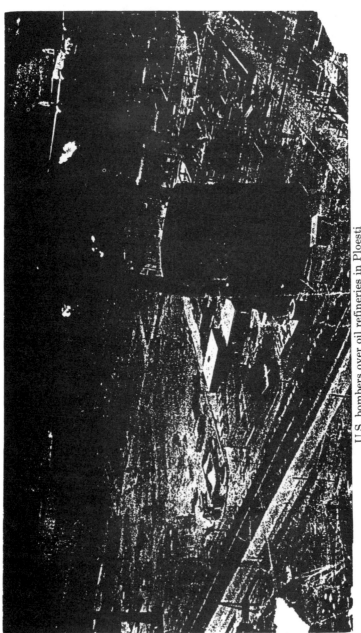

U.S. bombers over oil refineries in Ploesti

Giant B-24's flying through the fire and heavy black smoke—many of the 24's never made it through—they never had a chance.

Giant oil and gas storage tanks were all over the area—
every 3rd 50 caliber was armor piercing every 5th a tracer
shell.

An error in navigation was made by the lead ship we
turned in a south easterly direction too soon—headed for
Bucharest—50 to 60 miles south of Ploesti—roared over
Bucharest looking for oil fields—Bucharest was
headquarters for the German Luftwaffe for the Balken
countries—every fighter with 400 miles was alerted and
they came to fight—mistake was very costly—also used
up additional gas which was critical.

Feathered engine propellers were a positive indicator to
the German pilots that the B-24 was crippled and they
attack 'em 'till they shot them down.

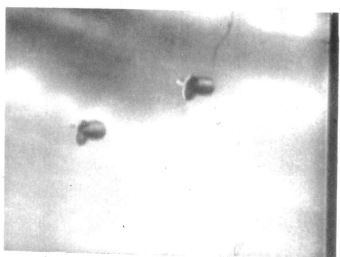

Over a 100 barrage balloons were floating throughout the
Ploesti area. The attacking B-24's were flying below
them—the cables that held them.

These two B-24's are about to crash land belly in—some of the crew members were lucky enough to get out alive—only to be taken prisoner.

The low (almost zero altitude) flying bombers were after cracking plants, distilling plants, power plants, dropping 500 pounders—delayed action from 45 seconds to an hour delay.

Oil and gas storage tanks exploding—burning throughout the area. In a matter of minutes the sky was filled with fire and smoke.

German fighters congratulating each other over their many B-24 kills—percent of aircraft dispatched the groups had the greatest loss of any mission ever flown in WWII.

Unbeknown to the Ploesti crews the Ploesti area had become the heaviest guarded target in all of Europe over 175 heavy Ack Ack guns.

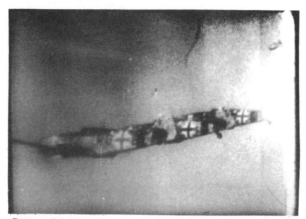

German fighters looking us over just before they attack us. They literally had a field day shooting down the crippled 24's that couldn't keep up with the formations.

B-24's approaching the Columbia Aquila Refinery. Many storage tanks already ablaze with 10 to 15 more B-24's approaching to finish off the target.

General Dolittle decorating "Ploesti" crews with "distinguished flying cross" for extraordinary achievement while participating in aerial flight—Sunday, 1st August 1943.

MONDAY, AUGUST 2ND

Recorded history will call Ploesti the greatest mass low altitude bombing mission in the history of heavy bombardment. Rumor has it that seven more low altitude runs were to be scheduled against the fields, but have been cancelled because of the heavy losses in men and ships. Looks like about 80 to 100 bombers have been lost. Bombers landed all over the Middle East—Greece, Turkey, Cyprus, Malta, Albania. Sea rescue crews have picked up about 25 fliers floating around the "Med" in dinghies. Bombers ran out of gas, bellied into the water. Each squadron has a ship searching the sea and the desert for crashed ships and crews. Group intelligence reports the mission, in spite of the mistakes, was about 75% effective. By the time the different groups have taken an accurate check on their missing ships, we'll have come close to losing about 60% of the striking force, maybe more. A hell of a high price to pay.

One can just imagine what the radio and papers are saying and printing about this history-making raid. Many folks back home are wondering, no doubt, who is alive and who is missing.

Looks as if the aerial bombing of Italy will get underway again. It's reported that the 98th lost over 25 ships. Hope Gaston and crew made it out, Dore and all the others. The official reports on all losses and other info should be out in the morning. Just laid around with the boys and naturally congratulated ourselves on still being alive. Believe me, I believe, as do all the survivors.

TUESDAY, AUGUST 3RD

The Egyptian Gazette (English version) headlines— "Ploesti Refineries Ablaze", "Third of Hitler's Gas Supplies Comes from Ploesti," "Peace Hint by Rome Radio." The official Air Force News of August 3rd headlines—"Roof Top Swoop on Oil Refineries." Official statements yesterday said the Astro-Romanian refinery, the largest in Europe, was heavily damaged. Many pipelines destroyed. Ploesti's newest refinery and the only one producing 100 octane gasoline, the Credit Minier Refinery, was showered by bombs. Many fires started.

The Air Force News goes on to say that at least 51 enemy aircraft were destroyed. The paper further states, "The airfields bustled with guns and the target is said to be one of the most heavily defended in the world." NOW they tell us!

British intelligence said resistance would be slight as the Romanians were tired of the war. Another interesting headline in the Air Force News states, "Italians Pray for Peace. Anxious-eyed crowds thronged Italian churches yesterday in fervent prayers for peace."

Of the five groups in the Ploesti raid, the 376th is in the best shape, B-24 wise. The heat today was stifling and no relief in sight. Wherever a couple of guys gather, the conversation is of Ploesti.

WEDNESDAY, AUGUST 4TH

The Officer's and Non-Com's Clubs at the 98th look like a morgue. Most guys stand around in shock. It's official— 27 of their ships failed to return. The 98th and 93rd are consolidating and bringing the 98th up to combat strength. The remainder of the 93rd will be returning to England in the near future.

Went to the dispensary and the Doc says I've got hemorrhoids and he wanted to operate on them. The hospital is full of this type of patient now and most wish they never had the operation. Think I'll sweat them out—don't want to miss any missions.

The five day rest period after the Ploesti run is about over and there is talk again of missions to Italy. Back to the high altitude again. What a blessing the 40 degrees to 60 degrees below temps will be compared to the heat of Ploesti. The mission hasn't been posted—just conversation. Went for a swim with the crew. Generally laid around trying to forget the Ploesti disaster and the loss of many good friends. The Egyptian Gazette (English version) carried the headlines, "Axis Northern Wing in Sicily Falling Back. U.S. Spearheads Cut Deep Into German Defense Line." Also showed a photo of B-24 tipping it's wing to keep from hitting a smoke stack. Stated that it was the greatest action bomber photo ever taken. Certainly brought back vivid Ploesti memories. Base security has loosened up somewhat as Wog kids are again going through our garbage cans. Poor kids. Can't help but feel sorry for them. Flies and heat will get you if the combat missions don't. Am positive none of the survivors of this group will ever eat "Bully Beef," "Rubber Pancakes," "Dehydrated Green Eggs," and marmalade again. No wonder everybody has hemorrhoids. A person has to eat to survive, I guess.

THURSDAY, AUGUST 5TH

Another long mission is in the making. A special practice run is scheduled for in the morning. After Ploesti who needs practice? Squadron leaders say the mission will go out the following day after the practice. This should put me over the 200 hour mark and will be sweating out the final 100 hours of combat. Seems a person gets more concerned with survival the more combat hours one acquires. One becomes more nervous. We all went for a relaxing swim and in general took things easy.

Rumor has it the great Jack Benny will be here shortly to give this group some much needed enjoyment to take our minds off the grim reality of combat. Word has just come through that Catania has fallen and that all of Sicily will shortly be in our hands. No more missions to Sicily. Lear just told us that he will probably make Squadron Operations Officer as Beck is going home. Lucky guy. Hope this doesn't bust up our crew.

FRIDAY, AUGUST 6TH

They gave a special edition of "Stars and Stripes" paper dealing just with the Ploesti raid—two pages with some print—eight super action photos showing the Liberators over Ploesti—a great collectors item. A headline stated, "Liberators Write Air History In Smashing Raid." Further states, "Coming in as low as 10 feet off the ground, the ships released over 600,000 pounds of bombs and hundreds of clusters of incineraries. It was the closest thing to Dante's Inferno anybody had ever seen."

Instead of going on the practice mission, I went to see the Doc, as did several other boys with the same problem— hemorrhoids. Not getting worse, but not getting any better.

Rumors concerning Italy and her role in the war are flying around again. Think maybe this time something will come out of them. We could be moving to southern Italy soon, or even to Sicily. Gaston and a few others from the 98th headed for home today. For them, the war is over—they survived. The lucky bastards. Wish we were going home with them.

The 98th requested from Air Force headquarters fifty more B-24's to be delivered immediately. Will be surprised if the request is honored.

Received a letter from my lovely wife and all the materials I've been sending with the boys returning home have been mailed to her. Good show! Many of the boys seem a little dazed since Ploesti, but that certainly is understandable. We've been burying our Ploesti dead almost every day. At least for them, the struggle is over. They've found eternal peace in the shifting sands of the desert. Most of the boys are ready to give it another go. Retired early.

SATURDAY, AUGUST 7TH

Again, nothing posted. Ground crews have been extremely busy patching up the ships. Many of them had hundreds of flak and bullet holes in them. Engines again in bad shape. Need extensive repairs. Major Nesbitt is flying this next mission and is taking Lear as his Co-Pilot and I'm to go along as Radio and Waist Gunner. After briefing, it was immediately cancelled because of weather conditions over target.

Recon photos of Ploesti reveal heavy damage to five of the seven major refineries. The other two were only slightly damaged. Intelligence tells us that the Germans have already felt the oil and gas shortages for their Panzers and aircraft. Some of us sat around at Squadron Headquarters and just chewed the fat about the war—missions to come—where the group would be moving and when. Enjoyed a swim and in general again took things easy. Seems like nobody is too eager to start the mission procedure again.

SUNDAY, AUGUST 8TH

We're beginning to hate the weatherman. Held the big ones on the ground again because of heavy cloud formations over the target areas. Most of us beat it to the beach and soaked up the sun. Later, five of us got a Jeep and went into Bengasi and the stench that hangs over the city isn't getting any better. Some poorly bottled soft drinks—none of them carbonated are making their appearance and the base doctors have warned against drinking them—could cause serious digestive problems.

The old-type fruit jar seal is used to keep the contents intact—served warm—doesn't even look refreshing. Kids are all over, begging for food, candy and money. If you give something to one of them, in a few seconds, there are fifty of them. Your heart really goes out to them—it's very sad.

MONDAY, AUGUST 9TH

Early this morning a very low flying bomber woke us all up and a few seconds later the ship's engines cut off and a tremendous splash could be heard near our shore line. Several seconds later, trucks of all descriptions were heading for the beach. The British crew all got out safely. The bomber was returning from a night mission over Italy when she ran out of gas. The bomber was a British Halifax. Took some good photos of her. She floated to shore. We climbed in and looked around—it was constructed of wood and fabric. The B-24's are all aluminum and sink in a matter of seconds. The British are very courageous fliers. they go out singly in their "Wimpys", "Lancasters" and "Halifax" ships every night. Some don't even have super-chargers on the engines. Altitude maximum would be about 12,000 feet— good targets for the searchlights and heavy Ack-Ack guns. The bombs they drop they refer to as "Block Busters". Must get damn lonely over Italy all by yourself. Our hats are off to them—they are dedicated fliers.

Weatherman says clouds still holding mission grounded. Here's a good rumor—mission could go to Hungarian oil fields near Budapest. Never realized they had any. Hope the high command doesn't make a habit of bombing oil fields.

TUESDAY, AUGUST 10TH

They woke us at midnight and said a mission was going out early in the morning—breakfast at 4:00 A.M.— briefing at 5:00 A.M. While eating, the word came down the raid was called off. Boy, were we all pissed off. All immediately went back to the sack and took things easy all day. After supper, they rounded us all up again and gave us a briefing update. The mission is to be an all-out effort again by all the B-24's in the area, and also by the Eighth Air Force B-24's in England. The target is to be the giant Folke Wolf aircraft plant at Wiener Neustadt near Vienna in Austria. Has to be a 10 or 11 hour run with most of it at high altitude. Wiener Neustadt compares to the German Air Force as does Wright-Patterson Field, Dayton, Ohio to the American Air Force. We'll be going up the Adriatic Sea, Italy to our left and Albania and Yugoslavia to our right. The city of Trieste, Italy will be a navigational check point. The return will be directly across the northern part of Italy to the Tyrrhenian Sea and then to Tunisia as we haven't the gas capacity to go back to Bengasi. Bomb bay tanks are in most ships. This time, by God, Fisher will see that ours are filled to capacity. We're in "Little Richard." Am beginning to love that ship.

We'll be dropping four 1,000-pounders. Only part of our crew is scheduled to make this run. Nesbitt and Lear flying, Gekas will be doing the bombing, and I'm on radio and waist gunner. Mac and Linderman are scheduled with another crew. Looks like our crew is busting up. Colonel Compton is also making the run. This is second in importance only to Ploesti.

Rumors are again around as to where the 9th will soon be moving. All of us who survived the Romanian Ploesti raid are to receive either the Distinguished Flying Cross or the Distinguished Service Cross—plus a Presidential Group Citation Award. A lot of Purple Heart Medals to be given out also.

WEDNESDAY, AUGUST 11TH

Again, weather forced the mission cancellation. this is getting to be a joke. Everything is on immediate go and another briefing is in the making for early morning. We're sweating this one out almost as bad as Ploesti.

We laid around on the beach and got a good burn—beet red. Played a little blackjack and did all right for a change. At dinner, they gave us the word—up at 4:00 A.M.—mission takeoff at 6:15 A.M. sharp. This is on again—off again. Finally weighs pretty heavily on your mind and attitude. Everybody seems plenty lonesome for the good old U.S.A.

THURSDAY, AUGUST 12TH

I'll be damned if they didn't do it to us again! Up early—rushed around—briefings—out to the ships—and cancelled because of weather. Somebody is going to kill that weatherman. All dashed back to the sack and slept till about 10:00 A.M. Laid by the beach and acquired a shade more tan. A colonel from Cairo spoke to us in the afternoon about the war situation in general. He predicted that Italy would be out of the war within a couple of weeks and that Germany could be out by this December. Time will tell. Think he is way off base reference to Germany. She's taking a hell of a beating but the war is far from over.

Played a little blackjack. Had a few at the club. Everybody early to bed as we're going to try again tomorrow.

FRIDAY, AUGUST 13TH

Friday the 13th. A bad sign. Hope it doesn't materialize that way before the day ends. Everything got under way before the sun began to rise in the east. The 376th had 24 ships in formation. The two flights immediately began to climb to altitude. Five groups were participating. Probably the second biggest mission reference to bomber numbers—second only to Ploesti. Nothing interrupted our flight. No fighters or Ack-Ack. Colder than hell out at 21,000 feet. Holbrook and I were back-to-back scanning the sky for fighters. About 100 miles from the target, because of a 100% cloud cover, the 376th turned back. The other flights continued on target course. The 376th headed for our secondary target—Turin, Italy, a huge steel mill.

Cloud conditions over the plants prevented us from dropping our payload. We headed out to the Tyrrhenian Sea and south to Tunisia. After 11 hours and 45 minutes, we landed at a base called El Bathan, a huge B-26 base. Those ships just returned from a mission to Rome and the huge marshalling yards as their target.

The 376th certainly screwed up the whole show today. The other groups managed to drop their bombs through the cloud cover without too much opposition. Don't know how much damage they did as of this writing.

North Africa is very picturesque. The foothills and lots of trees certainly add to the scenery. Bomber bases seem to be all over the area—B-17's, B-25's, B-26's and of course, fighters. This section of Tunisia is a great wine producing area. You can buy Vino (red wine) by the gallon for just a few pennies. Five gallons for about $1.25. Needless to say, we had our share. As a matter of fact, the whole crew got stinking drunk.

Because of lack of tents or sleeping quarters, we all slept in the bomber with our clothes on. Not too comfortable. It was quite a mess. Was a long, disappointing day. We'll probably receive no combat time for participation.

SATURDAY, AUGUST 14TH

After having gassed the ship and checked it all over, we ate a fast breakfast and with gigantic hangovers, we headed back to good old Bengasi. We were all pretty tired and after landing, headed for the medical tent and debriefing and then to the sack. Before leaving, they alerted us to another mission in the morning—details to come later. Hope the raid is not Messina. It's become the hottest spot in all the world as the Axis troops leave Sicily across the Straits of Messina to Italy. Traffic back and forth is extremely heavy. The whole crew is very weary.

SUNDAY, AUGUST 15TH

They woke us up again early. The mission is still 'go.' However, we're not scheduled. No time as yet posted. Most of the crews not on the run laid around and drank up some of the wine we took on board leaving Tunisia. Crew replacements should be coming soon as many of the oldtimers should be completing their 300 hours.

All hell broke loose early this morning. The British Ack-Ack gunners cut loose on a 24 coming in to land from Tunisia. The radio operator was off the ball and failed to send the proper identity signals which change almost hourly. Probably didn't copy 'em right at the radio briefing. The crew is lucky to be alive and that's for sure! The 514th Squadron lost a ship on takeoff at El Bathon. Don't know the status of the crew as yet.

MONDAY, AUGUST 16TH

Long before the sun rose in the east, ground crews were swarming over the ships. Combat crews had breakfast and briefings. Twenty-four ships of the 376th and the same number from the 93rd took off and headed for the big airdrome near Foggia, Italy on the east coast by the Adriatic Sea near the Gulf of Manfredonia. Some of our crew was not scheduled. We got up and ate together. Listened in on the briefing, then watched them take off, move in to specific locations in the formations out over the desert and then buzz the base, tipping their wings ina final salute. Gives a person a lonesome feeling—not being with them. Guess maybe you reach a point where this business of combat gets into your blood. You become sort of a fatalist. If you're going to get killed—so what? A kill or be killed proposition. Maybe you're just beginning to crack under the nervous and mental strain.

The 514th lost another ship. Crampton, radio operator, was aboard her. At the debriefing it was noted that all bailed out as she circled to earth. Maybe they were all alive somewhere. Hope so.

The days are getting somewhat shorter and the nights longer and colder. Last night we observed a full eclipse of the moon— beautiful and bright. Received several letters from Anne and a couple of packages. Had a feast in the tent.

TUESDAY, AUGUST 17TH

Received an anniversary telegram from Anne today—a touch of home. Very glad to receive it. Another mission is posted for tomorrow and, again, we're not scheduled. We're getting pissed off at this business of being left out of these missions. How in hell are we ever going to get our time in—300 hours. Complained to Lear and also to squadron flight leaders. Seems we'll never get our time in.

Rumors are again around that we'll be joining the 12th Air Force and moving shortly to Sicily. It's also rumored that we'll probably be going on every other mission as Lear now has officially become a flight leader. That's a step in the right direction. With Sicily almost out of the war, this means longer flights—probably eight to twelve hours to Italian targets.

WEDNESDAY, AUGUST 18TH

Late last night they informed us that the hottest spot in the world as far as Ack-Ack guns are concerned is in Allied hands. Messina is ours and the battle for Sicily has all but become history. A few local pockets of resistance still exist. We've lost a lot of our targets but they've added many new ones on our list in middle and northern Italy.

The 9th needs ships badly and we're hoping replacements come soon to bring our squadrons up to full requirements. The 376th will only be sending out 18 bombers instead of the usual 24— sometimes as many as 36. The ships are in bad need of repair throughout. Another reason for the everyother mission routine is to give all the crews a chance to get their hours in. Seems we have right now more crews than ships. With this routine, we'll still be here (or someplace in the Middle East) at Christmas.

The blowing dust was so intense you had to wear a dust mask if wandering outside the tent. Seems lately the wind is almost constant, multiplying the problems reference to engine maintenance. Fall and the rainy season can't be far off. Jack Benny should be here at the base tonight with his traveling artists. Should be a great evening.

THURSDAY, AUGUST 19TH

The old saying still is true—bombers die fighting as do the crews that man them. The mission again went to Foggia airdrome and again members of our crew missed the run. The debriefing report indicated as Friburg and crew came off the target flying "Little Richard," fighters jumped them and on the first pass of ME-109's they mortally wounded the "Little Richard." Seven parachutes were counted as the ship spun to earth. Somebody, again, was looking out for us. Lear's crew could just as well have been aboard her. It had to be the 15th mission for the "Little Richard." Our crew feels as though we've lost one of us. She was a great ship. Brought us to the target and back on many of our missions.

The 98th also lost a 24 on the raid due to fighters. The 513th Squadron has only six combat-ready bombers. A disastrous situation. The missions seem to be getting rougher as the air battle of Italy intensifies. Survival is becoming more questionable than ever. The crew's attitude still great—no real signs of anyone beginning to crack up from the strain. The crews keep hoping we'll have strong fighter support on future missions, giving us positive protective cover. Still very windy out and quite cold.

FRIDAY, AUGUST 20TH

Just checked at squadron headquarters and a mission is 'go' for in the morning. Lear is taking the 513th Squadron.

We're scheduled to make the run in a ship called "Barrel House Bessie"—17th raid for this veteran combat ship. The target is Naples, the huge airdrome nearby called "Cancello." We're dropping nine 500-pounders. The old wind and dust hit a new high today. The blowing dust was so heavy it was difficult to see the tent next to ours. Dust was all over—bedsheets and blankets. Sat around and wore our dust masks. If the damn Germans don't get us, the damn duststorms will. The food is lousy enough, and now the dust doesn't add a lot of flavor to it.

SATURDAY, AUGUST 21ST

The 513th lead the whole show this morning and Lear led the 513th and the other five groups participating in the run. The target finally turned out to be the huge marshalling railyards just outside of the city of Naples. As we approached the target from the Tyrrhenian Sea entering the Bay of Naples, the harbor was filled with ships of all description. Everything seemed to be going routinely—cold as hell. The Ack-Ack was extremely accurate and the big black 30-yard puffs of smoke appeared all over the sky. The fighters were waiting out of range of the Ack-Ack to attack us—both sides of the formation.

Gekas, the Bombadier, had control of the bomber and we were on the bomb run. All of a sudden, Gekas reported he couldn't see the target. Lear took all the ships in a huge circle for a re-bomb run and as we circled, we were directly over the heaviest defenses surrounding the Naples area. The Ack-Ack was probably the heaviest and most accurate we've run into for some time. The sky was literally one big black cloud. The sweat runs off your face. You stand—watch—and pray that the giant exploding shells miss your ship. A person lives a lifetime.

Several of the groups salvoed their bombs and headed for Bengasi. I witnessed a bomber take a direct hit in the Pilot and Co-Pilot area. The giant ship looped-the-loop and went into a slow spin towards the ground. It looked as though the Pilot and Co-Pilot were killed instantly as the ship was completely out of control. Luckily, it wasn't on fire as yet and one parachute was seen to blossom out before she crashed. We never did find the damn target. We all knew one thing—to survive, we had to get the hell out of these heavy Ack-Ack defenses. We headed for Cancello airdrome and salvoed the 500-pounders and headed for home. The 376th portion of this mission was a complete failure. Too bad the crew had to foul up a golden opportunity. Could go pretty rough on Lear. Hope not, for his sake. Gekas made the mistake in judgment.

It's a grand feeling to be heading down the home stretch—300 hour mark. Am far from finished yet and much can happen on future missions. We were 9 hours and 25 minutes in the air. Had to use the piss tube. As always, the damn thing freezes over and you've a mess on your hands. The crew was tired. Very dejected because of the series of events reference to the mission just completed. After debriefing, ate and to bed as another mission is 'go' for tomorrow.

SUNDAY, AUGUST 22ND

Mission rescheduled for tomorrow. Nothing cooking. Lear had quite a session with the big wheels of 9th Bomber Command regarding the run to Naples. He was made Squadron Operations Officer so he survived the ordeal. We were very happy for him. The crew's future as a crew becomes more uncertain. Hope Lear decides to make a lot of missions and takes us with him.

An all-out is posted for tomorrow. Mission to be the harbor of Bari, Italy, just up the eastern boot of Italy on the Adriatic. Intelligence states that the harbor is filled with German and Italian shipping. Should be a good 'go.'

MONDAY, AUGUST 23RD

As we prepared to taxi out for the mission to Bari, the top turret went haywire. Couldn't revolve and, of course, Lear scrapped out of participation. Couldn't risk the crew and ship with no top turret operating. Mac took a skeleton crew to Malta where we picked up a crew that had landed there on a previous mission. The ship they were flying stays there for repair.

We all went to Velleta and looked over Malta in general. Many things have changed here. Buildings have been generally repaired (not completely) and the people in general seemed to be a lot happier. They were not starving as was the case when we were here several months ago. Secured a "Times of Malta" newspaper, tabloid size. The harbor of Velleta was filled with battleships, cruisers, and warships of all descriptions. Much shipping activity in and around Malta. Germans made a big mistake by not capturing Malta when they had the golden opportunity.

Upon return,. the ships from Bari were also coming home. The mission was an easy one with little concentration of enemy action, Ack-Ack or fighters. Seems we always miss the easy ones.

"Times of Malta" headlines—"Great Allied Air Assault Severs Italian Rail Communications. Over 50 Axis fighters destroyed in bitterest battles of the war. Liberators battle through to Naples area." The paper further states in Africa and Sicily, Axis forces lost half a million troops. Malta Air Force flew 4,000,000 miles in Sicilian campaign protecting ships and beaches by day and night. Night fighters alone used over 200,000 rounds of shells and over 2,000,000 gallons of gasoline used in the campaign. Sicily is now history but the logistics of the campaign will be discussed for years, in terms of equipment and human lives. War is hell.

TUESDAY, AUGUST 24TH

Looks like another great mission. Target location is Foggia, the big airdrome near the Gulf of Manfredonia on the Adriatic Sea. We'll go up the sea into Foggia and back out to sea, head south across the "Med" for home. We're leading the 98th—the 376th, that is, and Lear is leading an element. The 93rd, 94th, 44th, 389th, and the 43rd are going back to England in a couple of days, leaving the bombing operations again to the 376th and the 98th for the Middle East.

Mission was scrapped because of weather moving in over the target area. Replacement rumors are floating around again that the squadrons will be brought up to flyable strength in the very near future. Looks like the invasion of Italy could be under way in the immediate future. The British are creating invasion noises around Greece. Could be interesting. Another eight or nine missions could put us over the magic 300-hour mark.

WEDNESDAY, AUGUST 25TH

Up and at 'em early. Breakfast. Up-to-date briefing info. Rushed out to aircraft. The green light was 'go'. Just a few seconds before leaving revetment, the Number 2 engine had fouled it's plugs. The ground crew swarmed all over it in a desperate attempt to correct the problem. Meantime, the ships keep taking off. Finally got the "go ahead" but we were about a half an hour too late. We could never catch up to the formations. Tried, but finally turned back to the base. Lost another 8 to 10 hours of combat time. What the hell else can happen to this crew?

Several new crews have arrived with new modified 24's. They've added a retractable belly-ball turret, replacing the 50-caliber you used shooting out of the belly fuselage entry door. The gun was absolutely worthless. The ball turret makes the 24 a well rounded out fighting ship. Four turrets plus two waist guns. The turrets have two 50-caliber guns each. Hope we're assigned one of these beauties.

THURSDAY, AUGUST 26TH

A quiet day. Nothing much of anything cooking. We worked around cleaning up our tent area inside and out. For a change, the wind was rather still so we hastily put of a clothesline and hung our dusty sheets and blankets our to soak up a little sun. No mail for quite a while. Bad for the morale of all the troops, especially the fliers. Mail from home seems to bolster up their morale and spirits. Little or no mail has arrived for several weeks.

We all went for a swim. The base security seems to be relaxing somewhat. The Wogs are going from tent to tent offering to launder your clothes for a nominal fee. They really are doing a landoffice business. We were trying to wash our shorts, socks, etc. using old 5 gallon gas cans and with no hot water. Not very effective. The Wogs promise two day delivery. What a deal!

FRIDAY, AUGUST 27TH

Berardi informed us that a mission is posted and Lear and crew are participating. No briefing time or target has yet been announced. Hope this time we're assigned one of the newly arrived ships with the retractable ball belly turret.

The damn heat again is almost unbearable. Around here, the uniform of the day is what's most comfortable— shorts—tee shirts—not very military but it's necessary to survive. We've cutoff our long G.I. pants and made a cool pair of shorts. No breeze at all. The flies seem to invade an area all of a sudden and there's a loud noise from their buzzing around.

All of the other groups have left the area. It's just the 376th and the 98th to carry on in the Middle East. We're a little battlescarred reference to fliers and equipment but somehow we'll survive the damn war. Replacements still arriving, being assigned to different squadrons by Group Headquarters. Those new ships are real beauties. In first-class shape compared to our old combat veteran B-24's.

It was crowded at the club. The missions—the air battles— the damned fighters and doomed bombers—the damn desert—the heavy Ack-Ack—all are the main topic of discussions between a few warm drinks. To bed early as 4:00 A.M. is just a few hours away.

FRIDAY, AUGUST 28TH

The target was Taranto, Italy—the harbor. Taranto is located in the top western inner portion of the heel of Italy. The 376th had 24 ships in the formation. The 98th was also participating. Headed for altitude immediately after takeoff in a north-westerly direction. Approached the general target area through the Gulf of Taranto. Cold—bitter cold. And then it happened to us again. About 40 minutes from the target, a supercharger on the Number One engine broke and our ship just couldn't keep up with the other formations. We were forced to turn back or go over the target by ourselves, which would be suicide.

We made a 'Gentleman's Agreement' that one ship in distress couldn't hold back and jeopardize the whole formation. This procedure we arrived at many missions ago. Seems like a hard and cruel method of doing things, but survival to fight again is the most important element. Slow moving bombers over the target or on the bombing run would become sitting ducks.

As we peeled off, we all silently wished them "God Speed." The crew was very upset. Probably we'll receive no combat time for this run. We seem to have a stretch of failures preventing us from going over the target.

We brought out bombs back, 500-pounders. Here's a good one—after every mission now the medical tent presents us all with a double shot of good old American whiskey to settle a person down a little bit. Really hits the spot on an empty stomach. Some of the crew don't drink—the writer took their allotment. Makes you sleep like a log and you don't worry about missions past, present or future. Maybe the medics are beginning to realize that some of the old combat veterans have breaking points beyond which it becomes difficult to continue. They now refer to this condition as "combat fatigue."

Another mission for tomorrow is posted and Lear and crew is scheduled. Here we go again.

SUNDAY, AUGUST 29TH

The run scheduled for today has been postponed. Weather again. At least this time they let us sleep. We've been given a new ship for tomorrow's raid. We should make it OK. Question is, who is going to operate the belly ball? No one on the crew is checked out for this type of turret. A person has to be quite small to fit into the ball. Lear is leading the 513th tomorrrow.

Several of us are going to try and check out the ball turret. Linderman, our top turret gunner, is really the only one that will fit into the ball. Immediately, I was told I was too tall, too big. Back to the waist 50-caliber gun.

Again, no breeze. Heat is stifling. Very depressing. Several more crews arrived with new ships. Great morale builder, these new super aircraft. Went for a swim. Just rested.

MONDAY, AUGUST 30TH

Instead of waking us up at 4:00 A.M. and going through all of the procedures before calling off the mission, they just let us sleep. Bad weather over target area. Heavy thunderstorms, high winds. The weather again plays an important role in the future—missions in the months to come. We all hope it doesn't deter us too much as many of the old combat veterans are eager to complete the 300-hour agreement and return to the Zone of the Interior—the U.S.A.

Went to Soluck with the Chief Chef today. We call him "Pierre." Went in a Jeep. He was on a scouting trip for eggs. Took along the camera and secured some interesting photos. Nomad tents dot the area between Bengasi and Soluck. Herds of camels and goats are quite picturesque. Soluck is like an undertaking parlor since all our ground troops moved north to Bengasi. Very little has taken place to rebuild the same settlement.

"Pierre" and I brought along chocolate bars and cigarettes for the Wogs. Very sad to see the little Arab children beg for chocolate and food in general. We did secure a large quantity of eggs. Boy! What a treat for all the troops in a day or so. Arrived back late in the afternoon. Weather over our base area looks bad. Maybe the mission scheduled for tomorrow will again have to be cancelled. A large group gathered at the club for a few, then to the sack.

TUESDAY, AUGUST 31ST

With a heavy local overcast sky and threatening rain, we finally got underway. The 376th with 24 ships in formation. The 98th was also with us. The target was Pescara, located about half-way up the eastern side of the boot of Italy on the Adriatic Sea. The ships were carrying 500-pounders. We were assigned "Daisy Mae," a new ship—first raid—Number 241031. She held ten of the 500-pounders. A great ship improvement over the combat ships we've been travelling in. The targets were railbridges around and near Pescara. Destroying these bridges would be very serious blow to the rail movement of German troops and military equipment.

The weather enroute up the Adriatic was the roughest we've encountered for many months. Formations became very spread out because of heavy turbulent cloud cover. Over the general target area, the cloud cover was about 80%. Little Ack-Ack fire and not too accurate. Very cold by the waist windows. All bombers salvoed their 500-pounders and many of the railbridges were destroyed. Such devastating destruction these 500-pounders cause. No fighters came up to intercept us—a pleasant surprise.

We were 11 hours and 33 minutes in the air—about 8 hours at altitude and on oxygen. Very tired. All ships returned safely. The two shots of booze certainly hit the spot to settle you down. Another mission is in process. Will be briefed on the details in the morning.

SEPTEMBER—1943

WEDNESDAY, SEPTEMBER 1ST

Some of the fliers are going home—they've completed the 300 hour goal—lucky bastards. Ken Snow, also Good is through. They'll leave Bengasi tomorrow. Another mission is posted—Suloma, Italy located southwest of Pescara. Scheduled for tomorrow. Should be about a ten hour run. Hope the weatherman cooperates. Most of the boys laid around, rested— some went for a dip in the "Med." Received a box of cigars from my darling wife. Worth their weight in gold. Some of the outlying tents still haven't got electricity, doubt if they ever will receive it while we're at Bengasi. Rumors again around reference to a move. This time to west Africa.

THURSDAY, SEPTEMBER 2ND

About midnight they cancelled the Suloma mission because of heavy cloud cover. Informed us to stand by as the raid will go as soon as weather breaks over the general target area. We just gathered in the tent and hashed over the war in general and our chances of surviving it. Several more crews arrived. These new crews are really eager beavers and just can't wait to get into combat. How fast that attitude will change after a few 90 MM Ack-Ack shells burst around 'em and an ME-109 or FW-190 shoots one of them down. It's rather cloudy and quite cool for a change.

FRIDAY, SEPTEMBER 3RD

The invasion of Italy has begun. News is scarce but guess things are going as planned. Early this morning, the 376th and the 98th headed for Suloma, southeast of Rome. We're in ship number 240209, "Wild Wolf", her 19th mission. We're carrying nine 500-pounders. The huge rail center is the primary target. We're on oxygen and at high altitude for over eight hours. As we turned west of the Adriatic heading over land approaching the general target area, fighters of all types intercepted us—ME-109's, ME-110's, FW 190's, MACHE 200's, and 202's. Our flight of twelve B-24's was in close combat formation, "B" Flight behind us and the 98th were all over the skies. The fighters hit the spread out 98th first and before anyone knew what was happening, four bombers were flaming. Their engines had been hit by incinerary high explosive 20-MM shells shot from launcher cannons mounted on the wings of the attacking fighters. Again, it seems giant B-24's die gracefully. It seemed they stalled for a few seconds (seemed like minutes), giving most of their crews a chance to bail out and the sky immediately was filling up with white parachutes. Then their wings dipped into a slow spin as they slipped away in graceful circles with flames shooting out all over them—wings—fuselage— waist windows. By now, the fighters were all over "B" Flight and the 98th. They also were beginning to encompass our close knit formation. All elements were now feeling their devastating attacks. The intercom blasted away— "Fighters 7 o'clock high"—Fighters 9 o'clock low"— "Fighters 6 o'clock"—etc. Two more bombers were fatally hit. The first one just exploded. Boom! She blew into a million pieces. No survivors and the other just seemed to slip away. The internal spinning forces pinned the fliers to the walls of the ship. No parachutes were seen as the ship spun towards earth.   We were beginning to think that this was finally going to be it. No more sweating it out. At least if we were going to go, the guns of "Wild Wolf" were blazing away at the attacking fighters. Seemed to us this could be the end of the 9th, 376th, and 98th. Ships were going down all over the skies, ours and theirs. Our "A" Flight was still in close combat formation— one could almost walk from one ship to another. We're taking a heavy toll as they keep attacking closer and closer to our ships. Our 50-calibers have a tracer shell one of every five—gives you a chance to adjust your fire at the attacking fighters. At least 16 to 20 of their ships have been seen going down. Not too many of them parachute out, indicating they've been killed. They were so eager, they followed us right through the Ack-Ack and over the target. Usually, they break off and pick us up out of the Ack-Ack gun range. Many of our ships have one or two feathered engines. Fighters swarm over them. The sweat just runs off your face. A person has no time to be scared. That comes later after the Ack-Ack, after the fighters. As fast as the great air battle started, it ended as we were southbound over the Adriatic again. Some of the badly damaged ships landed in Sicily and Malta. The availability of Sicily to our bombers is a great help. It seems to us the firepower of the bombers has to be increased—the fighters don't scare away as easily as they did in missions past. Their 20-MM, even 30-MM, launcher cannon is a powerful weapon and could attack us and stay beyond the reach of our 50-caliber guns.

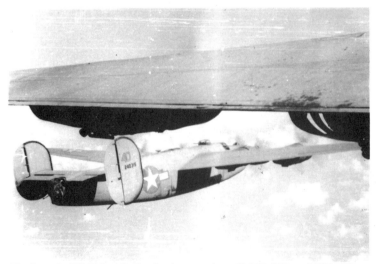

Number 40—"Wolf Pack" slips in close as about 30 ME 109's and FW 190's— German fighters approach to do battle. Photo taken from waist window.

Number 54—"Barrel House Bessie" with several other bombers enroute to target. Photo taken from waist window of our ship.

We're tired and very nervous. In the air over 11 hours. At the medical exam they gave us a couple of shots of bourbon— really hit the spot on an empty stomach—so the writer has several rounds. After the debriefing, which took an extremely long time because of ship losses, crews missing, fighter questioning, etc., we hit the sack. Hopefully, we never will have a run again like Suloma. We'll be a long time forgetting this mission. We are a tightly knit fighting machine—almost like brothers. Another six or seven missions should put most of the crew over the 300 mark.

SATURDAY, SEPTEMBER 4TH

The whole crew is hoping we'll never run into another situation mission-wise like the raid on Suloma. If we do, the consensus is we'll never survive them. Our luck would just run out. Another raid is in the making and I really don't know if I'm mentally able to take another long 10 hour run.

Again, the heat is unbearable. You'd think you could adjust to dry high heat. If the Germans don't get us, this damn heat will. The damn flies buzz around as though they are in formation. Seems like you swat one and fifty more appear immediately. A few of the boys went for a swim and just relaxed. No wind.

SUNDAY, SEPTEMBER 5TH

Weather is again holding the 'big ones' on the ground. Now that the invasion of Italy has begun, the crews should be getting in hours and hours of combat. Guess we'll be after all rail centers and bridges in northern Italy to stop shipment of supplies. Italy is very mountainous, and there must be hundreds of rail bridges to bomb out.

The nights seem to be getting considerably cooler. Lizards and scorpions seem to seek shelter from the cold early in late afternoon—more so than a month or two ago. It's necessary to keep the tent tightly closed and the sides and back flaps are firmly sandbagged down to keep 'em out of the tent. Scorpions can become killers if the sting is in the right place.

The rumor plot is boiling over again and that is we'll soon be moving to a new location. In spite of the heat, flies, lizards, and duststorms, Bengasi is not too bad a spot with the cool "Med" so close by. Two locations seem to predominate. Sicily and North Africa—Tunis.

MONDAY, SEPTEMBER 6TH

The old weather man again kept the heavies on the ground due to very heavy cloud cover over all of Italy. Heavy turbulence, violent thunderstorms also reported. This constant cloud cover could slow down immeasurably our mission hour accumulation time, keeping us here for a few extra months.

Berardi was taken over to the 15th Field General Hospital. His nerves reportedly causing him considerable difficulty. Not an unusual situation among the group personnel. The sky around Bengasi is filling up fast with heavy cloud cover. Hopefully it will clear away from our targets. Also an indication the rainy season here is not far off. The rain is confined to the "Med" coastal areas.

The invasion continues to progress. We've lost a few more of our bombing targets—Reggio—San Giovanni—and we'll probably lose a few more shortly in southern Italy. The missions should be in the 8 to 12 hour catagory. They are tough missions to pull but hours count up.

TUESDAY, SEPTEMBER 7TH

As Gabrial Heater used to say, "There's good news tonight!" It's rumored that American forces have invaded Italy in great strength just south of Naples in an attempt to cut the country in half and cut off at least sixteen crack German divisions and of this writing many Italian divisions would be affected. News of the operation at this point is very scarce.

Weather again is holding the 24's on the ground. We could be giving those troops some much needed heavy air support. This invasion could have serious repercussions as far as we're concerned. Could keep us here in Bengasi for the next three or four months. If Italy surrenders in the next week or two, we'll no doubt move to a closer target location and be inactive for some time. Many of us are hoping to finish our 300 hours before Italy throws in the old towel.

The mission is still scheduled and if the front moves east clearing skies over Italy, we'll be enroute to Foggia, the big airdrome. Six or seven good missions should see a few of us finish our time. God willing, that's the way it will be. These future missions are constantly on your mind—like an ulcer. One cannot help but think of the alternative--shot down—killed—with only a few more to go. There really isn't a positive tomorrow. Nobody plans ahead. It's one mission at a time.

WEDNESDAY, SEPTEMBER 8TH

We were up and at 'em at 4:00 A.M. Weatherman gave us the 'go ahead' and the 376th and 98th prepared for takeoff.

We're in "Daisy Mae". It's the ship's 3rd mission—still like brand new. Carrying ten 500-pounders and the target is one of the airdromes in and around Foggia, Italy. On a previous raid to Sulmona, the German interceptors came from the Foggia airbases. We headed for altitude almost immediately and flew up the Adriatic Sea. Cut inland north of Foggia. My parachute rip cord caught on a hook near the waist windows and the chute opened, filling the rear of the fuselage completely with billowing parachute. What a mess! Finally got it all gathered together. The chute was useless to bail out with as I would never clear the tail assembly with it. Even if this came about, probably wouldn't properly open. Holbrook agreed that if we bailed out, I'd just jump with him, literally wrapped around him, hoping that when his chute opened, I could still cling to him and we'd go down together. Fortunately, this didn't materialize.

Over the target we encountered very little Ack-Ack and only a few fighters. They were not too eager to do battle. Stayed out of our range about 800 yards and fired a few 20-MM cannon shells at us as we headed back to the Adriatic and south to Bengasi. All ships landed safely. Mission added 10 hours to our combat time list. After the medical debriefing, while eating supper, we were informed of Italy's unconditional surrender. The whole camp went completely wild. Many groups huddled together, talking things over and speculating what the future holds for the 9th now. It's hard to say. My guess is we'll either stay here, move to North Africa but will continue to bomb Italian targets as the Germans are still in this battle. We'll still bomb Italy, plus Greece and targets north of Italy near Germany.

We've been advised the whole group is to meet in our outdoor theater in the morning. Colonel Compton is to address the 376th as to what's what. Too early to tell what effect, if any, this will have on us, especially the combat personnel. The missions will continue-win, lose, or draw. As the old saying goes, "Anything can happen now—and probably will."

THURSDAY, SEPTEMBER 9TH

In spite of the fact that Italy has unconditionally surrendered, another mission was posted late last night and again, all those crews scheduled were up and at 'em at 4:00 A.M. Breakfast—briefings—and, at the last minute, Lear and crew were crossed from the listings. The crew was fit to be tied. All were damn mad. Mission went to Foggia again—airdromes— about a 10 hour run. Another mission is posted for tomorrow even before the crews return from this one and it's going again to Foggia airdromes.

The airfields surrounding Foggia are the largest the Germans have in all of Italy. These airfields must be made completely inoperable to give our fighters complete air superiority to protect our ground troops invading Italy. Lear and crew are scheduled for the raid tomorrow.

Windy and rather dusty out. Miserable. Several of us went out to the airstrip and watched the ships come in, circle the field and land. Really is a beautiful sight to see the big ones landing with wheels and flaps down, engines roaring. All were safe. At the debriefing, Ack-Ack and fighters were not too aggressive. Hope it's that way again tomorrow. Retired early.

FRIDAY, SEPTEMBER 10TH

Seems we just hit the sack and they got us up. Rushed around again. Mission to Foggia. Seven or eight hours at high altitude on oxygen. Lear and crew in ship "Let's Go" Number 124032. We're carrying 12 500-pounders. The 376th and 98th participating. It's critical on these long missions that everything possible is taken along from a dress standpoint to keep from freezing. As soon as the bombers take off, it's quite a process to get dressed. One certainly can't dress before takeoff—you would roast to death. With the heavy flying suit, pants, jacket, boots, helmet, heavy gloves, goggles and oxygen mask, it's difficult to move—very bulky but necessary to survive the sub-zero temperatures at 20,000 plus altitude.

We crossed the toe of Italy and the Messina Strait. Seemed strange—no Ack-Ack—and headed north along the Italian coastline in the Tyrrhenian Sea. As we approached the Bay of Naples, literally thousands of ships of all descriptions could be seen stretching in all directions almost as far as the eye could see. No wonder we needed to destroy German airdromes. These ships, men and equipment had to be protected at all costs.

Cloud formations all around were becoming very thick and heavy. Thunderstorms appearing in and around the entire area. Lightning flashed throughout the sky. As we headed inland towards Foggia, it became evident that 100% cloud cover would prevent us from dropping our payloads. We circled the general area over Foggia looking for a break in the cloud cover and finally headed south for Bengasi. Disappointment registered heavily with all of us as we'd probably receive no credit for the mission, or maybe half credit.

Allied fighters could be seen in the distance heading towards the invasion area. No doubt they were Sicily based. This air superiority has got to be the deciding factor for our troops on the ground. All ships landed back safely and again we brought the 500-pounders back with us. Preparations seem to be getting under way for the 376th in the near future to abandon old Bengasi. Truck convoys are arriving and staying. Pretty good indication we're to move soon. rumor again around that the move is to take place in a week or so and the destination is to be North Africa, Tunisia. They (headquarters) got very generous and allotted half time for the raid—4 hours and 25 minutes. After the Medics gave us a couple of shots to settle us down, some of us continued the activity at the club—slept it off.

SATURDAY, SEPTEMBER 11TH

Because of continuing heavy overcast skies over Foggia and other Italian targets—German held—nothing cooking at all. Just rumors. Everyone is on standby and told to stay on base as 'take off' could be on a moment's notice if the clouds disperse.

We're going to move—no question about that. Equipment is being packed and loaded into the convoy trucks. Am hoping we'll pull at least a couple more missions before the move as most of the crew has accumulated about 250 hours of combat time. These 8 to eleven hour runs add up in a hurry. Survival seems to be the predominate thought in all the minds of the old combat veterans.

Went to the hospital to visit Berardi and some of the other boys. Makes a person very sad and depressed. Poor devils. Hope everything turns out for the best for them. War is a lousy, dirty, rotten business.

Received a couple of shots in the arm while at the hospital. They just informed us she's 'go' for in the morning.

SUNDAY, SEPTEMBER 12TH

What a surprise. They let us sleep. Had a casual breakfast and then to briefing. We all figured the mission would go back to Foggia. Apparently the cloud cover is 100% over central and northern Italy. We're going to the Island of Rhodes near the country of Turkey. Our target is Maritza airdrome near the City of Rhodes. Rhodes Island is a part of a chain of islands called the Dardanelles. We've been assigned the ship "Wolf Pack." It's this combat veteran ship's 29th mission. She's in pretty good shape. We're dropping nine 500-pounders on the airdrome. The 98th was also on the raid and Lear and crew lead the 376th formations. We had 24 ships in our formation.

Enroute to the target, we passed over the eastern coast of the Island of Crete, a German-held fortification. Nothing of any importance could be observed. Several airfields stood out in the haze from 20,000 feet and it looked as though there were quite a few aircraft surrounding the runways. None came to intercept us.

As we approached the target, Turkey could be seen in the distance. Encountered no opposition whatsoever—no Ack-Ack— no fighters—this was probably the closest to a 'milk run' as we've participated in so far in over 30 plus missions.

As the formations headed back for Bengasi, history certainly was in the making. Two B-24's left the formation and headed for Cairo. Their mission was to load up with booze and beer and return to Bengasi. Upon landing at Berka Number 2, we were officially informed that the 376th and the 98th are moving and the mission we just completed was probably the last one flown against the enemy in this area of the "Med." The move is expected within the next several days and it's to be Infidiville, Tunisia, North Africa.

(Today), I was awarded the Distinguished Flying Cross for Ploesti. Most of the crew has about 40 hours to go to finish the 300 hour goal. Excitement is at a high pitch amongst the crews. Crews gathered in groups to discuss the move and another dirty rumor cropped up—that the 9th Air Force, heavy bombers, were no longer to exist. We're to join another Air Force. We all went to the club and hung on a good one.

MONDAY, SEPTEMBER 13TH

It's official—word was passed on down that the 9th is history. To state it mildly, the crews are stunned—speechless! How could they do this to us old combat veterans?

We've become part of the 12th Air Force and will be taking our orders from them. They are B-17's. Not much love lost between the crews. They seem to get the milk runs, short missions time-wise. The 24's, because of their increased gas load, are assigned the long hauls—hours and hours over enemy territory. Should develop into an interesting situation. The first ground personnel convoy will start westward in the morning. Squadron Headquarters has just posted another mission. Lear and crew not scheduled to participate in this one.

The crew spent most of the day trying to wash clothes out of old five gallon gas containers with the tops cut off. Not too efficient, cleaning-wise. Also began to assemble and pack all our gear as we could be leaving Bengasi in a few days. The Wogs are all around, picking up items we have already cast aside. Boy, what a field day they're having and it should get better as the deadline nears. Looks like our tents, etc. will go right into the bomber with us when we finally go westward. Excitement abounds all over the base as moving operations seem to be in full swing.

TUESDAY, SEPTEMBER 14TH

The base is beginning to look like a big city intersection—staff cars—trucks—jeeps are all over the place. The moving operation is in full swing as huge convoys leave continuously heading west with equipment and ground personnel. So far, aircraft maintenance personnel are still at work on the 24's—also armament personnel. An all out mission went to Pescara, Italy on the east coast on the Adriatic directly east of Rome. The 376th and the 98th, Lear and crew not participating. Really pisses us off as several of us, if we had made these last missions, would be right at the magic 300 hour mark. The 5th Army at Naples, just south of Naples, is in danger of being pushed into the sea if the German flow of men and equipment can't be stopped. All available aircraft—twin engine and four engine bombers are all out almost around the clock pounding the rail centers, bridges, troop convoys in and around this whole section of Italy from Rome south to in and around Salerno. Another raid is posted for in the morning and we're scheduled.

An amazing thing is happening. Our crew is actually eager to participate. Come hell or high water, we want to finish our time if possible before the whole base shuts down and we leave Bengasi. The blowing dust and high winds made operations almost impossible to day. The crew was supposed to receive decorations (medals) today, but due to the visibility situation, the ceremony was postponed. We've just received word that the British have taken Bari, Italy, located on the upper part of the eastern heel of the boot of Italy... An important harbor and airdrome facility. The food situation has deteriorated because of moving conditions. Personally didn't think it could get any worse but it has. Probably stay that way for some time—at least until we get settled in our new location, Enfidiville, south of Tunis. We all just sat around the tent enjoying a few snacks—too excited to sleep.

WEDNESDAY, SEPTEMBER 15TH

Up the east and west coast of Italy, the British 8th Army is racing in a desperate attempt to divert the full weight of the German attack against the extremely hard-pressed American 5th Army which practically has one foot back in the water at Salerno. At this point, the Germans could shove the 5th Army off the beaches of Salerno and a terrible catastrophe (American) in loss of life and equipment. Replacements are being landed continuously as wounded are being evacuated to waiting ships off shore. Hundreds of ships in the area are protected by British and American air cover.

All available aircraft are constantly on the go, bombing every available target to prevent reinforcements and supplies from reaching the German Army overlooking the beaches of Salerno. Immediately after the briefing, trucks rushed us out to the aircraft. We've been assigned "Wild Wolf", Number 240209, her 29th mission. Grand old combat veteran. We're carrying nine 500-pounders. The 376th and 98th in the mission. We have 24 ships in the formation and the mission is to Potenza, Italy. A large railway marshalling yard.

We headed again up the Adriatic to a point north of Bari and then headed west over land to a point north of Potenza, then south for the bomb run. Lear and crew again heading the 376th. Altitude about 21,000 feet. Colder than hell out. Wind factor by the waist windows like a great tornado. Never ceases. Picked up 'Axis Sally' on the radio and she's putting out the propaganda reference to the situation regarding the desperate position of the 5th Army at Salerno. She also has a good pipeline of information because she called us by name—the 376th—. Admitted she didn't know our destination but she sure as hell know we were in the air and over the Adriatic. She also told us to go home while we're still alive. Played beautiful music making the entire crew very lonesome. Also stated our wives and girlfriends were having the time of their lives dating 4-F's every night, etc. No Ack-Ack of any importance. No fighters at all. Dropped our bombs on rail yards and bridges. Italy is mountainous—very picturesque from the air.

We headed home to Bengasi and upon landing were informed of another mission for tomorrow. This run was 11 hours and 30 minutes—over 8 hours at altitude with oxygen, standing by the waist windows searching the skies, almost wishing you were dead— half frozen—difficult to move. At least if they shot you down, it would all be over.

Convoys are leaving Bengasi regularly heading west with all types of equipment. The highway runs along the "Med" shoreline—should be a very interesting drive. Almost wish the crew could leisurely drive to Enfidiville. That's wishful dreaming. Most of the crew has less than 30 hours to go.

After debriefing, a few shots from the medical tent, some tasteless food, and to bed. The crew is tired—worse than that— exhausted. We go again tomorrow.

Two little Arab children searching through our garbage cans for any food that's edible—survival for these children was tough.

Arab children near Bengasi constantly looking for food, hand-outs. The poor kids never had a chance, we kind of adopted them.

A few of the boys washing out their mess kits. Fires were built under the water container to heat the water. Water became greasy-dirty in a short time.

THURSDAY, SEPTEMBER 16TH

The situation still is in the critical stage as far as the 5th Army is concerned at Salerno. Reinforcements are constantly being landed and the all-out air offensive continues almost around the clock against the German forces throughout all of Italy. We've been assigned "Daisy Mae", Number 241031. It's her 9th mission and she shows the battle scars. We're carrying nine 500-pounders. The 376th has 24 ships in formation. The 98th also participating. The target is Potenza, Italy. British Intelligence informs us the Germans have huge munitions dumps in and around the Potenza area. We'll probably toggle the bombs out of the bomb bays one at a time to cover a larger ground area.

We immediately climbed to altitude, about 20,000 feet, and headed into the Ionian Sea approaching Italy through the Gulf of Taranto. Truck convoys could be seen slowly making their way through the mountainous terrain heading for Salerno supplying the German troops. Over the target area, much activity could be observed around Potenza. We ran into no opposition whatsoever. Gigantic explosions could be seen all over the target area as we headed in a southerly direction. No fighters could be seen anyplace in the skies. Usually they like to attack us flying out of the sun. It's extremely difficult to detect them until they are right on the formations.

As we headed south, we descended to about 8,000 feet, took off the oxygen masks and stretched our necks looking over the Italian toe and heel of Italy. Practically all of Italy is mountainous—beautiful country from this altitude. All 24's returned safely. We were a little over 8 hours in the air. The ground crew informed us another mission is scheduled for morning. Had a few at the medical briefing—really got relaxed.

MacDonald, our Co-Pilot, is scheduled to fly the raid. This will put him over the 300 hour goal and should be his last mission. We all wished him "God Speed" on the run tomorrow. The rest of the crew is not going to participate. Most of the crew have about 20 to 30 hours to go and

September should see us finish. Seems that's all we think about. What a disaster to get shot down—killed with only a mission or two to go.

FRIDAY, SEPTEMBER 17TH

The mission today went back to Pescara. Railyards and the many railbridges throughout the area were the specific targets. The British 8th Army has joined the hard-pressed 5th American Army and averted an almost certain disaster for the American troops.

Upon all the ships safely landing, the crew had a special farewell party for Mac. He should be leaving the squadron in a few days. We'll all give him letters to take back and mail in the States—no censorship. Am also giving him negatives— undeveloped film to take back and send to Anne—good deal. The farewell party was a joyous affair for Mac but an extremely sad affair for the rest of the crew. We were very happy for Mac, but guess we were also very sad for the rest of us yet to finish. Mac is the first to leave the crew. It's almost like losing one of the family. We finally called it a night as the rest of Lear's crew is flying in the morning.

Lt. DeJean is taking Mac's place on the ship. This business of acquiring 300 hours is becoming a great obsession with all of us. So near to completion, yet so far. All it takes is a 90-MM Ack-Ack hit or 20-MM shells from an ME-109 or an FW-190 to finish off all your dreams. Small wonder the more hours a person accumulates, the greater the mental stress and strain—even to the point of cracking up as a few of the boys already have—poor devils—they certainly aren't cowards. They just were forced beyond their mental capacity to continue this gruesome mission routine and all of it's ramifications. One wonders if there will ever be peace again.

SATURDAY, SEPTEMBER 18TH

The crew really doesn't require any one special to awake us at 4:00 A.M. It's almost automatic. We've been going through this process it seems forever. Mac was at the breakfast and we went through the final goodbyes again. This old veteran combat crew had tears in the eyes as we said our final 'goodbyes' and headed for the mission briefing. We all vowed to keep in contact after the war was over—either on earth or in heaven. We've already had our hell.

We've been assigned "Daisy Mae" carrying nine 500-pounders. The target is Pescara again—railyards—railway bridges. We have 24 ships in formation. The 98th is also with us with 24 ships. Altitude 20,000 feet. Again over the target area we ran into absolutely no opposition from heavy Ack-Ack guns or German fighters. Outside of the damn cold—freezing cold one could almost say, as missions go, this is probably as close to a 'milk run' as we'll ever participate in. The ships were almost 12 hours in the air. All landed safely at Bengasi as the sun was setting in the west.

The ground crew advised us another raid is in process for tomorrow. God! How tired we all are. Many of the crew are closing in on the magic number to survive all this combat mess— 300 hours. A couple more 10 hours plus runs should see us finished. The 12th Air Force has a 50 mission deal for their B-17 crews and the rumor is that is going to be applicable for us old 9th Air Force crews. The 300 hour deal is out. The 50 mission deal is in. God! What a blow!

Nothing cooking for our crew tomorrow. We can't sleep. If this deal goes through, it would mean another 12 to 15 more missions and they'd probably be 10 to 12 hours in length, while the 17's would be running the 6 to 7 hour missions. Are we ever pissed off! Hope and pray this rumor is way out—not true. No wonder a combat flier drinks to forgot the surroundings.

SUNDAY, SATURDAY 19TH

At the last minute they decided to keep Mac around for a few days, flying to Malta, Cairo, Sicily, etc. About 10:00 A.M., Fisher and I with Mac at the controls took a group of fliers who had finished their 300 hours and some ground personnel to Cairo on their first leg of a long journey to the good old U.S.a. What a happy group of guys. We landed late in the afternoon at 'Helio' airport just outside of Cairo. By the time we all got checked in at the Grand Hotel, it was quite late—time for supper. Several of us rushed over to the American Bar and sat on the balcony having a few cold beers and watching the passing parade. All of a sudden the war—missions—hours—was a million miles away. Had a great dinner then back to the hotel—a good shower and a very comfortable bed—clean sheets. You almost forget things like this existed after months in the desert. Cairo hasn't changed—noisy—dirty—and the foul odor still hangs over the city. It all quiets down about 2:00 A.M.

MONDAY, SEPTEMBER 20TH

Fisher and I were up early and walked around Cairo taking a few good pictures here and there. Bought a lot of booze, candy, canned fruit to take back for the boys. Had a few cold beers. What a treat after drinking 'em almost hot—really tasty. Fisher finally broke down and bought a camera. Coast him $60.00 American bucks. Wasn't worth $20.00. That's prices in Cairo. Sky high as long as there are soldiers around. About noon we took a cab back to 'Helio' and after checking everything over, we took off and headed for old Bengasi, our home. We asked Mac to buzz the pyramids so we could take some aerial photos of the giant structures. Landed back at the base late in the afternoon. Wrecked trucks—tanks—aircraft are still all over the desert. Still grim evidence of the great human struggles that took place in the African battles. Slit trenches by the thousands dot the land. The desert wind and blowing dust and sand will eventually take over and in the years to come historians will write the final chapter.

The mission situation at the base is bad. The 12th Air Force 50-mission program looks like what we're going to have to live with in place of our 300 hour agreement. Another several missions should finish most of the crew. If we don't get 'em here before we move, most of us will be looking at another 15 to 18 missions to reach the 50 deal. Some of us feel like telling 'em to go to hell. How can the 9th Air force treat its combat men in this manner? Some of the boys feel like throwing in the towel and quit flying. They'll bust them to Privates and give them menial tasks around the base. Don't know if I could take that kind of treatment. Think maybe Lear hasn't helped the situation any by holding us back mission-wise keeping us together as a crew so he would be in a better position to make Captain.

The whole base is in an uproar over the rumor. The next couple of days should bring the whole situation to a head one way or the other. The boys went to Pescara again today and all returned safely. That's the only good news. The enlisted men of the crew want me to talk to Lear about this whole damn mission and hour lousy mess at the first opportune time. Maybe a compromise could be worked out—somewhere in between the hours and the missions.

TUESDAY, SEPTEMBER 21ST

The main topic of discussion all over the base, mess hall, squadron headquarters, the 'Palm Room', is the 50-mission deal we're to receive under the 12th Air Force. The bigger question is, "Why should the old combat veterans continue to fly missions when the newly arriving crews fly 4 or 5 and then decide to throw in the towel?" Lear had no direct answer to that question. The rumor mill is really grinding 'em out and all of them are bad. Our crew is still hoping we can finish up in Bengasi before the move. Another mission is in the making for tomorrow. Have accumulated 281 hours. Several more raids would put me over the 300 mark.

A British invasion in the Balkans is under way. Information really scarce. Preparations at the base reference to the move are progressing full swing. Several more days should ring the curtain down on old Bengasi. Then the desert winds—blowing sand—dust, along with the Wogs will take over. All the heavy groups that were in this area several months ago are now in Tunisia. After they returned to England, their orders were changed and we'll operate out of North Africa together under the 12th in the very near future.

TUESDAY, SEPTEMBER 22ND

The main topic of discussion at the briefing was not the target or radio procedure, but the 50-mission deal from the 12th. If the General commanding the 12th was here, we would probably have buried him. We've been assigned "Daisy Mae," her 13th raid. Getting rather desert and battle scarred. Dropping none 500-pounders and the target is the big airdrome near Athens, Greece called Eleusis. The 376th has 24 ships in the formation. The 98th is not participating.

Ack-Ack over the target was very light—could be the Germans are moving their heavy guns to other more important targets as the war heats up in Italy. No fighters came up to intercept. All ships returned safely. One more mission should see several of the crew over the magic number—300.

After the medical and squadron debriefings, the club was full of fliers speculating on the future. Another mission is posted—no target as yet. This could see us through. Have acquired 288 hours of combat time.

It's interesting to observe the newly arriving crews— eager—filled with expectation—listen to every word the old combat veteran says. They've never seen a bomber catch fire and circle earthward with no parachutes blossoming out. They've never seen a big 90MM explode so close to the ship you can hear it over the noise of the engines. They've never seen a good buddy get killed fighting back at the enemy. They've never seen an ME-109 or an FW-190 coming at your B-24 with all their 20 MM cannon blasting away at your ship. They've never stood by the waist window with hands on the trigger of the 50-caliber for 8 to 11 plus hours—more frozen to death than alive—almost wishing you were dead—almost wishing they'd soot you down and it would be all over. One cannot help but wonder what it would be like six or eight months from now in the club listening. A person some day reading these diary entries would probably say, "If this was fiction, the writer certainly had an amazing imagination." The sad part of it all is—it's true.

THURSDAY, SEPTEMBER 23RD

Late last night orders arrived from the 12th Air Force Headquarters instructing us to move immediately to Enfidiville, Tunisia. The curtain has finally come down on Bengasi and the Middle East War. All that remains will be the tradition that the 9th Air Force never turned back because of enemy opposition, regardless of odds. All that remains will be the blowing, shifting desert sands— the sand fleas—flies— lizards and scorpions. Miserable blowing dust and terrific desert heat. But we'll all miss Bengasi and am confident those of us who survive this war will always have a warm spot in our hearts for Bengasi. We shall never forget those of our comrades we buried here. In these timeless shifting sands surrounding Bengasi.

We're dismantling the tent. Everything is being loaded into the bomber. We'll probably clear away from Bengasi this afternoon or early in the morning. If it's tomorrow, we'll all sleep with our clothes on in the bomber. The area is already looking like an uninhabited stretch of desert. Junk all around and the Wogs going through everything we toss out. The hourly situation is still the main topic of conversation and rumors are pro and con. Every flier is hopeful a satisfactory solution can be arrived at. Personally, I don't believe I could last another 16 to 18 missions. But believe I'd sweat 'em out one way or the other and pray for the best. The dust was almost unbearable today. Wore our dust masks as the packing procedure continues. This crew will never forget the dust storms.

Missions from Tunisia will probably carry us to portions of France, Northern Italy, Germany, Austria. Romania (oil fields)— all at high altitudes. No mail is being delivered to Bengasi— probably being held for us in

Enfidiville. Three British 'Whimpy's." two engine bombers, blew up in a nearby field. Sabotage is not ruled out. Don't have any further details.

FRIDAY, SEPTEMBER 24TH

Early this morning the first flight of 24's took off west to our new base. We still spent most of the day packing and loading the bomber. Some of squadron headquarters material is going with us. Reports are the new location is as bad or worse than Soluck. God! That can't be! That was the jumping off place of creation.

The mission situation is still the major topic of discussion amongst the crews still at Bengasi. The area looks desolate and by tomorrow should be completely deserted leaving only Wogs and stray camels. The Wogs have literally taken over—seems there are hundreds of 'em throughout the whole area. Looks like we'll be here another night.

SATURDAY, SEPTEMBER 25TH

We were all up and at 'em about 4:00 A.M. We're definitely leaving Bengasi today. By tonight all the ships will be gone from Berka Number 2 and should be safely parked in our new location at Enfidiville. We're really going to miss Bengasi and especially the beach by the "Med." A haven in the desert.

Early this afternoon we roared down the runway for the last time in our heavily loaded ship and headed west. But not before Lear circled old Bengasi several times in a final salute. Almost brought tears to your eyes. Hours later we landed on dirt runways at Enfidiville. The base is way out to hell and gone— away from everything. Seems muchmore so than at Bengasi. This area seems to be the real desert. Almost kinda leaves a person weak from the heat. Immediately unload the bomber and trucks delivered our tent and gear to the 513th combat area. We as fast as possible pitched the tent. No electricity again.

We're going through the same damn situation again. Soon as the tent was properly pitched, we moved inside out of the heat and just rested. This area seems to be right in the heart of grapes and wine country and the boys already are getting their share of 'vino' and 'cognac'. Earthen crocks in 5, 10 or 20 gallon capacity can be purchased for just a few dollars. Five gallons of 'vino' red wine costs about fifty cents. Many of the tents have 10 to 20 gallons of wine in them. The earthen crocks cool down the wine. What a celebration is going on. We're stationed just north of a coastal city called Sousse. The rumor factory is of course grinding 'em out. At this point, nobody seems to care a great deal. The wine is tasty.

SUNDAY, SEPTEMBER 26TH

The whole base has one big 'vino' hangover. Yesterday the writer had about one 12-hour mission to finish. Today—about 16 to 18 more missions. It's hard to believe what's happened to us. The disappointment is beyond measure. The crew is very bitter about the whole situation. If only they had offered us a compromise—a "We'll give— you give" type of situation. No one knows when we'll finish our missions. If ever. The new rumor is that we'll be stationed here a very short time and then go to southern Italy. With the rainy season not far away and dirt rock runways and taxi strips the heavy bombers could be bogged down for days at a time. Some of us have seriously thought about spending the rest of our overseas duty on the ground. Probably as privates. They can't take away from us the Soluck—Bengasi experience. Somehow I knew Anne wouldn't want it that way and I guess deep down in my heart I don't believe I could live with myself either. The good Lord will decide and take care of us one way or another. That's for sure.

The base is situated in a huge valley and that accounts for some degree the terrific heat. The flies are equally as bad as they were in Bengasi. We secured about 20 gallons of 'vino' and about 5 gallons of 'cognac'. Lots of hangovers and headaches.

Photo of tent area at Enfidiville, Tunisia—October 1943—big tent in center is the "mess tent" and that's exactly what it was.

Aerial view of harbor of Tunis in background—Tunis is a beautiful city. The city survived the war with little dammage.

MONDAY, SEPTEMBER 27TH

Discontent among the veteran crews is mounting at a fever pitch and where it will all end is difficult to project at this time. Morale is reaching an all-time low and the spirit of the crews is extremely negative. Some of us are beginning to sell ourselves on the idea to make the best of a damn lousy situation. Most of our biggest disappointments are that we're stuck here for an additional 4 or 5 months. Maybe longer.

Heavy rain. Thunder clouds are forming over the mountains surrounding our area. A mission is scheduled but Lear and crew are grounded. The writer has been assigned to Lt. Irvine of the 514th Squadron as radio and waist gunner. It's going to be another long one but hours don't seem to mean much anymore. Briefing and target information not yet posted. The boys are really missing the beach on the "Med." The gang has gathered around our tent and a 'bull session' is in full swing with plenty of great refreshments—'vino.'

TUESDAY, SEPTEMBER 28TH

Heavy rains came in the night and cancelled our scheduled mission. Target was Wiener Neustadt near Vienna in Austria. The whole base is swimming in a sea of mud. Also, some hail fell but not too heavy. It's very chilly and windy—a generally lousy day. At breakfast, all are complaining about the water and mud. Some tents have water standing all overinside and out. Rumors again around that we'll be in Italy in less than 6 weeks. Most of the crews don't give a damn anymore. Nobody, of course, is eager to fly the long hour missions to northern Italy, Austria, etc. The boys have pretty much accepted the thought that we're going to be here for months to come. If we survive the damn thing.

Played some poker and had a few 'vinos' with the gang. Thank God for the wine. It's more plentiful than water. Seems all the Arabs and French drink in this area is wine. Fresh water is rather on the scarce side.

WEDNESDAY, SEPTEMBER 29TH

Not too many moving around too fast this morning. Beautiful sunny day. The sun, heat and wind really vanishing yesterday's rain. Everything rapidly drying out. Word has just reached us that Lear has been taken out of the 513th Squadron and placed in Group Operations. The rest of the crew will be listed as spares in all squadron operation headquarters. Also a possibility some of us could become a part of other crews. Not a pleasant thought but guess that's the chain of events. Personally believe we're getting a rotten deal, but who in hell can a person complain to? The mission has again been posted. Target remains the same. Am still scheduled to go with Lt. Iovine and crew. Will see if he would accept me as his personal radio and waist gunner. Will check it out with Squadron Headquarters. Iovine is in the 512th Squadron. Several of us hiked into Enfidiville today and looked the little village over. It's really run own and conditions are very filthy. Worse than the old section of Cairo. The natives can't just comprehend what this is all about. They just stand and stare at the soldiers. We did barter for some wine and journeyed back to the base. Enroute to and from the road is lined with hundreds of crudely marked graves—Germans and Italians mostly. American graves are off the roadway and in closed off sections. A very depressing and gruesome sight. At least for them it's all over. The gang gathered by the tent and drank the wine. Good show.

THURSDAY, SEPTEMBER 30TH

Late last night the mission was cancelled because of adverse weather conditions over the target area. The 12th Air Force is really getting rough and they have laid the lowdown to all us reference to writing letters to family and loved ones. Because of security, about all you can say in a letter is that you are feeling fine and in good health and spirits. (The spirits are certainly true with all the vino in the area.)

The mission has again been posted for Friday. Doubt very seriously if it will materialize. We're all on immediate standby alert. Thank God for the relaxing effect of the 'vino.'

German JU-88—flew into our base with wheels and flaps down—from Crete—pilot gave himself up—American markings were painted on it and the ship was flown state side.

OCTOBER—1943

FRIDAY, OCTOBER 1ST

They gave us the mission to 'go ahead' by getting us out of the sack at 4:00 A.M. The usual—a quick breakfast—the briefing. They gave us survival kits consisting of maps, compass, American gold coins, American paper money and bills from the country we're dropping the bombs on. Am assigned to the 512th Squadron, B-24 ship "Miss Minervia II". The 98th is also on this raid. Lt. Iovine is in "A" Flight of the 376th. "B" Flight and the 98th follow us. We're dropping nine 500-pounders. Should be at least a 10 to 11 hour run. The ships had dust problems taking off and it slowed the procedure of getting the formations together to head northeast over the "Med" to Sicily. We got under way with no problems and passed just west of Sicily heading into the Tyrrhenian Sea passing east of Sardinia and Corsica. Hundreds of islands dot the area. Weather was perfect. A few convoys could be seen heading for Salerno. They were well protected by destroyers, cruisers, etc. We're at about 20,000 feet. We're going to Wiener Neustadt near Vienna in Austria. Giant german aircraft factories are the specific target. Apparently the Germans felt it (target) was out of our range. We had no Ack-Ack to speak of and no fighter intercepts.

We entered the Ligurian Sea and crossed the northern part of Italy in a northeasterly direction going over Bologna, Padua, Treviso and Austria. As we approached the target area, "A" Flight was in tight flying formation. We all thought Messina was a rough target because of heavy Ack-Ack but it was nothing compared to what the Germans threw at us as we approached Wiener Neustadt.

All of a sudden the sky in front, both sides and back became one big black cloud from exploding 90 MM shells.

The Germans had to have over a hundred guns below. You could hear the exploding shells over the heavy engine noise and expended Ack-Ack fragments falling to earth sounded like hailstones on the fuselage. The ships were taking a hell of a pounding. Many of the crews almost immediately had seriously wounded on board. The flak barrage lasted for over ten minutes. At the waist windows we just stood—watched—prayed. You can't fight back at the exploding 90 MM shells. "A" Flight was first over the target and we salvoed the bombs. We couldn't even see "B" section behind us because of the black cloud cover from the 90-MM's. Not one of the 12 ships in "B" section made it back to Tunisia. They all landed at different U.S. airfields in southern Italy. Most had feathered engines—electrical and hydraulic problems. The ships—all of them—took a hell of a beating.

Upon inspection, our ship had about 25 flak holes throughout. None of our crew was injured, thank God. Nothing official has come through yet. Major Knox had his left leg blown off from an exploding shell near the left front of their aircraft. Tomarhawski was blown completely out of the nose section and of course has to have been killed from the explosion. We were over 11 hours in the air. The 512th area looks like a morgue.

Lear and Hurd are flying to Italy in the morning to assess the damage to ships and get first-hand the condition of the crews. All in all, 13 bombers failed to make it back to the base—13 of 24. That's cutting it quite close. Thank God our ship was in "A" Flight. Something will have to be done now to change the 50-mission deal for the old B-24 crews that have over 300 hours. Had a few in the medical tent. Spent over an hour at the debriefing. Intelligence couldn't believe the intensity of the Ack-Ack. There is no question about it—the Germans are concentrating their heavy guns around their vital war operations. That has to be the reason on some raids, no Ack-Ack at all. The crew is dead tired. Most thankful to be alive.

We took time to bury our dead, at least for them the struggle was over. They have eternal peace in the timeless shifting sands of the desert.

SATURDAY, OCTOBER 2ND

It was pretty quiet at breakfast. Most of the fliers ate in silence. Sort of a stunned atmosphere. Rumor is a compromise is being made to the fliers that have close to 300 hours. The new hour attainment is to be set at 350 hours. Nothing official. We could live with that even after Wiener Neustadt. The only item everybody agrees with. There better not be another run like the last one.

Several of the ships returned. They landed at other bases in Tunisia. None from Italian-American bases have returned as yet. Reports from other squadrons are beginning to appear. Three men from Earl Zimmerman's crew bailed out over the target when they thought the ship was fatally hit and going down. A 90-MM exploded directly under the tail section of the ship, flipped the tail upwards and pointed the bomber nose down at a speed of about 200mph. After losing about 15,000 feet, they leveled the ship but the three men had already bailed out. The ship landed at Brindisi in the southeastern portion of Italy on the Adriatic. As of this writing, details are quite sketchy. Stout and Les were on that ship. Hope they stayed with her.

Another mission is scheduled for in the morning and she's reported to be another long one. Where in hell are we going to get together enough bombers to go out in any creditable numbers? Am scheduled to fly with Fogel and crew. The run could go to the Brenner Pass in northern Italy to shut down the flow of German war equipment and troops into Italy.

Drank a little 'vino.' Sat around and just counted our blessings. Really not many to count except we're still alive and in one piece. Amen.

SUNDAY, OCTOBER 3RD

Late last night Squadron Headquarters advised us the scheduled raid was cancelled and that we should standby with full flying equipment, along with a few daily essential items to leave Enfidiville in a moment's notice for as long as a week or so. Needless to say, sleep the rest of the night was impossible.

Early this morning I flew with Fogel on a practice mission with several new crews in other ships. Close formation flying. At noon they informed us that 24 crews would fly back to Bengasi and pull three or four missions to Greece, Crete and Rhodes Island to assist the British that apparently are having problems with their invasion attempt. A few ground maintenance personnel per ship will accompany us.

Took off early afternoon and headed east to old Bengasi. Landed late in the afternoon. Soon the Wogs were around selling eggs and looking for handouts—for food we had "C" rations or field rations in containers like Crackerjacks. All contents in cans. That's what we'll be eating for a week or so. Not too tasty but if you're hungry enough, you'll eat it and plenty of it. A mission is scheduled for in the morning to Athens, Greece. Tatoi airdrome nearby. The rumor around the fliers is the hour mission situation has been resolved at 350 hours for the old 9th crews. All the crew is sleeping with our clothes on in the bomber. We have "Mama Yokem," Number 272876. It's the ship's third raid. She's a beauty. The ground crews are checking over the ship, gassing her and loading the bomb bays with nine 500-pounders. Will try to sleep in the tail section of the ship.

Twin engine, twin tailed P-38 fighter being checked over, gased up at Bengasi base.

MONDAY, OCTOBER 4TH

The crews were up at daybreak. It was good to see the "Med" again. Nobody really slept too good. Personal hygiene—forget it. Fresh water is in very short supply—hardly enough for drinking purposes, let alone for shaving, brushing teeth or bathing. We're growing beards. If you have to take a leak, just whip it out and go. Same way if you crap. Only here, you cover over your deposit with sand.

After a short briefing, we took off, got into specific formations and headed for Athens. The 376th, the 98th, and the 93rd. Hopefully we can finish off this huge airdrome—at least for several weeks.

It was an easy mission. Ack-Ack was not too heavy and not too accurate. No fighters came to intercept. We all landed safely back at Bengasi. We were a little over 7 hours in the air—most of the crew is over the 300 hour mark. Rumor now has it that we'll be here for some time. Maybe three or four weeks.

About 40 P-38's arrived at a nearby field and we're hoping they are here to give us top cover. This would be a great comfort as they act as diversion when the Germans attack us.

Fogel told us a skeleton group is enroute here—more ground personnel, etc. Another mission is scheduled for in the morning— going back to Athens. This target is Eleusis airdrome near Athens. Crews just relaxed around the bombers. Ground crews busy. All turned in early. Am sleeping on the ground tonight. Not too comfortable. The "C" rations are not getting any tastier.

TUESDAY, OCTOBER 5TH

Moments before takeoff, they transferred the writer to another ship in the 'Purple Heart' section of the "B" Flight. Every indication pointed to another 'milk run' mission, if there is such a thing. Encountered no opposition enroute. Expected some fighters from Crete would intercept us. Ack-Ack over the target area was not accurate and not heavy. However, as we unloaded our 500-pounders and were turning in a southwesterly direction at about 21,000 feet, we observed vapor trails from fighters coming to intercept us. Called the pilot to advise the ships to close up in tight formation as about 25 to 40 fighters will be among us in a matter of a minute or two. We began to drop altitude to gain speed and head out over the "Med"— put distance as a factor in our favor. A few seconds later the sky was full of ME-109's and FW-190's—over us— around us—through us—all over guns were blazing on both sides. Looks like another Messina, Suloma or Wiener

Neustadt. These Germans come to fight. Almost in seconds, three of our ships were on fire—burning throughout the entire ship—fatally hit—slipping away from the formation. Captain Fallen's ship was the first one to slip away. That's the ship the writer was taken from. It carried the other four enlisted men of our crew— Linderman, Holbrook, Keller and Fisher. Keller's guns were pointing down indicating he was seriously wounded or killed. I'm stunned—shocked—in a total state of disbelief. By an act of God, I could have been going down with them. We try and keep track of the parachutes— one— two—three. The fighters are attacking with such vengeance. They practically collide with us, they are so eager for the kill. We don't know how many of the crews were able to bail out of the burning ships. Was credited with shooting down ne ME-109. Hope he's the one that shot down our crew. Came directly at the waist window. Pumped at least 150 to 200 rounds of 50-caliber at him. The ship burst into flames and the pilot ejected out of his aircraft.

As fast as the battle started, it ended. They broke off and headed for their base. Had the battle lasted any longer, chances are our ship would have gone down. They were swarming around us like flies.

We hope they all bailed out safely but that's wishful thinking. The Germans on our air frequency did advise us they would pick up the downed fliers floating in the water. Five men on Fallen's crew had over 300 hours and should have finished their combat. This is the thanks they get. We lost three bombers. Many of the ships were shot up badly from the attacking fighters. Upon landing again maintenance and armament crews immediately began to get the ships ready for a mission tomorrow. We can only put one section in the air because of the condition of the ships. They are all shot up. The 24 can really take a hell of a beating and still bring the crews back for another mission tomorrow. We're going to Rhodes, the Maritza airdrome is the target.

I find it most difficult to accept that my boys are gone. We were together practically 24 hours a day since we came together as a crew (the enlisted men)—like brothers in a large family. We sat around the ship in silence—ate our rations. Am sleeping in the back of the ship using the heavy flying equipment as a mattress. Am very tired and deeply saddened. War is hell.

WEDNESDAY, OCTOBER 6TH

The crews sat under the wings of the ships and had a very tasty field ration breakfast. Adverse weather over the target kept the ships grounded today. The mission should go out in the morning. A few more 24's arrived with skeleton ground maintenance crews indicating we'll probably be here for some time. Haven't had our clothes off for four or five days.

The topic of conversation amongst the old crews that have 300 hours, or close to it—what and when is the situation to be settled once and for all? Good or bad—for some peace of mind, we should be informed as to what's what regarding the mission hour deal.

It's still extremely hard to accept my boys are gone. I hope and pray they did have time to bail out of the burning ship and if they did, they were not burned. The salt water on the burns would finish them off.

We had another briefing. Target is Rhodes Island. They finally advised us we could maybe have fighter cover—P-38's. Christ! It's about time! Most of the missions we've battled it out by ourselves. The British seems like are serious about invading Greece. Could be just a clever diversion to tie up more German troops in Greece that are greatly needed in Italy. Also tying up a large number of fighter aircraft.

FRIDAY, OCTOBER 7TH

After much deliberation over the status of the weather over Rhodes Island, we finally got underway. We're in ship Number 111779, "Li'l Abner" carrying the old standby nine 500-pounders. The airdrome is the specific target. Out of only 18 ships that took off representing the 376th, only 11 of them reached the target area. The other seven had to abort the mission because of engine failure, mechanical problems, etc. The ships are in terrible shape, in bad need of complete overhauls. Thank God we ran into minor Ack-Ack shelling and no fighters came to intercept us. The ships were a little over 8 hours in the air. Now have over 325 hours of combat and over 40 missions. More than 40 if one could count the aborts where no time was granted.

Upon landing at Bengasi, the word was passed another mission is scheduled for in the morning. Target to be the airdromes on the Island of Crete. The main airdrome is Maritza. It's developing into a big contest—who's going to wear out first—the crews or the old combat-worn B-24's. Another night of sleeping in and around your ship. A person is so damn tired it doesn't make any difference where you put down.

FRIDAY, OCTOBER 8TH

With clear skies, a bright sunny day in the desert, the 376th with 18 ships. We were assigned "Mama Yokem" carrying nine 500-pounders. The bombs and gasoline are transported by British equipment and also some American that never left Bengasi when the group moved. The airdromes at Crete were Kastell, Pedidia fields. Looks like the British ae going to attempt an invasion. Many ships could be seen travelling in the direction of Greece.

Again, we ran into little opposition from Ack-Ack or fighters. Our P-38 cover never did materialize. As we headed back to Bengasi, huge dust clouds could be seen in and around Bengasi. We thought we'd seen dust storms before, but this was the king of them all. All returning ships had to be diverted to outlying air strips. Landing at Bengasi was impossible. We finally found one east of Bengasi. Landed and spent about four to five hours before we got the word to come home to Bengasi. It was still very dusty when we brought old "Mama Yokem" home to her parking strip. As seems to be the pattern, another mission was immediately announced for in the morning. Don't believe at this point I'm scheduled. We'll see.

Major Young, the group doctor, came over to visit me and after relating to him the whole story, Ploesti, Suloma, Wiener Neustadt, Messina, Athens, the hour-mission controversy, the Major said to me, "Would you like to go home?" I damn near fainted. Couldn't believe what my ears were hearing. He told me to be ready to leave in the morning as they are flying me back to Enfidiville. It's over. I've survived it. Can't believe it's happening to me. Why me? What's prompting this? The other crews heard the news and in a matter of minutes were congratulating me. The mission-hour situation has not been settled as yet. It's all too good to be true. Can't actually be taking place. The good Lord has really answered by prayers. As of now, the writer has more time and missions than any other person in the squadron. Have lots of things to do before leaving for Tunisia in the morning. Mainly shaking hands with many of the crews and wishing them 'God Speed." Am too excited to even think of sleeping. Probably will wake up and find out I'm scheduled for another mission and this is all a dream.

SATURDAY, OCTOBER 9TH

Needless to say, there was little sleep last night. Early this morning the base was an active beehive as crews prepared for today's mission. Target to be Rhodes Island again. Tried to say a personal final goodbye to many of the crews— wishing them well. Could read in their expressions the anxiety, their deep concern for their future. They all wished me the best and we promised to meet after the war was over. After the mission ships departed—we watched them go—gives one a lonely feeling. You almost wished you were participating. Our ship headed for Enfidiville. Certainly got a lonesome feeling again leaving Bengasi. This time, it's final. For Linderman, Keller, Holbrook and Fisher, I'll always think of Bengasi as their home— our home.

Have again talking with the group doctor and they have decided to take several of us before the 12th Air Force medical board. The doc is going along with us in case things don't progress in a beneficial manner. More than just us two are at stake here. It's all the old timers. Could change the whole situation. There is still a chance the board might decline to return us to the Zone of the Interior. We're sort of a trial run under this new setup. Have checked in my equipment. Have been grounded and have secured from Squadron Headquarters a clearance. At this point, don't think it means too much. Amongst the fliers in Enfidiville, our situation has become the main topic of discussion. The wine flowed freely.

SUNDAY, OCTOBER 10TH

Last night after everything had quieted down and the party ended, all of a sudden the grim reality of what happened at Athens hit again. I was alone in the tent. The boys were no longer with me. It's a very depressing deep feeling. It's so quiet. No one talking. No noise. Sometimes it seemed I could hear them talking, laughing, talking of home and loved ones. This atmosphere is going to drive me crazy. Finally dropped off to sleep.

At breakfast, the topic of conversation was our appearance before the 12th Medical Board. Galvin and Butcher are going to move into the tent. Sure welcomed that situation. They'll be great medicine for me. Went to church and communion this morning and am praying everything works out. Not only for me, but for the fliers in the weeks, months ahead on the hour-mission deal. Looks like we'll go before the medical board on Tuesday. Captain Nuttal of the group has decided to accompany us and plead our case. Every flier is sweating us out. Had a few vinos and played some cards. Won $20.00. Still hard to believe the mission ordeal is past. I've survived. Am very eager now to get this appearance over with one way or the other.

Left to right—Butcher, Phipps, Byers, Potenza, Fleming and Al Galvin. Butcher and Galvin moved into our tent to keep me company after our 4 crew member were shot down as we were leaving Athens Air Drome—Greece. They were great medicine as the loss of our crew members weighed very heavily on my mind.

MONDAY, OCTOBER 11TH

What a pleasant surprise. About mid-morning the bombers returned from Bengasi. Everything pointed to a long stay there. Apparently, the British changed their invasion plans. They pulled two more raids after the writer left. Both went to Rhodes. Tomorrow is the day we go before the 12th Medical Board. The topic of discussion all over is speculation on the outcome of our appearance. All the old timers are sweating us out. If it's 'no go' many of the enlisted old timers have indicated they would throw in the towel. Am really sweating this out but am also mentally adjusting to be prepared to take a negative answer. Galvin and Butcher moved in and they've already been a great assist. To top it all off, Base Supply was here (tent) and took all of Holbrook's, Keller's, Fisher's and Linderman's personal belongings to send home to their folks. Some of the items that were not personal or family related were divided up among a few of those close to them. Such as boots, shoes, soap,

257

toothpaste, etc. It's still most difficult for the writer to accept the fact that they are gone. Latest rumor is the group will very soon move to southern Italy. We have to get out of this large mud hole before the rainy season hits in force as the 24's will be really bogged down in the mud. From a new base in Italy, they'll be going to Ploesti at high altitude. With the long range of the Liberator, the missions no doubt will become a hell of a lot longer and rougher. Everyone wishes tomorrow was over. About 15 of us sat around our tent area and drank our share of the 'vino.'

TUESDAY, OCTOBER 12TH

Excitement at breakfast was at a high pitch among the veteran combat fliers reference to our appearance before the 12th Medical Board. We got under way for Tunis about 9:30 A.M., 60 some miles north of Enfidiville. The medical board consisted of two Colonels and a Captain. They were looking for information in general—how we felt, could we sleep nights, were we nervous, could we eat the food? They looked over the list of missions flown. The big question asked was, "How I felt, personally?" this developed into a lengthy give-and-take discussion. The writer informed the board, "I'd felt as though I'd done my part for awhile and that a change of events was necessary to rehabilitate myself and an opportunity to gather together my courage and a positive mental attitude." Indicated to the board after a reasonable length of rehabilitation that a tour of combat in the Pacific on B-29's would be acceptable, if needed. Further told the board many of the fliers were reaching a breaking point because of the mission-hour indecision situation. Guess we expected an answer right then and there, but none was forth coming. They instructed us to go back to the base and wait for the board's decision. They grounded us from further missions. They further advised a decision would be forthcoming in a few days.

We were mentally exhausted—let down. The interview lasted several hours. Reference to the questions, "how we felt," answered, "have had enough reference to the mission record—need a change—rest—relief from the stress." Question, "could we sleep nights?" Answer, "Not only can I sleep nights, but also during the day. Combat flying is extremely exhausting and literally drains the mental and physical strength out of a person." Question, "Were we nervous?" Showed arms stretched out with fingers spread apart. Answer, "all of the fingers are spread firmly and steady." Question, "Could we eat the food?" Answer, "Gained 20 pounds on the stuff." Told 'em point blank—"Have just had enough. Have reached the limits of endurance."

The road to Tunis is lined with wrecked equipment of all descriptions. Most bridges are still out or under repair from the engineers. Tunis itself is in pretty good shape, filled with moving transport equipment and soldiers. Wine is plentiful but food is very scarce. Am extremely nervous about this whole situation. If the decision is "No," don't know yet what'll happen. Don't believe I could set out the rest of my overseas duty on the ground. Believe I'd fly on one way or another. At least until a positive policy is arrived at. Time will tell. The boys at the squadron were disappointed at the information— felt not much was accomplished. The bombers are mud bound. No missions scheduled. We sat around and drank our share of the 'vino.'

WEDNESDAY, OCTOBER 13TH

This business of not knowing whether you're going home or staying is getting me down. Can't even write Anne what's happening or anybody else for that matter. The base security officer would not allow the letter to be mailed. Everytime a single engine or any aircraft comes into the base, am over to Squadron Headquarters asking if there's any information regarding our disposition.

A mission for tomorrow and for the first time in many months, I'm not a participant and not even considered standby. Sorta left out in the cold. The raid is going to Pescara, Italy—raid bridges and shipping. A group gathered in the tent. Had a few 'vinos' and discussed in general what the writer should do if the decision should be negative. Some are of the opinion, continue to fly, take the chance you'll make it and a mission-hour settlement has to be rendered soon and you'd be on your way home. On the other hand, some argue, you're still alive and in one piece—stay on the ground and live out the war—it can't last forever. Wish the answers would be that simple. Whatever the outcome, a person has to live a lifetime with whatever decision is reached. We drank a lot of 'vino.'

THURSDAY, OCTOBER 14TH

The big ones left their parking revetments and headed over to the main strip for takeoff early this morning. Pescara, the target. 24 ships in formation. 98th also on the mission. It's a wonderful feeling to know you're through but as they took off and formed into specific formations, it gives a person a deep lonesome feeling to be with them—to participate. No question about it, this grim business of combat gets into your blood. If the 12th Medical Board rejects us, am confident I'll fly on. Reinstate myself and take the chance. Might say the indecision is driving me to a nervous breakdown.

Major Young assured us we'd be on our way home in a few days. All that's holding us up is the orders from Group Headquarters. The paper work.

Rushed out to the air strip and watched the big ones come back. All returned safely. A huge group gathered around the tent after debriefing. Drank a lot of 'vino' and hoped for the best. After the group busted up, Galvin, Butcher and I sat in the tent and had a few cognacs.

FRIDAY, OCTOBER 15TH

It looks as though preparations for a move to Italy are beginning to get underway. The group has to get away from the mud here or the bombers will be grounded for weeks at a time. The long talked about and hoped for B-24

Brand new B-24 arriving at Enfidiville base—with new front turret—also new retractable ball belly turret— top and tail turret—plus the waist window 50 caliber machine guns—sand colored for easy camouflage—combat crews really fell in love with this fighting beauty.

has arrived on the base. Nose turret, top turret, retractable belly turret and tail turret. Was assigned to the 513th Squadron. What a beauty. Would almost reinstate if you could be assured of being assigned to her. Another raid is in process for tomorrow. No target as yet. Nothing from group regarding the medical board's decision. Maybe tomorrow will be the big day.

SATURDAY, OCTOBER 16TH

This morning right after breakfast, Colonel Compton, Major Cox and Major Smith and the writer flew to Tunis. They had business with 12th Headquarters. Guess it could be our move to Italy. Bari seems to be the selected spot. We've got to move within a couple of weeks to avoid mud disaster with the 24's. They'll become immobile. Clouds up heavily in the surrounding mountains—threatens rain—does rain some—everything turns to mud—shoes grow to about four times their size because of the sticky mud. What a mess. Some of the new crews are quitting, and Hurd, Squadron Headquarters, has got to do something about this situation before the whole mess gets out of hand.

Combat morale is at a new low. Can't really blame the old timers from feeling that way because of all they've been through during the last six or seven months. No news regarding our situation. The crews are sweating this out almost as if they were the ones to be affected, and guess maybe they will be in the final end.

Watched the natives stomp the grapes for vino at Enfidiville today. Went there to purchase 10 or 15 gallons of wine. Almost threw up. They unload huge quantities of grapes in a large cement round container, about 15 feet across and several feet high. The natives then enter the grape container and begin a systematic foot stomping process to extract all the juice from the grapes. Their feet become permanently discolored a dark purple. Guess if you're desperate enough a person will drink anything. After a few vino's, somehow the process was not that distasteful.

SUNDAY, OCTOBER 17TH

Everything very quiet around the base. The usual rumor reference to the move to Italy. Went to church this morning. The tent was filled with combat men. There are no non-believers in this grim business of kill or be killed and that's for sure. Squadron Headquarters also very quiet. Wrote a few letters home. Can't say anything.

MONDAY, OCTOBER 18TH

The orders finally arrived from 12th Headquarters for T/Sgt. Bill Jordan and the writer to return us to the Zone of the Interior dated October 15th and marked 'confidential', by command of Major General Doolittle. Preparations are being made for us to leave the squadron and base first thing in the morning for Tunis and then heading west. There is a chance we could go back by boat. The orders state we can go to the Zone of the Interior (USA) any way we can get there. The time involved at any one stop not to exceed 15 days. This could add up to two or three months in the return places. Nobody is going back— 99% of troop movement is coming over. We have no specific priority travel-wise. The word spread rapidly throughout the squadron and the next thing we knew a big party was under way with many gallons of vino. The boys were bringing over sealed letters they wanted us to smuggle into the States and mail. Must have had 35 to 40 of them before things quieted down. It was an evening of great jubilation and yet one of sadness. The troops were happy the decision was in our favor and the both of us were saddened all of them couldn't go state-side with us. Much toasting of the vino. Packed what had to go with me and the rest was left behind to divide amongst the fliers. It's difficult to drop off to sleep. A mission was posted late this evening for early morning. The target, railroad bridges along the eastern coast of Italy.

TUESDAY, OCTOBER 19TH

Bill Jordan and I had an early breakfast—final one— with the gang going on the mission. Lots of conversation about a multitude of subjects. We also attended the briefing, then watched them go in trucks to the big ones. A few minutes later, the ships were in the air maneuvering into "A" and "B" Flights. They circled the base, the usual tipping of the wings, and they headed northeast for their targets. This would be the last time I'd witness such an awe-inspiring sight. Huge B-24's in close formation— beautiful!

We gathered our brief belongings together and walked over to Squadron Headquarters for a final farewell goodbye and to wish everyone 'God Speed.' There is a possibility we could go back by boat. The Queen Mary is docked at Casablanca taking on wounded from the Italian campaign.

263

We walked off the base and hitched a ride to Tunis, our first stop enroute to La Salamander. We'll be spending the night at El Aauena, a large air base near Tunis. We'll leave in the morning by DC-3 to La Salamander for scheduling to the USA. Seems we've been away from the base for days. Already the war seems distant. Bill and I are really excited about the marvelous change of events in our lives. To get home, I believe we'd row an old flat bottom across the Atlantic if we had to.

WEDNESDAY, OCTOBER 20TH

Bill and I early this morning were at base operations, eager and ready to travel west when we were informed our flight was cancelled. We were determined, one way or the other, to proceed. Finally, a good Captain listened to our story and we were stowed away on a DC-3 heading for Algiers. We boarded the DC-3 about 45 minutes before takeoff. Landed at Algiers around noon and immediately started proceedings to go to Oran. La Salamander is near by. Left almost immediately for Oran and landed there late afternoon. Checked in at Operations Headquarters and were advised we were to by-pass La Salamander and travel to Casablanca as a large oceangoing vessel is sailing in several days for the USA. We're spending the night on the base and hope to leave early in the morning for Casablanca. Bill and I will have to pinch ourselves to be sure all this is happening to us and is not just a beautiful dream.

THURSDAY, OCTOBER 21ST

The situation at base operations looked as though we may spend a couple of days here. All westbound aircraft were scheduled to capacity. We had no priority whatsoever. If there was room, we'd go. Fortunately, we fastened ourselves to a westbound B-26 (my first ride and it'll be my last). This twin-engined ship is all engines, very little wing, that was heading for Casablanca.

Casablanca is a beautiful city—quite modern—on the shores of the Atlantic in the country of Morocco. Felt good to see the ocean again after looking at the "Med" for months. Kinda gave us a feeling of being closer to home— the good old USA—Anne and family. Landed at Casablanca around noon and again immediately made preparations for continuing the journey. Looks as though we can make arrangements to fly back rather than on the Queen Mary. She was taking wounded aboard for the journey home— thousands of 'em. Not a pleasant surroundings. Operations placed us immediately aboard a B-34 and we headed for Marrakesh, French Morocco. The heat is almost beyond endurance and seems to become more intense the further south we travel. Landed with no problems. We happened to get on a C-54 in the morning for Dakar and then west across the Atlantic to South America. The PX on the base has everything—even cold Coca Cola, but we were too late—they had already sold out the allotment for the day. Believe me, the boys that fight this war have very little. These troops have all the comforts of home. Kinda makes you mad. Should be the other way around. We are anxious to be on our way and with any luck could arrive in the U.S. by October 26th or 27th. Had a few cold beers—what a treat.

FRIDAY, OCTOBER 22ND

We had high hopes of leaving Marrakesh today and continue our journey to Dakar but this was not to be and resigned ourselves to the fact we may spend a few days here before being scheduled on a westbound transport to South America. The food on the base is just great. Olive and date trees are in abundance throughout the whole area. Bill and I made sure we got a cold Coke today and it really hit the spot after months of drinking hot water and a few warm beers. .Kinda made a person feel that civilization was not too far away.

Sleep at night almost impossible as one constantly thinks of home and the anticipation of arriving there shortly. Am trying to hide all the negatives I have, also photos so the censor in the U.S. can't find them. Also have two Italian pistols, one German and a 45. These may present some problems as also the 45 to 55 letters I'm carrying to mail for the boys back at Enfidiville.

SATURDAY, OCTOBER 23RD

Late last night, base operations informed us we were scheduled to leave early in the morning and after much confusion, we got under way for Dakar. A General, a couple of Colonels, and a couple of Captains were on the C-54 with us, lots of cargo also. Enroute to Dakar, we made two stops at desert outposts for gas and oil—Atar and Tindouf. At Tindouf our right landing wheel had to be changed because the tire developed a blister on it. These outposts are in the French African desert where nothing grows—just sand—more sand—wind—heat and dust. Landed at Dakar in the day and probably be here for a few days. The ship we take from here should take us all the way to Florida via South America. The heat is out of this world and the mosquitos are the worst I've ever experienced. Natel, Brazil should be our next stop. The PX here is also well stocked with all kinds of goodies.

SUNDAY, OCTOBER 24TH

While sitting at the PX, who should walk in by Markus Joyer? He was at Smoky Hill Air Base in Salina, Kansas while we were there picking up our B-24 for overseas. He's been fooling around in the States ever since going from base to base. We really had a good old bull session. He, of course, wanted to know all about combat—changes of survival—getting shot down, etc. We had a few mugs of cold African peanut beer. There is a chance his crew will be assigned to the 376th or the 98th. Gave him a list of names to look up if assigned the 376th. Will probably be here for a few days. The list of travelers going west is quite long and we have no priority. Malaria is quite prevelant here and all precautions are taken that we don't catch it

266

while we're here. Haven't heard any war news in over a week. Seems like the war is a million miles away! The troops here are very indifferent to the war. Almost an attitude of "We can't be bothered." As always, heat here is terrific and of a rather damp kind for a change. Negroes here work all over the base. Guess the government has to feed them to keep 'em from starving, so they put them to work doing odd tasks around the base. We check base operations frequently to see if there is any status change regarding flights west.

MONDAY, OCTOBER 25TH

How many days we'll be here depends on the transports that are traveling west. The waiting list is quite long. Laid around most of the day. Thought about our first meeting— Anne and me. How much have I changed and how difficult it will be to convert to another life style after all these months in the desert in an atmosphere of "killed or be killed." I'm hopeful it will be kinda a heaven on earth. B-24's keep coming on the base enroute to the front, the bomber front. They all have the latest improvements— turrets all around. The boys in the 376th and 98th will welcome them with open arms.

TUESDAY, OCTOBER 26TH

Late last night, operations informed us we're scheduled on a C-87, a converted B-24 from combat to cargo carrier, that will be heading west early. It was a great feeling to see the African coastline disappear in the east as we headed west over the Atlantic towards Natel, Brazil which we left about eight or nine months ago heading into the combat struggle of war. Seems like it was years ago. The trip across was long, uneventful and all were glad when we touched down at Natel. The base has been improved considerably since our last visit. There's a good chance we may head north tomorrow for Belem, Brazil. We'll probably be on a C-54 transport. Am really getting the fever for Anne and the good old USA.

WEDNESDAY, OCTOBER 27TH

Laid around base operations all morning and about noon got under way on a C-46 heading for Belem. This ship is destined for Miami and a couple of more days should see it touch down at Miami or West Palm Beach. Belem is in the heart of rubber country and dense jungles surround the city and the airbase. The tropical rainy season is on and during the day on and off it rains. Almost like turning off and on a faucet. At the PX, had some good old American ice cream and just sat around and talked of home and of course the bomber war. All to bed early as we're getting an early start for Florida. The good Lord willing, we'll touch down in the USA late tomorrow night. Wow!!

THURSDAY, OCTOBER 28TH

It's almost like being in combat. At 4:30 A.M. this morning we rolled down the water-gutted runways of Belem, Brazil and headed north—destination Miami, Florida. The good old USA. There is no place on this earth to compare to America. I've seen the other side. Weather over the Amazon River was very turbulent as usual. No big problems. We refueled at Georgetown, Trinidad and finally at Puerto Rico and then the final step—Miami about 8:30 P.M.

It was magnificent to look out the window of the aircraft and see the beautiful night lights of the city. It could only happen in America. No wonder we fight so vigorously to preserve all of this.

After landing, went immediately to customs. They searched my baggage very thoroughly but not my personal clothing. Had all the photos, negatives, etc. strapped around my belt line and the guns were all taped to the bottom portion of my legs. All got through safely. Am scheduled to leave by train in the morning for Chicago and then to St. Cloud, Minnesota for several weeks before reporting to Salt Lake City and reassignment.

I guess there is a question that never will be answered to my satisfaction as long as I live. It'll no doubt have a profound effect on my future life almost to the point of being an obsession—"Why was I chosen to survive?"

EPILOGUE

For generations, historians will continue to evaluate the vital role of the United States 9th Air Force in the defeat of the Axis powers in Africa and the Middle East during World War II.

Since it's inception in early 1942, the 376th Liberando Bomb Group flew a total of 451 combat missions in Africa, Sicily, Italy, Crete, Greece, Romania, Austria, Dodecanese Islands, France, Bulgaria, Germany, Hungary, Yugoslavia and Czechoslovakia. Italian and German convoys in the Mediterranian were also attacked.

The complete dedication of the ground personnel to keep the giant B-24's mission-ready remains unequaled in the annals of heavy bombers. This aircraft maintenance was carried out under extremely difficult conditions in the African desert where blowing dust and intense heat were as great a deterent as the enemy.

There were many times when combat crews flew their missions, knowing full well that the aircraft was not mechanically sound. Nevertheless, every man had a strong desire to launch as many ships as was possible in the raids against the Axis. Very often, missions were airborne with as few as 18 planes in formation. On almost every raid flown, a percentage of the aircraft were forced to abort due to mechanical problems, thus increasing the danger for the remaining target-bound ships.

In the early days of the war, Allied fighter cover was not available. The B-24's fought off the attacking German and Italian fighters alone, sustaining heavy casualties in aircraft and personnel. The bombers could have turned back—but they did not. In spite of the devastating Ack-Ack and attacking fighters, the ships steadfastly flew on, fighting their way in to the target and during their return trip home.

Young men, in the prime of their lives, knew that the odds of surviving were stacked against them. And yet, mission after mission, they gallantly flew against the enemy to preserve our American way of life. They fought and died so that we, our children and our children's children might live in freedom.

It may never be possible to record the incredible courage and daring of these young men—nor to accurately explain to others the deep and total regard for their fellow combat crew members.

The following Memorial Day verse, "Come Visit My Grave," By Commander Jim Rolfes, of Plymouth County, Iowa, a member of Wasmer American Legion Post No. 241 of Le Mars, Iowa says it all.

Those of us who survived will never forget our comrades who fly forever in the African skies.

Come Visit My Grave

By Jim Rolfes, Commander
Plymouth County American Legion
Wasmer Post No. 241
LeMars, Iowa

I am a veteran laid under the sod,
   I'm in good company, I'm up here with God.
Come to my grave and visit with me,
   I gave my life so you could be free.
Today is Memorial Day throughout this great land
   There's Avenues of Flags, parades and bands.
I can hear the music, the firing squad and taps
   Here come my comrades, the Legionnaires, the Bluecaps.
One of them just put a flag by my stone.
   Some day he'll have one of his own.
Some think of this day as just a day free from toil,
   While others are busy working the soil.
They say they have plans, other things to do.
   Don't put us aside as you would an old shoe.

Come visit my grave in this cemetery so clean,
This is what Memorial Day means.
There are many of us lying in wakeless sleep,
In cemeteries of green and oceans of deep.
It's sad that for many who fought so brave,
Now no one comes to visit their grave.
They died so you could have one whole year free.
Now can't you save this one day for me?
There are soldiers, sailors, airmen up here,
Who went into battle despite of their fear.
I've been talking up here to all of those men.
If they had to do it over, they'd do it again.
Look; someone is coming to visit my grave.
It's my family, for them my life I gave.
My wife; I remember our last embrace,
As I left the tears streamed down your face.
I think you knew the day I shipped out,
I wouldn't return, your life'd be turned about.
There's my daughter that I used to hold.
Can it be that you're nearly twenty years old?
Next month is to be your wedding day,
I wish I could be there to give you away.
My son's here too, Dad's little man,
Always love your country, do for it what you can.
There is one thing that really did bother,
Is seeing you grow up without the aid of a father.
I wish you could all hear me from up above,
That's a father's best gift to his children is love.
And what better way to prove my love to the end?
Is that a man lay down his life for his friends.
I see it's time for you to go home,
Your visit made it easier to remain here alone.
Don't cry hon, you look so sad,
Our children are free, you should be glad.
Daughter, thanks for the bouquet so cute,
Thank you son, for that sharp salute.
Come again; I forgot; you can't hear me from up here.
But I know you'll come visit me next year.
I hope all veterans are treated this way,
On this day to remember, Memorial Day.

World War II Leaflets

ALLONTANATEVI DALLE FABBRICHE.

I BOMBARDIERI ANGLO-AMERICANI VERRANO A POLVERIZZARLE

In Italia, fabbriche, porti e ferrovie servono alla guerra tedesca e sono perciò obiettivi militari

---

Nel 1940

"Ho chiesto ed ottenuto dal Fuehrer una diretta partecipazione alla battaglia contro la Gran Bretagna con velivoli."

RISULTATO . . .

Nel 1940/41

100.000 uomini, donne e bambini uccisi o gravemente feriti — una casa su cinque danneggiata — in INGHILTERRA.

Nel 1943

Ogni fabbrica, che lavora per questa guerra tedesca, — ogni obiettivo militare — in procinto d'essere polverizzato — in ITALIA.

Valeva proprio la pena di chiedere il permesso del Fuehrer per questo ?

GET AWAY FROM THE FACTORIES.
THE BRITISH AMERICAN BOMBARDERS WILL COME TO PULVERIZE THEM

In Italy, factories, harbors and railroads serve the German war and are therefore military objectives.

In 1940
I asked and obtained from the Fuehrer a direct participation in the battle against Great Britian with sea planes.   Mussolini

Result . . .

In 1940/41
100,000 men, women and children killed or seriously injured—one house in 5 damaged in ENGLAND.

In 1943
Each factory that works for this German war—each military objective—on the verge of being pulverized—in ITALY.

Was it really worth asking the Fuehrer's permission for this?

POI

PRIMA

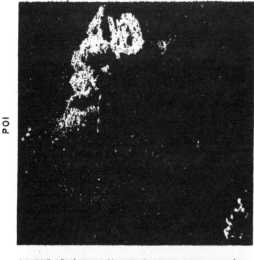

MARINAI ITALIANI !   ECCO QUELLO CHE VI ASPETTA !

La prima fotografia mostra due navi mercantili italiane di un convoglio diretto verso la Tunisia, il 6 Aprile 1943.

La seconda fotografia mostra le stesse due navi, alcuni secondi dopo, in seguito al bombardamento delle forze aeree degli Alleati.

Questo convoglio era "protetto" dai caccia tedeschi, i quali pero' si sono sottratti al combattimento : tutti i nostri aeroplani da bombardamento sono tornati indisturbati alle loro basi.

MARINAI ITALIANI !   NOI VI ASPETTIAMO !

ITALIAN SAILORS! HERE IS WHAT AWAITS

ITALIAN SAILORS! HERE IS WHAT AWAITS YOU!

The first picture shows two Italian freighters, part of a convoy headed to Tunisia on April 6, 1943.
The second picture shows the same two freighters a few seconds later after aerial bombardment by Allied forces. This convoy was "protected" by German fighters, which however disengaged from fighting: all our bombers returned untouched to their bases.

ITALIAN SAILORS! WE ARE WAITING FOR YOU!

INGHILTERRA 1940

Bomba da 500 kg. con cui, allora l'Inghilterra è stata...

COVENTRIZZATA

ITALIA 1943

Bomba da 4000 kg. con cui l'industria di guerra fascista sarà...

POLVERIZZATA

Inutile resistere contro la nostra Superiorità Schiacciante...

Churchill

(discorso del 28.11.1942)

"Già i centri dell'industria bellica dell'Italia settentrionale ricevono un trattamento più aspro di quello ricevuto dalle nostre città nell'inverno 1940.... Ma se potessimo a suo tempo riuscire a cacciare il nemico dall'estrema punta della Tunisia, come intendiamo fare, allora tutte le città dell'Italia meridionale, tutte le basi navali, le fabbriche di armamenti ed altri obiettivi militari, ovunque siano situati, saranno soggetti ad un prolungato e scientifico attacco aereo.

E questo è solo il principio

Un uomo, ed il regime da lui creato, hanno portato queste immense disgrazie al popolo italiano.

Sta ai 40 milioni di italiani il dire se è loro desiderio che al loro paese tocchi questa sorte tremenda."

(Speech delivered on 11.29.1942) CHURCHILL

Already the industrial war centers of Northern Italy have received harsher treatment than that received by our cities during the winter of 1940.
But if we can, in time, succeed in turning back the enemy to the extreme tip of Tunisia, *as we intend to do*, then all the cities in Southern Italy, all naval bases, armament factories and other factories objectivs, wherever located, will be subject to a prolongued and scientific air attack.
AND THIS IS ONLY THE BEGINNING
A man and the regime created by him, brought these great misfortunes to the Italian people.
It is up to the 40 million Italians to say if it is their wish that their country have this awful fate.

England 1940
A 500 kg. bomb with which England has then been
"coventrizzata"

Italy 1943
A 4000 kg. bomb which will reduce fascist industry
to dust

It is not worth resisting our
OVERWHELMING SUPERIORITY

AVVERTIMENTO!

PORTUALI! OPERAI!

Nel 1940 Mussolini ci ha dichiarato la guerra.

Nel 1940 Mussolini ha insistito per partecipare ai bombardamenti sull'Inghilterra.

Cosi facendo, Mussolini ha seminato vento ed ha condannato VOI a raccogliere tempesta.

Una tempesta di bombe - che vanno fino alle 4 tonnellate ciascuna - sta per scatenarsi sui porti e sulle fabbriche e basi italiane di sommergibili. Vi avverte la R.A.F. —

EVACUATE SUBITO!

EVACUATE SUBITO TUTTI I PORTI!

Voi ci attaccate sui mari e sotto i mari. Noi stiamo per contrattaccare.

Nell'ottobre 1942, prima di bombardare le industrie dell'Italia settentrionale, vi abbiamo avvertiti. Oggi la R.A.F. vi avverte di nuovo.

La guerra marina e sottomarina sarà combattuta d'ora innanzi anche nei vostri porti e nelle vostre fabbriche e basi di sommergibili, a COLPI DI BOMBE ANGLO-AMERICANE.

PORTUALI! OPERAI!

Evacuate le vostre famiglie! Evacuate voi stessi! Chiunque rimane presso un obiettivo militare è in

PERICOLO DI MORTE!

WARNING!
DOCK WORKERS!   WORKERS!

In 1940, Mussolini declared war on us.
In 1940, Mussolini insisted on particpating in the bombardment of England.
In doing so, Mussolini seeded the storm clouds and comdemned YOU to reap the tempest.
A tempest of bombs—weighing up to 4 tons each—is going to be unlieshed on the harbors and on the factories and on Italian submarines bases. The R.A.F. is warning you.—

EVACUATE IMMEDIATELY!

EVACUATE IMMEDIATELY ALL THE HARBORS!

You attack us at sea and under water. We are going to counterattack.
In October 1942, before bombarding the industries of Northern Italy, we warned you.
Today, the R.A.F. warns you again.
The war at sea and under water will be fought from now on, even in your harbors and in your factories and submarine bases with BRITISH AMERICAN BOMBS.

DOCK WORKERS! WORKERS!

Evacuate your families! Evacuate yourselves!

Anyone who stays near military objectives is in
DANGER OF DEATH!

L'AVIAZIONE
ANGLO-AMERICANA
VI AVVERTE

Mussolini, dimentico dei 12 milioni d'italiani d'America, dimentico della pace millenaria tra Inghilterra e Italia, al rimorchio di Hitler ci ha dichiarato la guerra.

Perciò, i vostri porti, fabbriche e ferrovie lavorano oggi nell'interesse tedesco non meno di quelli in Germania, e d'ora innanzi saranno bombardati non meno sistematicamente.

E, oggidì, tutto il Mezzogiorno è a 2 ore di volo dalle nostre basi in Africa!

ABITANTI DEI PORTI E DELLE ZONE INDUSTRIALI!

PERICOLO  **DI MORTE!**

Per salvare le vostre famiglie dal pericolo di morte basta allontanarle subito da ogni obiettivo militare.

In campagna non c'è pericolo.

I/11

125,000

aeroplani
americani
quest'anno....

THE BRITISH AMERICAN AIR FORCE WARNS YOU

Mussolini forgot the 12 million Italian Americans, forgot the thousand year peace between England and Italy and towed by Hitler, declared war on us.

Therefore, your harbors, factories and railroads are working today for the German interest no less than those in Germany, and from now on they will be bombarded no less systematically.

And today, all Southern Italy is at two flying hours from our African bases!

INHABITANTS OF THE HARBOR AND OF THE INDUSTRIAL ZONES
DANGER OF DEATH

To save your families from the danger of death, all that needs to be done is to immediately remove them from military objectives.

IN THE COUNTRYSIDE, THERE IS NO DANGER.

**125,000
American
planes
this year . . .**

ΜΗΝΥΜΑ ΤΟΥ ΠΡΟΕΔΡΟΥ ΡΟΥΣΒΕΛΤ ΠΡΟΣ ΤΟΥΣ ΕΛΛΗΝΑΣ

ΟΥΑΣΙΓΚΤΩΝ, Πέμπτη
Ὁ Πρόεδρος Ροῦσβελτ ἀπέτισε φόρον τιμῆς εἰς τὸ Ἑλληνικὸν Ἔθνος κατὰ τὴν διάρκειαν τελετῆς εἰς Ἀμερικανικὸν ναυπηγεῖον εἰς τὴν ὁποίαν ἡ κυβέρνησις τῶν Ἡνωμένων Πολιτειῶν παρέδωσε νεότευκτον πολεμικὸν σκάφος εἰς τὸν Ἑλληνικὸν Στόλον.

Ὁ Πρεσβευτὴς τῆς Ἑλλάδος καὶ ἄλλοι ἐπίσημοι Ἕλληνες καὶ Ἀμερικανοὶ ἤκουσαν τὸν Πρόεδρον νὰ ἐκφωνῇ τὸν ἀκόλουθον λόγον:

«Εἰς τοὺς περισσοτέρους ἀπὸ ἡμᾶς, οἱ ὁποῖοι ἔχομε συγκεντρωθῆ ἐδῶ ἐπὶ τῇ εὐκαιρίᾳ ταύτῃ, τὸ ἔτος 1940 φαίνεται ἀρκετὰ ἀπομεμακρυσμένον. Μολαταῦτα κατὰ τὸ ἔτος ἐκεῖνο συνέβη ἕνα γεγονὸς τὸ ὁποῖον θὰ διακηρύξῃ εἰς ὅλας τὰς ἐποχὰς τὸ γεγονὸς ὅτι ἡ βία καὶ μόνη δὲν ἀρκεῖ διὰ νὰ ἐξαλείψῃ τὴν ἐπιθυμίαν καὶ τὴν ἀποφασιστικότητα τοῦ ἀνθρώπου νὰ ζήσῃ ἐλεύθερος, οὔτε τὴν προθυμίαν τοῦ ἀνθρώπου νὰ θυσιάσῃ καὶ τὴν ζωήν του ἀκόμη διὰ νὰ ἐπιζήσῃ ἡ ἐλευθερία.

Ἡ 28η Ὀκτωβρίου 1940 θὰ παραμείνῃ εἰς τὴν ἱστορίαν ὡς ἡ χρονολογία τοῦ γεγονότος αὐτοῦ. Ἡ θέσις τῆς νοτίου χερσονήσου τῶν Βαλκανίων, ἴσῃ εἰς ἔκτασιν πρὸς τὴν Πολιτείαν τῆς Νέας Ὑόρκης, μᾶς εἶναι γνωστή. Ἐπὶ δύο χιλιάδες χρόνια καὶ πλέον οἱ ποιηταὶ ἔψαλλαν τὴν γῆν αὐτὴν ποὺ λέγεται Ἑλλάς.

Μολονότι εἴχαμε ἀρχίση νὰ προετοιμαζόμεθα διὰ τὰ δεινὰ ποὺ ἐπρόκειτο νὰ ὑποστῇ ὁ κόσμος κατὰ τὸ 1940, αἱ Ἡνωμ. Πολιτεῖαι παρηκολούθουν τὸ τρομερὸν δρᾶμα τῆς ἱστορίας κυρίως ὡς ἀνήσυχος θεατής. Τὸν Ἀπρίλιον τοῦ ἔτους ἐκείνου παρέστημεν μάρτυρες τῆς δολίας ἐπιθέσεως κατὰ τῆς Νορβηγίας, καὶ ἀκολούθως τῆς ἀπροκλήτου ἐρειπώσεως τοῦ Ρόττερνταμ, τῆς πτώσεως τῆς Ὁλλανδίας καὶ τῆς συνθηκολογήσεως τοῦ Βελγίου. Τὸν Ἰούνιον τοῦ ἔτους ἐκείνου αἱ ὁρδαὶ τοῦ Ἄξονος εἰσῆλθον εἰς τὸ Πα-

ρίσι καὶ ἡ σημαία τῆς ἐλευθερίας ἐκυμάτιζε με-
σίστιος ἀνὰ τὸν κόσμον. Τὴν 27ην Σεπτεμβρίου
τοῦ ἔτους ἐκείνου, ἡ Γερμανία, ἡ Ἰταλία καὶ
ἡ Ἰαπωνία ὑπέγραψαν σύμφωνον μὲ σκοπὸν νὰ
ἐπιβάλουν διὰ τῆς βίας τὴν Νέαν Τάξιν των
ἐπὶ τοῦ κόσμου, τὸν ὁποῖον θὰ διεμοίραζον με-
ταξύ των. Καὶ τότε ἦλθε ἡ 28η Ὀκτωβρίου 1940.
Εἰς τὰς Ἀθήνας ὁ λαὸς καὶ ἡ κυβέρνησις
ἔλαβον τριῶν ὡρῶν προθεσμίαν διὰ νὰ ἀποφα-
σίσουν ἐὰν θὰ δεχθοῦν τὸν ζυγὸν τοῦ ἄξονος; ἤ
ἐὰν θὰ ἀντισταθοῦν ἐναντίον τῶν ἀεροπορικῶν
ἐπιδρομῶν τοῦ ἄξονος.
Ἐπαναλαμβάνω ὅτι εἰς τὸν λαὸν καὶ εἰς τὴν
κυβέρνησιν τῆς Ἑλλάδος ἐδόθη προθεσμία τριῶν
ὡρῶν καὶ ὄχι τριῶν ἡμερῶν ἤ τριῶν ἑβδομά-
δων. Ἀλλὰ καὶ ἐὰν ἐδίδετο προθεσμία τριῶν
ἐτῶν, ἡ ἐκλογὴ των θὰ ἦτο ἡ ἴδία.
Σήμερον ἡ Ἑλλὰς ἀπογυμνωθεῖσα ἀπὸ κάθε
πόρον ζωῆς. παρουσιάζει εἰκόνα ἐρειπώσεως.
Χιλιάδες Ἑλλήνων ἀπέθανον τῆς πείνης καὶ
χιλιάδες ἀποθνήσκουν. Σήμερα ἡ Ἑλλὰς εἶναι
σῶμα ἀδυνατισμένον καὶ ἐξηντλημένον, δεῖγμα
τοῦ συστήματος ποὺ ὁ ἄξων ἐπιθυμεῖ τόσον ἀνυ-

πομόνως νὰ ἐπιβάλῃ εἰς ὅλον τὸν κόσμον.
Ἀλλα μέσα εἰς τὴν χώραν των καθὼς καὶ
εἰς ξένας ἀκτάς, οἱ Ἕλληνες ἐξακολουθοῦν νὰ
πολεμοῦν. Οἱ Ἕλληνες δὲν θὰ νικηθοῦν ποτέ.
Καὶ θὰ ἔλθη ἡ ὥρα ὁπότε οἱ Ἕλληνες ἐλεύ-
θεροι πλέον θὰ διατηρήσουν τὴν ἰδικήν των
κυβέρνησιν ὑπὸ τὴν σκιὰν τῆς Ἀκροπόλεως καὶ
τοῦ Παρθενῶνος. Εἰς ἔκφρασιν τῶν ἐλπίδων
καὶ τῶν προσευχῶν μας ὅπως ἡ ἡμέρα αὐτὴ
ἀνατείλῃ τὸ ταχύτερον, ἡ κυβέρνησις καὶ ὁ λαὸς
τῶν Ἡνωμ. Πολιτειῶν προσφέρουν τεκμήριον
τῆς ἐνθέρμου φιλίας των πρὸς τὴν κυβέρνησιν
καὶ τὸν λαὸν τῆς Ἑλλάδος.
Τὸ πολεμικὸν αὐτὸ σκάφος, ναυπηγηθὲν ἀπὸ
ἀμερικανοὺς ἐργάτας εἰς ἀμερικανικὸν ναυπηγεῖον, παραδίδεται δυνάμει τοῦ νόμου δανει-
σμοῦ καὶ ἐκμισθώσεως πρὸς τοὺς μαχομένους
Ἕλληνας ὁπουδήποτε καὶ ἂν εὑρίσκονται. Εἴθε
ἡ μονὰς αὐτή, ἡ ὁποία θὰ φέρῃ τὸ ὄνομα «Βα-
σιλεὺς Γεώργιος ὁ Β΄.», ὡς τμῆμα τοῦ Βασιλι-
κοῦ Ἑλληνικοῦ Ναυτικοῦ, νὰ προσθέσῃ νέας
λαμπρὰς σελίδας εἰς τὴν δόξαν ποὺ λέγεται
Ἑλλάς.

Η ΑΦΡΙΚΗ ΑΠΕΛΕΥΘΕΡΩΘΗ
ΕΠΕΤΑΙ Η ΣΕΙΡΑ ΤΗΣ ΕΥΡΩΠΗΣ

PRESIDENT ROOSEVELT'S MESSAGE
TO THE GREEKS

Washington, Thursday

President Roosevelt paid dues of honor to the Greek Nation during ceremony in American shipyard, when the government of the United States delivered new-built war vessel to the Greek Fleet.

The Greek Ambassador and other Greek and American honorary guests heard the President deliver the following speech:

"To the most of us who gathered here on this occasion, the year 1940 seems rather remote in the past. Nevertheless, during that year occured an event which will declare to all generations that violence alone is not enough to erase man's wish and determination to live free or man's willingness to sacrifice his own life for the survival oa freedom.

The 28th October 1940 will remain in history as the date for such an event. The location of the southern peninsula of the Balcan, equal in size to the State of New York, is well known to us. For more than two thousand years, poets have sung of this piece of land called Greecè.

Although we had started to prepare ourselves for the adversities that the world would be subjected during 1940, the United States observed this terrible drama of history mainly as a worried spectator. In April of that year, we witnessed the sky attack against Norway, followed by the unreasonable and unprovoked decapitation of Rotterdam, the fall of Holland and the Treaty of Belgium. In June of that year, the hordes of Axis entered Paris and the flag of freedom was raised half-masted around the world. On the 27th of September, Germany, Italy and Japan signed treaty aiming to the imposition of their New Order upon the world, which intended to distingute among themselves afterwards. Then came the 28th of October 1940.

The people and the government in Athens were given a three-hour waiting period to decide whether to accept the occupation by the Axis or to resist against the air raids of the Axis.

I repeat, the people and government of Greece were given a three-hour deadline, not three days or three weeks. Had it been three years, their choice would still be the same.

Today, Greece, deprived from every resource presents a picture of desolation. Thousands of Greeks died of starvation, and thousands still do. Greece today is a weakened and exhaused body, sample of the system that the Axis eagerly wishes to impose upon the whole world.

However, the Greeks continue to fight whether on their own land or on foreign shores. The Greeks will never be defeated. And the time will come when the Greeks, freed, will support their own government under the shadow of Acropolis and the Prthenon. Expressing the hope and prayer, that ths day may arrive the soonest, the Government and the people of the United States offer token of warm friendship to the Government and the people of the United States offer a token of warm friendship to the government and people of Greece.

This warboat, built by American labor in American shipyard, is delivered by the loan and rent legislation policy, to the fighting Greeks, wherever they may be. May this unit that will wear the name "King George the 2nd", as a part of the Greek Royal Fleet, add new gilded pages to the glory called Greece.

AFRICA IS LIBERATED
EUROPE IS NEXT

Names of a few of
the B-24's, 376th Group
Liberandos, Africa

Barrel House Bessie
Blue Streak
Coral Princess
Daisy Mae
Elsie
Fertle Mertle
Flak Sack
Lady Be Good
Let's Go
Li'l Abner
Little De Icer
Little Richard
Mama Yokum

Miss Minerva II
Oh Kay
Old Spare Ribs
Pappy Yokum
Patches
Pink Lady
Strawberry Bitch
Tangerine
Tail Wind
Teggie Ann
The Duchess
Wild Wolf
Wolf Pack

ABOUT THE AUTHOR

On December 7, 1941, the war clouds that had darkened the skies of America finally burst. Thousands of young men immediately rose to the defense of our country and enlisted in our armed services.

Richard G. Byers of St. Cloud, Minnesota chose to enlist in the Army Air Corps and was sent to Ft. Snelling, St. Paul, Minnesota for induction procedures in January 1942. From there, he proceeded to Sheppard Field, Texas for basic training where, it seemed to him, all they did was stand in line or do close-order drill.

From Texas, a troop train took him to Yakima, Washington for a three-month course in aircraft maintenance. The train trip took almost a week to go from Texas to Washington as it was side-tracked many times for high priority trains.

At Yakima, the men were housed, six to a cabin, in a large transient labor camp near the beautiful apple orchards in the Yakima Valley. Unfortunately, a horde of bedbugs had arrived at the cabin before them and it was necessary to fumigate everything. The troops were marched to and from the camp to the college campus, a distance of eight miles. Aircraft maintenance classes were conducted 24 hours a day in three 8-hour shifts. America needed trained men in a hurry.

Upon graduating, Byers was shipped to Salt Lake City for assignment to an overseas outfit. While there, volunteers were requested for B-24 and B-17 radio school. Byers volunteered, passed the test and shortly thereafter found himself on the college campus at Walla Walla, Washington.

After three months of intensive schooling, he was returned to Salt Lake City once more. He was informed he would be going to gunnery school at Las Vegas to gain experience with the 50-caliber machine gun. However, after some time had passed, he was sent, instead, to Davis Monthan Air Base at Tucson, Arizona where he met the men of the B-24 crew who were to be his constant companions for the next year (for the rest of the war). The crew consisted of:

LEAR, DEAN E.   2nd/Lt.   Pilot
MacDONALD, JOHN O.   2nd/Lt.   Co-pilot
GREGG, WARREN H. 2nd/Lt.   Navigator
GEKAS, JOHN N.   2nd/Lt.   Bombadier
FISHER, LOUIS G.   T/Sgt.   Engineer-Belly Gunner
BYERS, RICHARD G.   T/Sgt.   Radio-Waist Gunner
KELLER, ROSCOE L.   S/Sgt.   Tail-Gunner
HOLBROOK, MELVIN B. S/Sgt.   Waist-Gunner
LINDERMAN, BURDETTE V.S/Sgt.   Top-Turet Gunner

The crew soon became a tightly-knit group who liked and trusted each other. The many hours of flight training drew them together and they became as brothers—loyal and eager to fight for their country and one another.

From Davis Monthan, they went to Briggs Field, El Paso, Texas and then to Smoky Hill Air Base, Salina, Kansas for more extensive training. While stationed at Smoky Hill, Byers was married to Anne Resebrook of Hibbing, Minnesota, making a total of three married men on the crew—Lear, MacDonald and now Byers. The crew transferred to Topeka, Kansas where they were assigned their own ship. The B-24's were affectionately referred to as "Lister Bags", "Flying Box Cars" and "Hopping Grasshoppers." Several months were spent at Topeka, flying their ship and becoming familiar with every aspect of her. Early February 1943 brought orders to proceed to Morrison Field, West Palm Beach, Florida—their Port of Embarcation.

Enroute, the crew landed at San Antonio where Lt. Lear briefly visited his family. While there, a cadet in a single engine trainer taxiied too near their ship and clipped the right wing section, requiring minor repairs. The crew promptly christened their ship, "PATCHES".

"PATCHES" was patched and the crew flew to Morrison Field where they were given a schedule of meetings and briefings to attend during their short time before departing for overseas. The three wives had driven to Florida in Byers 1940 Oldsmobile sedan and were waiting for them when they arrived.

One of the items Richard Byers bought at the PX on February 24, 1943 was a small 5" x 7" dark blue, hardbound book entitled, "My Stretch in the Service." He had determined to keep a daily diary of the events to come—and he did.

One can only wonder and be amazed at the discipline and dedication of this young man to have faithfully recorded every single day's happenings—the strange sights of new and far away places, the warm affection and abiding friendship for his fellow airmen, the gruesome scenes of destruction and the terrifying reality of death of comrades.

Through this diary, Richard G. Byers has given us a gift of history.

Sue Ruehle